REBUILDING
THE INNER
CITY

REBUILDING THE INNER CITY

A HISTORY

OF NEIGHBORHOOD

INITIATIVES

TO ADDRESS POVERTY

IN THE

UNITED STATES

ROBERT HALPERN

COLUMBIA UNIVERSITY PRESS *NEW YORK*

COLUMBIA UNIVERSITY PRESS

NEW YORK   CHICHESTER, WEST SUSSEX

Library of Congress
Cataloging-in-Publication Data

Halpern, Robert
Rebuilding the Inner City:
a history of neighborhood initiatives
to address poverty in the United States/
Robert Halpern.

p.   cm

Includes bibliographical references
and index.

ISBN 0-231-08114-6.

ISBN 0-231-08115-4 (pbk.)

1. Community development,
Urban—United States.
.   2. Inner cities—United States
3. Urban policy—United States
4. Urban poor—United States
5. United States—Social Policy.
I. Title.

HN90.C6H334   1995
307.3'362—dc20   94-27659
                                    CIP

This book is dedicated
with love and
affection to Shirl,
Anna, and Eli
and
to my parents

C O N T E N T S

ACKNOWLEDGMENTS

I would like to acknowledge the helpful feedback of Mary Larner, Harold Richman, Alice O'Connor, Claudia Coulton, and an anonymous reviewer on earlier drafts of the manuscript; the expert and sensitive editing of Susan Pensak and the guidance and support of Gioia Stevens, both of Columbia University Press; and the assistance of Maija May on many aspects of the book. The Foundation for Child Development provided invaluable financial support during a critical phase of the writing, but just as important was the personal encouragement and support of Barbara Blum, the foundation's president, and Sheila Smith, director of research.

REBUILDING THE INNER CITY

After establishing that a community has died . . . we must ask who has been served by its death. —WENDELL BERRY, *Does Community Have a Value?*

The neighborhood has long been an important locus for efforts to address the causes and consequences of poverty in American society. Over the course of the past century neighborhood-based initiatives have been called on to reduce class conflict, counter feelings of anger and alienation, localize control of social institutions, create jobs and reverse neighborhood decline, and address a variety of specific poverty-related problems ranging from infant mortality to juvenile delinquency to overcrowded housing. As I write the Clinton administration is proposing to establish ten "Empowerment Zones" and one hundred "Enterprise Zones" in poor neighborhoods. In each selected neighborhood the federal government will concentrate a variety of categorical waivers, regulatory relief, tax breaks and incentives, and funding for new social services. Objectives are to create jobs, draw existing jobs from elsewhere, address individual and communitywide obstacles to employability and business creation, and generally revitalize the neighborhoods economically, physically, and socially. The Clinton administration's proposals are just the tip of the iceberg: there are probably some three or four dozen sizable neighborhood initiatives and scores more smaller initiatives underway in inner-city neighborhoods across the country.

In this book I discuss the historical experience with neighborhood initiative as a strategy for addressing poverty-related social problems. I will explore how changing social conditions and preoccupations, and accumulating experience, have shaped each subsequent generation of neighborhood-based initiatives. At the same time I will use the history of this particular strategy to point up inherent dilemmas and contradictions in American society's efforts to address poverty and its correlates. In that sense I will be examining neighborhood initiative not only as an important strategy in its own right but also as a metaphor for how American society addresses its most important social problems.

The Natural History of a Social Movement

At one level this book constitutes the "natural history of a social movement" (Janowitz 1978:459). It is a history marked by the continuous invention, and later reinvention, of new neighborhood institutions: settlements, school social centers, neighborhood councils, public housing, community action agencies, neighborhood service centers, community development corporations. In each era these institutions have been used both to meet immediate needs and to achieve certain broader social purposes: individual adjustment, social integration, and social reconstruction; countering the disintegrating and alienating effects of urban life on individuals, families, and neighborhoods; urban renewal, collective self-help, community control, economic redevelopment, rebuilding community spirit; most recently comprehensive neighborhood renewal.

The history of neighborhood initiative has also been shaped by the evolution of poor urban neighborhoods themselves. This evolution has been marked by shifting ethnic composition, and struggles over ethnic succession. It has been shaped by the priorities and preoccupations of neighborhood residents. It has been shaped by the evolving concerns of municipal reformers and, in parallel, by the evolution of local machine politics itself. In recent decades the history of poor urban neighborhoods has been marked by a dramatic loss of manufacturing jobs, and a pattern of decisions by outside public and private institutions not to invest in, insure, support, or interact with those neighborhoods and their residents. These decisions in turn have heightened the vulnerability and isolation of inner-city neighborhoods, contributing to a deterioration in the social fabric, thinner associational networks, fewer social and institutional resources, and a growing sense of anger and betrayal. They have also contributed to a growing determination among inner-city residents to be the authors and owners of local efforts to improve their well-being.

At least since the 1950s neighborhood initiative has been shaped by and sometimes acted as a function of federal government initiatives, and local government responses to them. The Federal Housing Act of 1949 set the stage for a decade of policies and programs that exacerbated (rather than buffered) the effects of both changing economic and residential patterns and the migration of large numbers of poor African Americans to the North and Midwest. Slum clearance led to the loss of hundreds of thousands of units of substandard but affordable housing that were never replaced. Federal mortgage subsidy programs promoted suburban residential development at the expense of the cities, exacerbating the effects of the shift in manufacturing to the suburbs. These programs also permitted suburban governments and developers to exclude African Americans, cutting them off from the most powerful wealth generation machine the middle class has ever known (i.e., the appreciation of those homes over the decades). The injurious effects of federal and local urban renewal policy, particularly their tendency to reinforce urban racial segregation, were further exacerbated by the location and design of public housing projects.

The 1960s was a decade of unprecedented federal activism in neighborhood initiative. Service programs such as Head Start, community health centers, neighborhood service centers, the Neighborhood Youth Corps, and Community Mental Health Centers helped to renew a severely depleted human service environment. The Community Action Program provided a vehicle for organizing discrete initiatives into a coherent local poverty-fighting effort and assuring community residents a voice in use of public resources. Yet Community Action and its accessory programs, and then Model Cities, struggled with a variety of crosscurrents and contradictions: a population in inner-city neighborhoods that was ill-prepared for an economy that was receding into the distance, the Civil Rights movement, fighting for integration, equal opportunity, and inclusion, and its foil in black separatism and community control. The federal initiatives of that era struggled to figure out what they should be about and how they should relate to mainstream institutions.

The 1980s proved that lack of federal initiative and financial support could be as powerful in its effects on inner-city neighborhoods as misguided initiative (in the 1950s) or overwhelmed initiative (in the 1960s). The decision to leave rapidly deteriorating neighborhoods to fend for themselves proved devastating to housing stock, local social institutions, and not least to residents themselves. The 1990s once again bring a federal government that is activist in spirit, if not in capacity. For the first time in over a decade the Department of Housing and Urban Development is struggling to figure out how to help inner-city neighborhoods and their residents. Should it focus on neighborhood revitalization per se; on providing inner-city residents the skills, transportation links, and job information that will improve their access to suburban jobs, but leave them the option of staying or leaving; on directly trying to "disperse" inner-city residents to other neighborhoods and communities; or perhaps on all three?

A History Repeatedly Constrained

The history related in this book reflects not just an evolutionary process but a repetitive one, a process repeatedly constrained. New initiatives emerge regularly, especially during periods of heightened social tension and concern about poverty and poor people. Each is believed by proponents to reflect unprecedented ideas and to contain uniquely promising solutions to problems associated with urban poverty. Nonetheless, many seemingly new ideas are actually old ones reinterpreted in light of the social and intellectual preoccupations of the moment. Both resurrected ideas and genuinely new ones seem to take a predictable course, first generating interest, then questions (and self-questioning), and then a loss of commitment. Rather than reshaping the larger social context, each new initiative is progressively shaped by that context. Each is accommodated in ways that preserve existing arrangements and interests. This process is not necessarily one-sided, as the comments of a community action worker interviewed by Coles (1969: 118) illustrate.

I think something happens to you, no matter how radical you are, when you work to change a political system. Some of the system's values rub off on you—you can't help it—even when you're fighting them. . . . In a way the more you fight the more you become entangled in what you're fighting.

Each new generation of neighborhood initiatives has had to cope with a larger legacy of unfinished tasks and unfulfilled promises from prior ones. This is in part because reform impulses in American society are so short-lived, and are often undermined by contradictory impulses. Discussing the War on Poverty, for example, Gans (1991:326) likens it "to a plant which impatient politicians pulled up every six months to see if it was growing." The legacy of unfinished tasks is also due to the lack of consonance between ends and means, to Americans' preference for trying to accomplish a lot with a little in the arena of social problem solving. There has been a tendency to use relatively modest intervention strategies as the primary—often the only—means for addressing deeply rooted problems such as persistent inequality or social exclusion. The result of this preference has been growing pessimism about solving problems when modest interventions do not prove adequate to the task.

Neighborhood-based initiatives in poor neighborhoods have always been forced to struggle with the individual and local consequences of national problems whose causes lay outside their purview. They have been shaped by, and at the same time been asked to reconcile, the discrepancy between American ideals and American social realities. Neighborhood initiatives have often been viewed as a kind of antidote to the casualties of capitalism, including its tendency to undermine local communities. The history of neighborhood initiative also reflects American society's persistent tendency to ask those who have the least role in making and the largest role in bearing the brunt of society's economic and social choices to deal with the effects of those choices.

Neighborhood Initiative and American Responses to Poverty

Neighborhood initiative has played an important role in efforts to address poverty in part because it is consonant with the ways in which Americans have preferred to think about and deal with poverty. In spite of evidence to the contrary, Americans have preferred to view poverty as an individually and locally rooted problem, a product of individual weakness or unhealthy community environments rather than inadequate wages, a shifting labor market, or deliberate exclusion from social and economic opportunities. Poor people, separated from the social, economic, and political contexts that shape their lives, "are presented as a mere aggregation of personal cases, each with its own logic and self-contained causes" (Wacquant and Wilson 1989:9).

Certainly poverty is locally rooted in the sense that particular local groups and communities get caught up disproportionately in larger historical processes (Jones 1992:19). Certainly people who have had, and continue to have, difficult lives make their share of mistakes and bad decisions, in part a residue of such lives. People eventually internalize social neglect, discrimination, and depredation in their outlook and behavior. (So-called social conservatives unwittingly illustrate this in their harsh attacks on the "unwillingness" of today's inner-city poor to work.) The primary difference between poor people and others is in the much greater effects of mistakes when there is so little room for error. Further, as Katz (1989:7) notes, "Descriptions of the demography, behavior, or beliefs of subpopulations cannot explain the patterned inequalities evident in every era of American history."

Public debate about poverty occasionally acknowledges the role of broader causal factors. Even during our most moralistic historical periods, such as the first half of the nineteenth century, there have been some who argued that poverty is primarily a problem of political economy. For example, Klebaner (1951:15) discusses the work of Mathew Carey, a Philadelphia pamphleteer who in the 1830s presented data demonstrating the inadequacy of wages to support families, for many classes of laborers. Carey "cited the specific case of a canal laborer who, assuming no illness or unemployment, would average about $136 a year, including $26 as his wife's earnings, but a family of four, he calculated, needed $166 as a bare minimum." During the depression of 1893–94 newspaper editorials asked "if it made sense to talk of the virtues and rewards of industry to people who had been thrown out of work" (Shelton 1976:157). During the present century a steady stream of social observers and writers have struggled to keep poverty discourse out of the narrow historical ruts in which it was inclined to run (see, for recent examples, Bowles and Gintis 1986, Katz 1989). But such struggles have had little influence on the dominant belief in individuals' personal responsibility for their well-being or lack of it.

There are a number of reasons for Americans' preference for focusing on poverty and its correlates as individual and local problems. One has been a reluctance to acknowledge that American society's collective economic and social choices bear inherent costs—in hardship, inequality, and social marginality—as well as benefits. Acknowledging these costs presumably would threaten the ideals and myths underlying American culture, and perhaps exacerbate an already chronic sense of insecurity that itself is a product of societal choices.

Even during periods of heightened concern about predominant economic and social arrangements, such as the 1890s and early 1900s, the 1930s, and the 1960s, there has been a reluctance to grapple with their implications for basic reform. One reason for this is that such reform would require significant state intervention in American social life, and Americans are reluctant to involve the state in contentious social issues (as opposed to issues about which there is consensus, such as social insurance for the elderly and handicapped). A second reason is the segmented and fragmented quality of American culture, which undermines the sense of common identity and destiny that would be needed to support a common reform project (Wiebe 1975). Related to these constraints to basic reform is Americans' strong identification with church, family, and neighborhood, which weakens class identification, and makes market inequities more tolerable (Birnbaum 1988:52).

Distancing as a Response to Poverty and to Difference

Americans also have always tried to distance themselves from poverty-related social problems, and from those who experience such problems, in the hope that distancing would provide immunity and protection. Distancing has been expressed in a strong tendency to view and to treat vulnerable individuals and groups, including poor people, as different and as lesser in some way—also as outsiders. This tendency itself has been made possible by who it is that has been disproportionately vulnerable and poor: early in the century immigrants from Southern and Eastern Europe, more recently African Americans and Hispanics. Distancing has been expressed concretely in the historic and intensifying tendency for particular groups of people to be segregated geographically and socially within larger urban areas. As Perrin (1977) notes, locality development practices are a "shorthand" for the expression of societal norms and beliefs. Distancing also has been expressed concretely in the development and maintenance of separate social welfare systems for poor and nonpoor families.

The history of efforts to segregate particular groups of poor and minority families from others in the community is interwoven with the history of neighborhood initiative itself. In the early decades of the century settlements and other community agencies refused to fight or condemn, and often supported, the color line that separated African Americans from others in most cities. In the 1950s and early 1960s the government destroyed established neighborhoods in the name of urban renewal, but in the service of segregation and exclusion (Gans 1991). In recent decades residential segregation, and the social disinvestment that accompanies such segregation, have been key causal factors in the escalating deterioration of the ghetto, multiplying the effects of long-term economic trends. As Massey (1990:350) notes, residential segregation "is the structural condition imposed on blacks that makes intensely deprived communities possible, even likely." It is also the main reason for the growing tendency of poor people to be concentrated in particular neighborhoods: "In a racially segregated city, any increase in poverty is confined to a small number of minority neighborhoods" (Massey 1990:337).

The damaging effects of racial and social class exclusion have provided Americans an excuse to reconfirm in their minds the individual and local nature of poverty. Social observers since the Progressive era have noted a strain of circularity in the tendency to neglect, and sometimes isolate, poor people and their neighborhoods, and to then point to the results of that neglect and isolation (e.g., overcrowded, dilapidated housing, high concentrations of problems) as inherent qualities of poor people themselves. In discussing the persistence of racial segregation in housing and schooling, Anderson and Pickering (1986:395) write that "separation and subordination seem to justify the denial of ordinary status, and the denial of ordinary status, in turn, seems to justify the dynamics of fear and avoidance, and so on." The circularity in our analyses derive in part from a continual effort to interpret hardship, inequality, and social exclusion in terms that do not raise questions about basic societal values. But neglected and isolated neighborhoods have not somehow created themselves. The residents of inner-city neighborhoods in the 1950s did not direct the federal government to isolate their neighborhoods with highways and tear down hundreds of thousands of units of housing. They did not send hundreds of thousands of manufacturing jobs to the suburbs over the past thirty years. Nor did they direct the federal government to dramatically reduce its expenditures on urban problems during the 1980s.

Americans' reluctance to face structural causes of poverty and social isolation has sometimes also been expressed as perplexity about the persistence of poverty and the disaffection of poor people, particularly in periods of economic growth. (The preamble to the Economic Opportunity Act of 1964 described poverty as a paradox.) Yet poverty has seemed a paradox primarily to those observing it from a distance, not to those experiencing its hardships day in and day out. Indeed in many ways the paradox is that "most poor Americans historically have kept their faith in the promise of opportunity long after it was clear to observers that they had no realistic chance to improve their circumstances" (Hochschild 1989:146).

Neighborhood Initiative and the Renewal of Community

Reliance on neighborhood-based initiative to address poverty-related social problems also derives from Americans' preoccupation with the the idea of community, its importance as a social organizer, its loss during the twentieth century, and its mythic power to renew itself and address various social problems. The loss of community has been attributed most commonly to the fragmenting effects of ethnic pluralism and urban life; the shifting of social functions from "primary institutions," such as family, church, and neighborhood, to bureaucratic ones (Nisbet 1953, Berger and Neuhaus 1977); and, in the past thirty years particularly, inordinate attention to individual rights and liberties, at the expense of social responsibilities. It has also been attributed to the values and demands of corporate capitalism, for example the emphasis on mobility of both capital and labor, and on financial profit as the only objective of economic activity. As Berry (1987:182) argues, "The way that a national economy preys on its internal colonies is by the destruction of community."

At the same time that they have mourned the loss of community, reformers have relied on the idea of community as the vehicle through which they could compensate for and counteract the costs inherent in American social priorities and arrangements. They have believed that local communities can be somehow different in values and dynamics than the larger society in which they are embedded (Wiebe 1975:chap. 6). Thus, for example, it has been presumed that in a society driven by self-interest it would be easiest to identify common interests within a local community. In an individualistic society feelings of responsibility for others' well-being would be strongest within a local community. In reality, as discussed above, Americans have been far more likely historically to use the idea of community to exclude and divide than to include, as illustrated by efforts to segregate poor and minority families in ghettos geographically and socially isolated from the larger communities of which they are a part. Suttles (1972:267) argues that the value of local community "is defended according to what it might become rather than for what it is or has been. Such utopias are a powerful lure tempting us to reconstruct history and dismiss the past."

Indeed another, and related, theme that threads its way through this book is a persistent tendency for the core precepts of American society to become inverted, to be used in ways opposite to the ideals they embody. Both the ideal of community and that of pluralism have been used to argue that those from different groups in society should not be forced to live together, support, or relate to each other against their will. Americans historically have turned the imperative for addressing poverty that is found in basic, shared ideals and beliefs back on the poor themselves; for example, arguing that if the poor want access to the American ideals of equal opportunity and social mobility they must try harder, and must behave in ways prescribed by those who are not poor.

Americans struggle to find approaches to addressing hardship, inequality, and marginality that allow basic myths—for example that ours is an open society with few impediments to social mobility or social integration—to be maintained. Strategies for addressing poverty-related social problems have reflected the enormous efforts we've had to make to adjust our lives and social institutions to the demands and inequities of capitalism, and to hold on to our ideals about ourselves as a society, in the face of numerous contradictions.

Neighborhood Initiative as Both Promise and Paradox

There is no more powerful image in American society than that of the people getting together to address their collective concerns (Morone 1990:5–8). Neighborhood initiatives in poor neighborhoods have done what they could to support the validity of this image. Whether externally or internally generated, they have mobilized existing latent resources and drawn new resources to their communities. They have helped revitalize primary institutions. They have provided residents of poor neighborhoods a voice in defining important issues in their lives and a vehicle for acting in concert to gain a measure of control over these issues. The health, social, and educational services they have created have provided poor people critical support in coping with poverty-related stresses. They have brought people and groups together who otherwise would not have come together. In cities in which there has been a vacuum in city-level leadership with respect to poverty-related problems, neighborhood initiatives occasionally have assumed that leadership, developing innovative problem-solving approaches in the process. (One example is Buffalo in the late 1970s, in which the Model Cities program stimulated the creation of ten neighborhood citizens committees, which in turn led to the creation of an overall board that developed a citywide economic redevelopment plan.)

Neighborhood initiatives often have provided the most holistic, if not always coherent, approaches to problem solving in their particular era. They have been distinct in their understanding of economic, social, and political concerns as linked, and in their struggle to address these concerns together. They have struggled to address simultaneously both the structure of opportunity and individuals' ability to take advantage of opportunity. They have been distinct in their recognition of children's and adults' welfare, and general family welfare, as linked, and in their struggle to address these three together. They have been in the forefront of efforts to find a useful basis for redefining and operationalizing the meaning of community in a time when the principle of economic interdependence no longer serves that purpose.

Nonetheless, because of the paradoxes in the way American society deals with poverty and marginality, what in most circumstances is a characteristic strength of American society, in poor, excluded neighborhoods becomes itself a paradox. In a society characterized by social and racial segregation, the people coming together to address poverty and its related problems become the poor and excluded coming together to address these problems. The history of neighborhood initiative reflects a persistent tendency to ask those with the fewest capital, institutional, and human resources to draw on those resources to better their lives; to ask those whose trust has been betrayed over and over—notably African Americans—to join a process requiring significant trust; and to ask the excluded to be responsible for finding a way to become included. We simultaneously assume that poor people, particularly poor minorities, cannot govern their own lives, thus caseworkers, case managers, and so forth, and then ask them to solve their own problems. Reformers repeatedly have encouraged the residents of poor, excluded communities to organize, and to pressure the larger society for resources and a voice in institutions affecting their lives. But in most cases when they have done so they have received little support from the very people encouraging them in the first place.

One of the central arguments of this book is that what for most American communities is a genuine choice can become for poor and excluded communities a false choice. Members of neglected and depleted communities have not only chosen, they have had no choice but to rely on their own efforts to counter the effects of their exclusion—to make something good of marginality. They have done so in response to the indifference of the larger society, in an effort not to let that indifference destroy their communities. They have done so to counter hopelessness and anger, and to secure a modicum of self-determination. The logic of neighborhood initiative, its consonance with American culture, can become illogic under conditions of resource scarcity and social exclusion. For one thing it is difficult to define a sensible function for neighborhood initiatives when little is owned or controlled by the community. Indeed, even the "basic stuff" of the poor residential neighborhood—domestic property—is owned by people and institutions located outside the neighborhood (Davis 1991). How can market mechanisms be made to work in communities that are outside the market? Where there is little at stake community residents' already over-taxed energies can be absorbed by activities that offer little potential to improve their lives. While participation nurtures democracy, it does not necessarily lead to increased opportunity or resources for one's community. This has become especially true in an era of retrenchment in both the public and corporate sectors.

Dilemmas in Neighborhood Initiative

The lack of consonance between the nature of neighborhood initiative and the social tasks that have been imposed on it, and the contexts of scarcity and exclusion in which it has had to operate, have contributed historically to a variety of philosophical and practical dilemmas in neighborhood work. Perhaps the central dilemma is what Minow (1990) calls the "difference dilemma," the question of how to address one's own social depredation and exclusion. On the one hand it is not possible for the excluded and neglected to solve these problems by creating a separate local society. As Kenneth Clark noted almost thirty years ago in *Dark Ghetto*, focusing on separate development implies a degree of acceptance of the permanent nature of one's exclusion. A particularly cruel effect of segregation, he wrote, "is that its victims can be made to accommodate to their victimized status and under certain circumstances to state that it is their desire to be set apart" (Clark 1965:63). On the other hand efforts to integrate into the larger society offer "no solution unless the majority itself changes by sharing power, accepting members of the minority as equal participants and resisting the temptation to attribute as personal inadequacies the legacy of disadvantage experienced by the group" (Minow 1990:25).

This dilemma has found expression in almost all aspects of neighborhood work in poor urban neighborhoods. It has been expressed first as a tension between striving for integration in the larger community and an emphasis on separate, autonomous community development (community control), and as a question of whether to focus more on community building or on addressing inequality (Posner 1990). It has also been expressed as a tension between reconciliation and confrontation, or between pragmatic or more radical aims. Ironically, for outside proponents of particular local initiatives this dilemma has been reflected in a tension between commitment to popular action—encouraging residents of poor neighborhoods to mobilize to help themselves—and wariness of the demands (for both more resources and social justice) resulting from such mobilization. That wariness often has been reflected in an effort to channel participation in predefined ways, and to direct reinvestment in a particular neighborhood to externally sanctioned or created neighborhood organizations.

Another expression of the difference dilemma has been the historic expectation that neighborhood initiative itself would somehow contribute to reform of social institutions and arrangements in the larger society. In the Progressive era this expectation was based on the idea that the healthful values and improved group relationships found in settlements and similar neighborhood institutions would spread to larger and larger social units, eventually infecting the whole society. In the 1960s and 1970s the thought was that a stronger disenfranchised neighborhood, acting as a coherent social and political unit, would be in a better position to negotiate for institutional reform and a greater share of societal resources for the community. Nonetheless, it is not clear what sources of influence neighborhood initiative can draw on to reform the larger society, particularly to influence the behavior of large corporations and government (Birnbaum 1988).

A different type of tension in neighborhood initiatives in poor neighborhoods has been that between concern for individual progress (and choice) and concern for community development. Should community residents be encouraged to defy their fate, or should they be encouraged to see fates as somehow bound together? What kinds of investments in a community make the most sense—those likely to benefit community residents selectively but powerfully or those likely to spread modest benefits more widely? The community economic development movement, which emerged in the mid-1960s, in particular has struggled with whether it should and can be an ideological alternative to capitalism, historically so dependent on mobility of capital and labor, on the need for both winners and losers. Some of those involved with this movement have tried to define a middle ground, arguing that individual and community success should be viewed as interdependent (Sclar 1970). Nonetheless, local experiments with alternative approaches to economic relations, such as cooperatives, have proven difficult to sustain, in part because the larger culture continues to promote, seek out, and recognize individual achievement. Further, the fragile nature of economic success in inner-city communities decreases the likelihood that individuals who manage to succeed will feel the luxury to invest in the community as a whole. Some have asked why inner-city residents should have to live up to communitarian ideals that few other Americans live up to, especially when for them mobility and choice are so hard won.

Dilemmas in defining purpose, role, and stance have been ubiquitous to neighborhood-based initiative. The struggle to find an appropriate and reasonable level of focus and set of tasks when there is too much to do, when there are many problems that all seem connected, has marked neighborhood initiative from the Progressive era, to community action, to the neighborhood revitalization efforts underway today. In a late chapter I examine how this struggle has shaped the history of neighborhood-based services. Such services have chosen for themselves, and had forced upon them, a variety of tasks, from altering individuals' life chances to rebuilding the social fabric of depleted and disorganized neighborhoods, serving as a stepping-stone into the labor market and reforming the larger human service system. In addition they have struggled with the paradoxical consequences of being so closely tied to and rooted in their neighborhoods, including a tendency simultaneously to alter and to incorporate the difficulties, stresses and vulnerabilities of their surroundings.

In another late chapter I will discuss the efforts of a new generation of neighborhood initiatives to address neighborhood renewal wholesale, to link physical, economic, and social strategies into a coherent effort. It is clear that that individual and collective, physical and social well-being are especially closely linked in inner-city communities. When housing is neglected by landlords it leads tenants to do so. People will not start new businesses in neighborhoods full of deteriorated, abandoned, and burnt out houses. Children will not struggle to succeed in school if there seems to be no purpose for doing so. Lack of opportunity, density and dilapidation of surroundings foster depression, which fosters substance abuse, inattentive parenting, and so forth. The linkage among domains is reflected in the televised image of an older black man standing in front of his burnt-out store during the Los Angeles riots, asking community youth why they did this to him, a minority business owner in his own community. Though the connectedness of things is clear, it is less clear how those formulating local intervention strategies should take this linkage into account. The emerging neighborhood initiatives generally are being started by forging discreet programmatic and organizational linkages (for example including social services in new housing developments, linking police and youth-serving organizations). They are also developing more holistic plans that strive to address a critical mass of the things that constitute a community. A key unanswered question is whether the proponents of the new, more holistic strategies have arrived at their understanding and commitment in time.

In the summer of 1965 the Watts neighborhood of Los Angeles exploded in anger. Thirty-four people were killed, nine hundred were injured, forty-three hundred were arrested, and millions of dollars of property was destroyed. Davis (1991:745) notes that a "core grievance fueling the Watts riots . . . was rising black unemployment in the midst of a boom economy." After the riots one resident of Watts noted that "the only way we can get anybody to listen to us is to start a riot" (Haar 1975:9). Upon reading the report of the McCone Commission, created to make sense of the riot and recommend actions, Hardwick (1993:6) noted that "society is calmed, and not so much by what is found in the study as by the display of official energy. For we all know that little will be done, nothing new uncovered." Two years and scores of riots later Kenneth Clark commented on the similarity of reports of the Watts riots to those of the Chicago riots of 1919 and the Harlem riots of 1935 and 1943: "It is a kind of Alice in Wonderland with the same moving picture reshown over and over again, the same analysis, the same recommendations and the same inaction" (Kerner Commission 1968:265).

As I was writing this book Americans were once again being reminded of the consequences of the way in which they have chosen to understand and address poverty and discrimination. Riots in South Central Los Angeles, precipitated by the first "Rodney King" verdict, took scores of lives and caused hundreds of millions of dollars in damage: 4,000 businesses were destroyed, 52 people died, 2,383 people were injured; property damage and loss came to almost $1 billion (Oliver, Johnson, and Farrell 1993:118). In response to the riots newspapers and magazines were full of articles about the need to rebuild and renew inner-city neighborhoods, through tax incentives and regulatory relief for businesses, tenant ownership of public housing, summer employment programs for youth, and expanded social services. The Bush administration pulled together a loose set of ideas that had been floating around Washington for years—tenant ownership of public housing units (Project HOPE), extra funding for law enforcement and social services ("Weed and Seed"), and Enterprise Zones—and presented them to Congress as an urban policy. As much as anything, this belated and modest response highlighted the lack of serious federal attention to the situation of the inner cities since the late 1970s. But it also signaled the beginning of another round of federal policy initiative.

During the first year and a half of the Clinton administration the Department of Housing and Urban Development has indeed focused attention (although not yet significant resources) on the inner city. Secretary Henry Cisneros's public comments, and the ongoing discussion within HUD, have tried to place the situation of inner-city neighborhoods in a larger historical context of disinvestment and deliberate residential segregation. For the first time in decades inner-city neighborhoods and their residents are being thought about in relation to the larger metropolitan areas of which they are a part. Planners and local officials are trying to imagine and create connections. Yet the bulk of actual initiative—as opposed to proposals and ideas—remains local, limited both symbolically and practically to the boundaries of inner-city neighborhoods. (Melvin Oliver [1993] reports that some 250 local initiatives have been started in South Central since the recent riots.)

Surely the desires embodied in neighborhood initiative—for self-determination, inclusion, an open future for community residents—are healthy ones. At its best neighborhood initiative combines the symbolic with the practical in a very helpful way, both recreating meaning through rituals and structure—strategic planning, community meetings, resident participation—and concretely improving the physical and social neighborhood—rehabilitating housing, cleaning up garbage-strewn lots, developing after-school programs. Yet why must this essentially modest approach carry so much of the burden of addressing social problems?

This book, really, is an effort to struggle with the question of what reasonable expectations and tasks are for neighborhood initiative, given its history and context. Neighborhood initiatives in poor neighborhoods have always been asked to perform a kind of alchemy: to make a lot happen with a little, and to make something positive out of despair and anger. It would seem to require enormous energy and imagination to overcome reality. Yet even these intangible resources are often depleted in low-income communities. How should we understand the assets of poor communities? They would appear to be more in relationships than in institutions, but even these appear to be very fragile.

As Belmonte (1989) illustrates so beautifully in his ethnographic account of a poor neighborhood in Naples, although there is much that is human, there is little that is redeeming about the need to cope endlessly with hardship and social depredation. Rather such pressures pit people "endlessly against each other in competition for the scarce and irregular resources from which they must derive their livelihood. . . . Every actor must seek his own personal compensations for the defeats suffered at the hands of life" (Eric Wolf, cited in Belmonte 1989:xx, introduction). A reporter visiting a South Bronx housing projects puts it more succinctly: "In Mott Haven the strongest community is one defined by hardship" (Gonzales 1991:A14). While neighborhoods cannot escape their history and their situation, neighborhood initiative nonetheless represents an effort to renounce and to seek mastery over that history and situation. Ultimately, it is this effort itself, more than the forces arrayed against it, that makes neighborhood initiative so interesting.

THE EMERGENCE OF NEIGHBORHOOD INITIATIVE

In the last decade of the nineteenth century it was not yet settled "on what terms, and on whose, the nation would be industrialized" (Kaminsky 1992:187). The questions of what kind of society the United States would be and what kinds of communities would constitute that society were still open ones. At the same time social trends were foreclosing options rapidly. What was euphemistically called the business cycle was wreaking havoc on the lives of millions of wage laborers. A series of violent confrontations between capitalist entrepreneurs and workers was shaping a pattern of labor-management relations that would last until the 1980s. Rapid, chaotic urban growth, the influx of millions of immigrants, and the liberalization of Protestantism combined to undermine feelings of social order and cohesion. The United States seemed less and less an "ever-expanding composite whole," a country creating unity out of diversity, and more and more a country becoming fragmented by numerous social forces (Melvin 1987:12).

While many were celebrating mass production and consumption as the highest ideals of a future society, others were concerned that emerging patterns of production and consumption associated with corporate capitalism (particularly with the great industrial monopolies) were undermining traditional ideals of behavior such as local civic responsibility, self-restraint, and prudence (Lears 1983). Writers such as Henry George, in his *Progress and Poverty,* warned of a widening gap in relations between the wealthy and the rest of the population. Corporate capitalism also created unprecedented problems, not susceptible to traditional explanations for and responses to poverty. First among these was widespread unemployment during increasingly frequent and severe cyclical depressions. Unemployment reached 50 percent in some cities during the depression of 1893–1894 (O'Neill 1990). Other problems included inadequate wages to support family well-being, debilitating and in some industries dangerous employment conditions, and chronic job insecurity. As Dawley (1991:339) notes, for industrial workers "hard times were like good ones, only worse." Even during "boom" years a third of the industrial workforce experienced several weeks of unemployment during the year (Sugrue 1993:91).

Even "as it created its own casualties" corporate capitalism was undermining the traditional means families and communities had always had available to cope with problems (Katz 1981:73). A family in distress was less likely than historically to be living in the same community as its extended network of kin, and was more likely to be surrounded only by other families experiencing the same difficulties as it was. Families coped in part by trying to organize themselves as economic units, each family member—children included—playing an important role (Coontz 1988:294). Immigrants strove to recreate elements of their communities of origin in their new neighborhoods, and developed new support mechanisms, such as mutual assistance associations, that fit the new circumstances. When informal coping mechanisms proved inadequate, families were forced to turn to organized charity, often at a cost to their privacy and sense of dignity.

Prevailing explanations of poverty were rooted in a belief that for the most part individuals "chose" their fate, through their backgrounds, habits, and predispositions. Prevailing responses to poverty were designed to weed out those undeserving of support, and to make sure the deserving were not corrupted by whatever relief was provided. Both explanation and response were incommensurate with the realities of millions of families' lives. Speaking of the response of Buffalo Charity Organization Society (C.O.S.) volunteers during the 1893–94 depression, Shelton (1976:144) notes that "nothing in their experience enabled them to comprehend the situation of people with no earnings, no savings, and no family or friends with the means to help them." They refused to acknowledge the evidence that for many families no amount of effort by children and adults could assure adequate income to meet even the most basic needs. During that same depression New York City's C.O.S. criticized the various newspaper relief funds that were trying to provide rapid, accessible relief to thousands of families, noting that "the results of years of work by the C.O.S. may be swept away in one season of unusual distress by sentimentalists" (Olasky 1992:127).

In the face of abundant evidence to the contrary, C.O.S. leaders continuing insistence on attributing hardship to individual behavior, for example arguing that the working poor needed to learn greater household economy in order to save a few extra pennies in anticipation of downturns in the business cycle, sounded increasingly hollow. (The Chicago C.O.S. established the Penny Savings Society in 1897 to encourage "thrift, self-denial and independence" among the poor, as if lack of these qualities was responsible for their poverty [Kusmer 1973:664]). C.O.S. leaders' continuing worries that "careless" generosity would engender dependence, and that dependence was contagious (spreading from household to household), sounded like rationalizations; so did their argument that providing material assistance to poor families caused the separation of society into classes (Kusmer 1973:661). Their continuing insistence on trying to sort out the deserving from the undeserving poor through objective analysis of individual causal factors seemed increasingly impossible. At any rate C.O.S. case records "often amounted to little more than a systematic listing of middle-class platitudes about the vices of the poor" (Kusmer 1973:668).

More than a few questioned the right of the Charity Organization Societies to make themselves alone responsible for deciding how American society would interpret and address poverty. Bremmer (1972:54) cites a letter received by Frederick Howe, a trustee of the Cleveland C.O.S., from a local clergyman, raising just this issue:

Your society [wrote the clergyman], with its board of trustees made up of steel magnates, coal operators, and employers is not really interested in charity. If it were, it would stop the twelve-hour day; it would increase wages and put an end to the cruel killing and maiming of men. It is interested in getting its own wreckage out of sight. It isn't pleasant to see it begging in the streets.

The Emergence of Progressivism

It was in this context of change, upheaval, and conflict in many spheres of society that a new reform movement emerged. Progressive reformers questioned, without entirely rejecting, the assumptions, analyses, and methods of the C.O.S.'s so-called scientific charity. It was apparent to them that "individuals suffered as often from the misdeeds and calculations of others as from their own failings" (Bremmer 1972:21). A new type of reform activity, social research (which in some respects was scientific charity's family investigation turned on its head), was demonstrating that unskilled and even moderately skilled wage labor was inadequate to meet basic family needs (Freeman 1992), that millions of families lived constantly on the edge of dependency, and that families usually sought relief from charity organizations or public relief authorities as a last resort (see Katz 1993:48, 56, Polsky 1991:46).

Nonetheless, it was not America's ideals that were perceived to be the problem, but the corruption of those ideals. It was not individual acquisitiveness per se that was the problem with the new corporate capitalism, but excessive acquisitiveness. It was not corporate profit per se that was the problem, but excessive profit. Competition was fine; not so unfair competition. Inequality was natural; it was extremes of inequality that were problematic. Thus, the Progressives sought explanations for poverty that were not as harsh and moralistic as those predominating during the nineteenth century but that did not raise questions about the basic tenets of American society. They sought responses to poverty that protected individuals, families, and local communities from the worst effects of corporate capitalism, but that did not directly contradict its imperatives of plentiful, cheap wage labor and concentration of capital in the hands of a few.

Progressive reform derived energy from growing popular anger at the rationalizations for economic exploitation offered by industrialists; for example their argument that child labor was healthy because it "gave boys and girls a chance to learn a trade" (Philpott 1978:65). It also derived energy from a growing popular anxiety at the realization that the majority of Americans were being turned into "wage slaves," an anxiety fueled further by the widely promoted "fiction that wage labor was merely a temporary condition" for most individuals (Lasch 1991:206).

Progressive reform embodied diverse, and in some cases contradictory, beliefs and concerns. Their approaches reflected an ambivalence that would characterize efforts to address poverty throughout the twentieth century. Progressives had a bias against public social spending, and at the same time rejected charity as the basis for dealing with poverty (see Skocpol 1992). They looked at causal relationships from both ends: "A disorderly family could `unmake' a decent house . . . but a congested tenement could destroy a good family too" (Philpott 1978:4). Their concern about the horrendous living conditions of tenements and the horrendous working conditions of sweatshops was based in part on the harm these conditions imposed on children and adults, in part on their contagious effects on the local community and on society as a whole (Shelton 1976). Overcrowding, constant exhaustion leading to inattentive parenting, fighting for a toehold, were viewed both as a consequence of economic organization and of social disorganization. Poor people simultaneously needed liberation from social oppression and guidance in desirable norms of conduct (Kirschner 1986). Progressives believed in the need for specialized knowledge in explaining and addressing problems and, at the same time, in the importance of citizens getting together on their own to define and address their concerns and problems. They mourned the passivity of the poor and, at the same time, "marvelled at the heroism of housewives who lugged water by the bucket load up two or three flights of stairs in the battle to keep things clean" (Philpott 1978:64).

Many of the concerns of Progressives had a strongly restorative character, and this was related partly to the backgrounds of the reformers involved. A majority of the early Progressive reformers were "descendants of long-established families [who] felt that their status was now being usurped by new industrial entrepreneurs" (Freeman 1992:199). Many Progressives believed that "urban industrialism had shattered the bonds that secured the preindustrial order and produced a morally vitiated urban society" (Bauman 1987:8). Some social historians have suggested that Progressives felt not only socially displaced but psychologically alienated from the new corporate culture, with its exploitive relations and its disregard for community (Chambers 1963:111). If they could reconstruct through deliberate effort the locally rooted social world that used to exist naturally, this then could be a vehicle for improving and reunifying society, and helping them reassert their role as stewards of that society. Among the artifacts of earlier eras Progressives sought to restore were the presumably unconflicted relations between more and less advantaged citizens, rooted in part in the carefully constructed paternalism of small community life, and the active expression of local democracy—citizens of each local community getting together to "meet, deliberate, decide and implement," in the spirit of Thomas Jefferson's hundreds of "little republics" (Morone 1990:6).

The restorative instincts in Progressive reform were also a response to massive immigration, which was changing the whole fabric of American society. Immigrants were a ready target for the frustrations, disappointments, and anxieties of growing numbers of Americans. Even the more sensitive reformers felt uneasy about the immigrants, "so different in manners, customs and beliefs from old-stock Americans" (Kirschner 1986:31). The size and social background of the immigrant population was seen to pose a major threat to the stability of the social order. Its "ignorance" of civic duties was viewed as an obstacle to the practice of local democracy (Addams 1965 [1893]:46). Bremmer (1972:10) notes that that "not only pauperism and crime, but hard times, political corruption, intemperance, and pestilence were laid at the door of the newcomers." Not least immigrants were indicted for creating their own little separate communities and for sticking with their own kind (Handlin 1951:273). The neighborhoods in which immigrants concentrated were perceived by those outside and by residents themselves as separate from the larger society of which they were supposed to be a part. One contemporary reformer wrote that "the great mass of immigrants who come to America settle first in urban `colonies' of their own race" (Daniels 1920:89). This suggested linking poor immigrant neighborhoods to the larger society as an important task.

A Reform Agenda

Progressives sought reforms that were socially conscionable yet realistic alternatives to the social Darwinism of the nineteenth century. They defined as a key problem the loss of constraints on individual acquisitiveness traditionally provided when economic activity had been embedded in a local, self-governing community (Bellah et al. 1985:43). As such, they sought reforms that addressed rampant greed and the decline in social cohesion rather than reforms that addressed the discrepancy in the influence and voice of different economic and social groups. The perceived need for social reconstruction and reunification encompassed almost every societal institution, including corporations, municipal government, neighborhoods, and families. Lack of organization and capacity to address problems was a concern that pervaded all these domains. Jane Addams (1965 [1893]:46) argued that the "policy of the public authorities of never taking an initiative, and always waiting to be urged to do their duty, is fatal in a ward where there is no initiative among the citizens." Another writer plaintively asked, "Must we look forward to an indefinite future of tame submission to saloon-keepers and actual or probably convicts?" (Storey 1969 [1892]).

The Progressive agenda was shaped in part by the struggle of a growing group of publicly active women to find an effective way to relate to economic and social change. Theda Skocpol (1992, part 3) sees a significant thread of what she calls "maternalism" in Progressive reform, which included a focus on protecting women and children, a glorification of mothers, healthy homes and neighborhoods, and maternal values. She points out (1992:2) that

the United States . . . did not follow other western nations on the road toward a paternalistic welfare state, in which male bureaucrats would administer regulations and social insurance "for the good" of breadwinning industrial workers. Instead America came close to forging a maternalist welfare state, with female-dominated public agencies implementing regulations and benefits for the good of women and children.

Baker (1984:640) on the other hand argues that the imperative for state action to regulate working and living conditions encouraged activist women to break out of traditional boundaries for female reformers. For example, women played key roles in efforts to push for laws to compensate victims of industrial accidents as well as laws for factory and tenement inspection. In a sense both Skocpol's and Baker's perspectives are correct. Female reformers were seeking both to regulate the corporate marketplace and to reduce its emerging dominance of American life by creating a renewed "social" realm to balance its influence (see Dawley 1991:99). They reinterpreted the city as a large, interdependent family rather than a giant marketplace. They redefined services such as garbage collection, formerly seen as one form of economic activity, as domestic activities (Flanagan 1990).

Progressive agendas ranged broadly from banning alcohol and saloons, to women's political suffrage, to the aforementioned laws to compensate victims of industrial accidents, to laws restricting immigration. The nineteenth-century preoccupation with physically removing children from unhealthy circumstances was gradually transformed to a new commitment to family preservation. This commitment was reflected in efforts to promote mothers' pensions and the Juvenile Court, and in a concerted campaign for various public health reforms, including pasteurization of milk, compulsory vaccination, and expansion of maternal and child health clinics. Central concerns included regulation of tenement living conditions and regulation of child labor, both of which appeared to offer means of attacking capitalist excesses without questioning capitalism itself.

Tenements and tenement districts in different cities presented distinct problems, all related to the cumulative effects of the economic interests of builders and landlords and the economic goals of immigrants. In New York City the principal tenement design was known as the dumbell. In the mid-1890s dumbell tenements housed over half of New York City's population. Dumbells were long, narrow buildings (typically ninety by twenty feet) that narrowed in the middle by about two and a half feet, so that when two building were side by side, as was common, a space of five feet was created between buildings. This space provided the only light and air for most of the 150 to 200 people who might live in a building (Wright 1981:122). In describing tenement life Handlin (1951 151–152) writes that the simplest tasks, such as garbage disposal or going to the bathroom, often became complex and disorganizing. For example, people living on the top floors might have to take themselves and their children down five or six flights of stairs to use a filthy backyard privy. There often was too little space for even a basic family ritual such as eating. DeForest and Veiller, New York's premier tenement reformers, described the suffocating atmosphere of many tenements, not only the lack of light and air in apartments, but the noise, the pitch-black hallways, and the constant smell of garbage thrown down the narrow air shafts (DeForest and Veiller 1969 [1903]). They argued (98) that "unrestrained greed has gradually drawn together the dimensions of the tenements, until they have become so narrowed that the family life has become dissolved."

Child labor frequently provided the modest additional income that kept families out of dependence, but at great cost to children's own future. Katz (1993:56) notes that most children accepted this role "with remarkable willingness." Conditions of child labor varied enormously. Some children helped with piecework at home; others made their living in the street trades, selling newspapers, shining shoes, doing odd jobs. Children's small size was often specially exploited to put them in the most physically exhausting and dangerous jobs in factories, mills, mines, and other settings. Descriptions and photographs of the more abusive work situations were among the most compelling tools in the arsenals of reformers, reinforcing the poignancy of lost childhoods and the pitiful wages children received in relation to the amount of work they did.

During its early years Progressive reform was built on the assumption that many problems were not solvable at the local level, and therefore that problem solving required a significantly expanded role for the federal government in economic and social life. The "municipal housekeepers needed the help of the state" (Baker 1984:640). Over time the relative emphasis on broad-scale legal and political reforms diminished, and that on poor neighborhoods and their residents increased. In a few cases, such as that of women's political suffrage and public health reforms, this was due to the eventual achievement of reform objectives. More commonly it was due to frustration with, compounded by an inherent distaste for and lack of skill in using, the interest-driven political process. Efforts to goad federal and state government into an active regulatory role with corporations "frequently perished in the legislatures or the courts at the hands of due process, which had become the legal instrument of individual rights" (Kirschner 1986:22). Owners and managers of the large industrial trusts turned the arguments against their monopolistic practices inside out, for example criticizing the attempts of workers to organize as monopolistic itself. Municipal government reform was complicated by the fact that municipal governments were weak, and the locus of political power diffuse and decentralized.

Tenement reform remained a major focus of the Progressives, because it combined the concerns of, and therefore could be sustained by, diverse interests. It provided a focus for the communitarians among the Progressives, with their concern for creating healthful environments. Tenement reform also was argued by reformers such as DeForest and Veiller to be in the self-interest of the upper classes. It provided a focus for responding to a variety of fears about the effects of slums on the larger society; in particular the fear that the diseases bred and nourished in the slums would spread to the neighborhoods where wealthier people lived. Fogelsong (1986:75) argues that concern about poverty and the poor in American society has often been based more on the calculation of its social costs than on concern for the welfare of the poor themselves. He notes that the "problem of disease was one of the earliest recognized `externalities' of the slum."

While Progressives were able to locate and argue for the public interest in tenement reform, their reform efforts were hampered by reluctance to look to the public sphere (i.e., government) as an alternative to the marketplace in the area of housing. Regulation and inspection, the two principal strategies for tenement reform, could not counter the market forces that shaped housing conditions for poor families. The landmark New York Tenement Law of 1901 set strict standards for ventilation, overcrowding, fireproofing, sanitary facilities, and basement apartments. At the same time these high standards discouraged speculative builders from using their money for tenement construction, worsening the housing shortage for poor families (Wright 1981:129). The Progressive era also saw the first efforts at slum clearance as a solution to the overcrowding and apparent depravity of tenement life. As would be the case (although on a far greater scale) in the 1950s, thousands of families were displaced as blocks of tenements were razed, with no new housing built to accommodate them. This furthered the overcrowding in nearby tenements and in other poor neighborhoods (Wright 1981:131).

Both tenement and child labor reforms proved to be closely tied to reform in other less malleable areas: "Every housing survey and each investigation of working children forced some consideration of the entire labor problem; every serious attempt to improve the home or save the children turned attention toward low wages, unemployment, industrial accidents, sickness, and the general atmosphere of economic insecurity" (Bremmer 1972:228). Poor families could not afford the higher rent that would accompany better housing, and they needed the income their children provided merely to afford their existing housing. In spite of compulsory education laws, over half the children in poor neighborhoods did not go to school (Wenocur and Reisch 1989:23).

Neighborhood Renewal as Theme and Practice

Neighborhood improvement had been part of the Progressive agenda from the outset. But it increasingly seemed the most manageable, and therefore natural, vehicle for addressing poverty-related social concerns. Neighborhood renewal seemed neither too trivial nor too radical as a response to poverty. It encompassed many of the Progressives' basic concerns, but at a level that did not appear overwhelming. When progressive reformers looked at poor neighborhoods they saw not only horrendous living and working conditions but ethnic and religious conflict, lack of neighborliness, and lack of social and physical order. Daniels (1920:161), reflecting the views of his contemporaries, wrote that "properly speaking, a `slum' is not a neighborhood at all. . . . It has no organic unity; rather it is a human conglomeration of which the outward shell may have a neighborhood look, but in which real neighborhood substance and organization is lacking." Robert Woods, a leader in the settlement movement, argued that the impoverished inner-city neighborhood represented the "microcosm of all social problems," and was therefore the "ultimate testing place of all social reforms" (cited in Melvin 1987:18).

Progressive reformers tended to believe that the best way to help integrate poor neighborhoods and their residents into the larger society was to first strengthen these neighborhoods and then try to link them to the outside world. Societal reconstruction would start with individuals and small groups in local settings. These would gradually be linked to each other, thus organizing the community: "Through the multiplication of individual reactions, the neighborhood is infused with new sympathies, new ideals, and new motives for action" (Daniels 1920:212). The new sense of community presumably would then spread to the city as a whole, and to the larger society, eventually altering the values of those who held economic and political power. It was a somewhat indirect strategy for addressing inequality.

If the neighborhood was going to be "the unit of civic and national reconstruction," as Robert Woods (cited in Chambers 1963:116) argued, something had to be created that symbolized and represented the neighborhood as a whole. The settlement, already emerging in many poor neighborhoods to provide specific services to neighborhood residents, seemed well-suited to this purpose (Chambers 1963). Settlements were the first institutional response to poverty shaped at least in part by the needs of poor families and neighborhoods rather than purely by the predispositions of reformers. Nonetheless, settlement leaders did not always or even usually trust neighborhood residents to determine their own needs and interests. Further, they had their own vision for the settlements, one not necessarily shared by other neighborhood institutions and residents themselves. Settlement leaders viewed the settlement as the potential hub and nerve center of the whole neighborhood—in other words, as a neighborhood center in the broadest sense. Settlement leaders saw the settlement as the vehicle for smoothing over and containing, if not integrating, the variety of separate group beliefs, interests, and behavioral patterns that made up poor neighborhoods (Kirschner 1986).

The primary attraction of settlements to neighborhood residents was the assistance provided in coping with the endless difficulties of everyday life, the specific skills taught, and the wide range of supportive services and recreational activities. Common elements included day nurseries, kindergartens, after-school programs, sports, sewing, hobby, and other kinds of clubs, and summer camps (outside the city) for children; equivalent clubs as well as day and evening classes of all sorts for youth and adults; theater, folk dancing, art classes, and art shows; primary health care, help in finding jobs, legal assistance, counseling, information and referral, emergency food, fuel, clothing, and bedding. Milk stations located themselves at settlements, as did visiting nurse associations and social workers charged with visiting families to determine eligibility for relief. (Settlement staff, called "residents," themselves were sometimes deputized as city or county relief workers, visiting homes to gather information and assess support needs.) Describing the University of Chicago settlement near Chicago's stockyards, Slayton (1986:174) notes that "people came for advice, for help in getting children out of jail, and especially to use the showers."

Settlements' staff tried to make the settlement a second home and family for tenement dwellers—also a model home, reflecting middle class "values and techniques" (Warner 1962:10). The settlement house itself was set up like a home, with kitchen, dining room, and living rooms as well as gymnasiums, club rooms, and workshops. Some settlements, in larger buildings, included apartments that were rented out. Settlement staff believed that the good things they had to offer inside the settlement were often in competition with the unhealthy (but attractive) things found outside, in the streets, and even in some homes. Especially with children, the settlement's job was "to compete . . . for first place in their secret minds" (Hall 1971:xi). Children indeed often found their way to settlements first, bringing home ideas from the settlement, as they did from school, and placing these ideas before their parents, to be digested by the family. (Men, perhaps being the most insecure about their position in the new world, were generally the most suspicious of the settlements, with their interest in family life and relationships.) Staff sometimes acted as surrogate parents for children, for example assuming a probationary function for children who ended up in court. Speaking of her childhood experience at Hull House, Dorothy Sigel (interviewed by Silberman 1990:54) notes:

You didn't realize that you were being observed or that someone was really caring about you personally. There must have been, in all of the residents' duties, sort of an unspoken assignment, each of them choosing a few [children] that they were following up on. There were always these little things going on, where someone who needed that extra dollar or two, somehow it just happened.

Like many indigenous neighborhood organizations, settlements and their staff viewed themselves as mediating institutions, both interpreting immigrants to America and its mainstream institutions and vice versa. Jane Addams (1965 [1893]:54) noted that it "sometimes seems as if the business of the settlement were that of a commission merchant. . . . It constantly acts between the various institutions of the city and the people for whose benefit these institutions were erected."

Settlement leaders and staff played an important role in a wide variety of neighborhood improvement campaigns and initiatives, advocating for "pocket" parks, playgrounds, public baths, and branch libraries, for closed sewers and adequate garbage collection, police and fire protection (Chambers 1963). They used clubs, lectures, forums, and other activities to mobilize and organize community residents around specific issues and also to educate residents as to their civic responsibilities (Bremmer 1972). They gathered data to provide an objective foundation for their campaigns. For example, the research of a Hull House resident revealed that there were over twice as many school-age children in the local district as there were places for these children in local schools (Addams 1965 [1893]:57). Settlement staff also stimulated innovations in other social institutions, such as the idea of school nurses, originated by Lillian Wald of the Henry Street Settlement (Hall 1971).

Polsky (1991) argues that at least in the early years of Progressive reform a few reformers, most notably Robert Woods, founder and director of Boston's South End House, had an explicitly political agenda for the neighborhood work of the settlements. This agenda focused on two interrelated activities. The first was "the dramatic expansion of neighborhood self-government as a device for linking marginal populations to the social order. . . . If given real political autonomy, a social space in which to generate their own collective identity, they could bring themselves into the social mainstream" (Polsky 1991:120). Self-government would provide poor, marginal populations a voice, provide valuable lessons in civic education, lead to more responsive services, and strengthen community identity. The second agenda, a prerequisite for the first, was unhooking immigrants from their dependence on the local political machine. This dependence was perceived to individualize and privatize people's concerns, and therefore to undermine the solidarity crucial to neighborhood self-governance. The machines were also seen to share the narrow self-interest and unrestrained acquisitiveness of the new giant corporations, contributing to the loss of the "older virtues" (Greenstone and Peterson 1973:115).

It was not clear in Woods's proposals what specifically would be governed by neighborhood government, how exactly the citizenry would be mobilized and organized to govern themselves, and how they would gain control over public resources. Still, as circumscribed as it was, proposals for self-government did not get very far, running into predictable opposition from established sources of neighborhood power, especially the political machines themselves but also such institutions as the Catholic church (which sensed correctly that it was also viewed by settlement leaders as an obstacle to neighborhood unity). Neighborhood residents viewed the settlements more as a service institution than a political one. Moreover they tended to appreciate the local ward system, depending on it to meet various concrete needs, including the not infrequent need for a job, albeit for the quid pro quo of votes. As one local Tammany Hall boss himself described it:

If a family is burnt out I don't ask whether they are Republicans or Democrats, and I don't refer them to the Charity Organization Society, which would investigate their case in a month or two and decide they are worthy of help about the time they are dead from starvation. I just get quarters for them, buy clothes for them if their clothes were burned up, and fix them up till they get things runnin' again. . . . Who can tell how many votes one of these fires bring me? (IRVINE AND LEVINE 1992:69)

The political potential of the settlement movement was constrained as well by its leaders' view of the settlements as neutral organizations, as integraters and conciliators in an increasingly segmented, conflict-ridden society. The majority of men and women associated with the settlement movement disdained politics, especially electoral politics, and felt uncomfortable with the conflict potentially resulting from the political empowerment of the poor and excluded. Morone (1990:114) argues that at heart most Progressives were "suspicious of the Immigrants who gathered in the eastern cities, nervous of the farmers that flocked to the populist party in the midwest, unsympathetic to the blacks and poor whites In the south." Indeed, they seemed uncomfortable with the whole idea that there were constituencies with genuinely different interests. As such there was little effort to link local organizing efforts to a larger political constituency, such as that represented by the emerging trade unions, although a few settlement leaders argued in public forums that such unions were a legitimate new form of American association.

Robert Woods did not envision neighborhood self-government as a vehicle for organizing the working poor to make demands on the more advantaged members of society. He warned settlement workers against promoting conflict-oriented tactics—such as those used by trade unionists—in neighborhood mobilization work (Woods 1902). Jane Addams's response to the Pullman Car workers strike of 1894 reflected the fine, and in some cases untenable, line Progressives tried to walk when it came to social and economic conflict. Between May and December of 1893 George Pullman lowered the wages of the workers who built his Pullman Cars five times, the last almost 30 percent (Freeman 1992). Meanwhile he refused to lower rents or food prices in the company town on Chicago's South Side, where most of the workers lived. When the workers, under impossible strain, went on strike, residents of the nearby neighborhood (in which Hull House was located) urged Jane Addams to side with the strikers. She refused, arguing that if Hull House took sides in the strike, "it would fail in its responsibility to reconcile capital and labor" (quoted in Philpott 1978:77).

Addams, generally sympathetic to unions, clearly identified with the objective injustice done to the workers. But she seemed most disturbed by her own realization that paternalism was an inadequate basis for labor-management relations—indeed for social relations generally—and that workers themselves had developed an alternative, solidarity, which was in many ways the opposite of paternalism. In "A Modern Lear," her reflection on the strike and George Pullman himself, she wrote: "A movement had been going on about him [Pullman] and through the souls of his workingmen of which he had been unconscious. . . . Outside the ken of this philanthropist, the proletariat had learned to say in many languages that `the injury of one is the concern of all' " (Addams 1965 [1893]:115). Not all settlement leaders were so torn by the dilemmas presented by militant trade unionism, with its assumption that workers and owners (and their managers) had fundamentally different interests. Addams's colleague Mary McDowell, of the University of Chicago Settlement, located near the stockyards, provided various kinds of support to the union organizers and meat-packers in their ongoing efforts to organize, and during their 1904 strike (Chambers 1963:114).

Another problem with neutrality and ecumenism in what were sometimes heterogeneous neighborhoods was that "no group could regard the settlement as its own. Since it belonged equally to everybody, it belonged to nobody, except the settlement residents themselves" (Philpott 1978:75). Settlements reportedly made only modest effort to reach out, relate to, and support the churches, the indigenous mutual assistance associations, and the trade unions that provided social structure and social support in poor neighborhoods. In some neighborhoods the local Catholic church actually discouraged parishioners from using the local settlement, citing its ecumenism and, in an ironic twist on the label applied to residents of poor neighborhoods, its alien origin (Slayton 1986; in some neighborhoods the presence of a settlement spurred the local church to begin providing services that it should have been providing already). For its part, the formal settlement movement, as represented by the local and national federation of settlements, did not accept settlements created by community members, especially those linked to particular ethnic or religious affiliations. Daniels (1920:146) cites the example of a priest who developed and directed a Ukrainian social center in New York, and who decided to call it a settlement house because "we wanted to be like the Americans." The priest reported that his settlement had "never been invited to join the federation of settlements in our city. Apparently only American settlements are admitted to that federation." Some black churches, especially the old-line churches, acted as settlements; but these also were excluded from the formal movement (Borris 1992:219; more on this shortly).

The community's sense of ownership was also undermined by patterns of settlement governance, financing, and staffing. Far from the ideal of neighborhood self-governance, most settlement leaders did not even support self-governance for the settlements themselves. Settlement boards were usually composed of people living outside, and often far from, the neighborhood, and residents had little say in how settlement funds were used. The bulk of financing came from wealthy, and generally conservative, individuals and philanthropic organizations upon whom settlement leaders always had to keep a solicitous eye. The settlements rarely hired neighborhood residents as staff, particularly in positions of authority (Philpott 1978:285). Settlement leaders and staff were confident that they knew what was most needed in the neighborhood, and felt that it was more efficient for them to make decisions about how resources were to be used (Daniels 1920:218). Nonetheless, neighborhood residents inevitably used the settlements for their own purposes, not for its purposes. When it was not helpful they stayed away.

Even when the purposes expressed by settlement leaders coincided with those of residents of poor neighborhoods, the consonance of purpose did not run deep. One domain of overlapping concern was "Americanization."

Settlement staff saw "expanding the horizons of the poor"—in terms of cultural awareness, knowledge of civic responsibilities, child-rearing beliefs and practices, and middle-class values generally—as critical to social membership, if not to economic progress (Husock 1992:57). Immigrants themselves recognized that mastering American ways was one ingredient in escaping poverty and entering the mainstream of society. But to the extent possible, it was to be Americanization on terms that respected their cultural heritage and traditional practices. Immigrants sought a middle ground between self-segregation and assimilation. Even as they "built institutions to preserve the solidarity of their particular group and to provide a measure of personal security, they tried to fit these institutions into the American social landscape" (Goren 1970:2).

Settlement leaders and staff appreciated immigrants' efforts to maintain a measure of continuity and control over their new lives. Nonetheless, in interpreting the behavior and practices of different immigrant groups they drew on decontextualized symbols as evidence of family disorganization and misguided cultural practices. For example the "family portraits, religious mementos, and objects the residents had brought with them from their former homes" were disparaged as debris, and even viewed as a sanitary threat (Wright 1981:131). Practices such as nailing windows shut or feeding infants wine and garlic water to ward off disease were criticized as precisely what was standing in the way of Americanization (Kirschner 1986). From reformers' perspectives other imperatives overrode the importance of traditional objects or practices as sources of continuity and security for immigrants in the face of a new and largely unpredictable world.

Many of the adaptations to poverty made by residents of poor neighborhoods were also viewed as examples of self-destructive or alien behavior that had to be altered if immigrants were to become successful Americans. They were viewed as evidence of the slum's harmful effects on people's morals and behavior as well. The practice of keeping children out of school to work was one common target of reformers, the practice of boarding was another. From families' perspectives child labor was critical to family survival (although families were acutely aware of the costs as well as the benefits of choosing survival over schooling; Butts 1989:113). Boarding was a way of using the family's resources to the fullest, and also of providing badly needed housing to immigrants (Slayton 1986:33).

From the perspective of reformers keeping children out of school was self-defeating; boarding was viewed as a major contributor to overcrowding and an important source of contagion of communicable disease.

The struggle between immigrants and those who would help them by reforming them constituted the "difference dilemma" of that era, for to gain access to the means of Americanization meant giving up a key part of one's identity. Historically, the argument has been made that immigrants, unlike African Americans, came here voluntarily, thereby choosing implicitly to "abide by the rules" and mores of American society in order to gain access to its benefits (Hacker 1990:1990). This argument presents only half the story, ignoring the need of many American industries of the time, such as the garment industry, for a large supply of unskilled labor, which could only be met through immigration. Regardless, it remained the responsibility of immigrants alone to cope with the difference dilemma, not immigrants and society together. As Wolin (1989:15) points out, acceptance into the collectivity or mainstream was "predicated upon acceptance by [immigrants] of mainstream institutions and their prerequisites. This results in a paradoxical situation in which the newly arrived group unintentionally connive at their own repression—and by repression here I mean no more than the ability to express difference freely."

One group for which the settlements' efforts to promote social integration was irrelevant was African Americans, whom most settlements simply refused to serve (Philpott 1978). By the early part of the century much energy was already being devoted to keeping a relatively small urban African American population segregated from other groups in clearly defined physical ghettos (Osofsky 1964, Spear 1967:91). Common techniques included restrictive covenants, steering, violence (including bombings of peoples' homes), and chronic low-level threats (such as sending anonymous notes detailing adverse consequences if a family did not move). In Chicago train tracks were used as physical barriers to segregate African Americans of that time, much as highways would be used in the 1950s and 1960s (Philpott 1978:147). African Americans were constantly pushed into the most marginal neighborhoods, with the most overcrowded and neglected housing, and then charged higher rents than whites in better neighborhoods. (In buildings that went from white to black, real estate agents demanded rents 10 to 15 percent higher than they had previously for the same apartment; Spear 1967:23). In 1917 the Chicago Real Estate Board, alarmed by the growing numbers of African Americans filtering into predominantly white subneighborhoods, appointed a commission to devise a segregation plan (Anderson and Pickering 1986:46). The plan developed was based on the principle of concentrating African Americans on particular blocks, and then on contiguous blocks as their numbers grew. Committee members sounded out influential blacks, hoping that they "would volunteer to segregate themselves" (Philpott 1978:162)

Settlement leaders supported the maintenance of "the color line" when they could. Nonetheless as more African Americans moved north they overspilled the boundaries of designated black districts, and many lived in the catchment areas of particular settlements. In response settlement leaders simply reconstructed the color line in their own policies, refusing to serve African Americans in existing settlements. Christamore House in Indianopolis defined its mission as uplift of white people "and moved—rather than desegregate its facilities—when the surrounding neighborhood became predominantly black" (Borris 1992:219). The more moderate among settlement leaders argued that racial integration would engender racial conflict. They argued that white neighborhood residents would not use the settlement if African Americans were present (in roles other than cook, cleaning person, or janitor). Since the whole aim of neighborhood work was to bring people together voluntarily, if one group objected there was nothing that could be done (Philpott 1978:311). The assertion by what constituted the leadership of the Progressive reform movement that in fact "whites just do not like blacks and there is nothing to be done about it," has been described as "racist realism," an effort to reduce a moral problem to a social fact (Anderson and Pickering 1986:7). It was an attitude that would define later efforts to address racial discrimination.

Settlement leaders and other Progressive reformers did provide some financial and technical support for settlement work in African American neighborhoods—just enough reportedly "to ensure a margin of safety in in neighborhood relations" (Philpott 1978:314–315). But with only limited financial backing and staff resources, few African American settlements survived long. In Chicago two settlements that were begun on the South Side, where many of the poorest African Americans lived, quickly failed, and one started on the West Side in 1908, the Wendell Phillips Settlement (funded in part by Sears's Julius Rosenwald), survived until the

1920s (Spear 1967). Those trying to develop settlements in racially changing neighborhoods faced similar housing problems, including exhorbitant rents and outright refusal to rent, as individual African Americans trying to find a place to live. Celia Parker Wolley, a white woman who started the first deliberately interracial settlement house in Chicago, had trouble obtaining property for the venture. Realtors " `were not averse to Negroes living on the premises if they were servants,' " she reported, " `but so soon as they heard that the Negroes were to be on a par with white people they refused to lease the property' " (Tuttle 1970:161). She was able finally to open the Frederick Douglass Center, located on the dividing line between white and black neighborhoods. While its interracial principles worked, it did not reach many poor blacks, being located too far from poor black neighborhoods on the South Side.

Other Neighborhood-Based Approaches of the Era

While settlements were the paradigmatic neighborhood initiative of the Progressive era, other institutional innovations also emerged in response to the same concerns as those driving the settlements. Some of these other innovations, for example the playground movement, with its clubhouses and youth workers, had close ties to the settlement movement. "Organized" playgrounds shared staff with settlements, and some were sponsored by settlements. Other innovations, such as school community centers (sometimes called social centers) and neighborhood improvement societies (often sponsored by local businesses), were developed independently but provided similar services. Most such innovations, other than school social centers, grew on a far smaller scale than the nationwide settlement movement, and some lasted only a matter of years.

By the second decade of the twentieth century the school had come to complement the settlement as the focus of neighborhood initiative in poor neighborhoods. The visiting teacher emerged as a new form of community worker, responsible for mediating between immigrant children and their families and the often alien public schools. Visiting teachers were encouraged by the leaders of their modest movement to view children's school-related problems as rooted in school practices and neighborhood conditions, as well as in children's home and basic life situation. Visiting teachers provided homework help and established clubs. They tried to get parents involved in school activities. A few tried, with modest success, to provide advice to teachers on curriculum and teaching methods. When a child was having problems at school or in the neighborhood they observed that child in the classroom and at home, discussed that child's home situation with his or her teacher, and school situation with his or her parents (Levine and Levine 1992). They intervened on behalf of children with the courts and other social welfare agencies, and through individual attention and relationships helped children through difficult periods (Levine and Levine 1992:86). Common problems addressed by visiting teachers included parents' need or preference for their children to work rather than attend school; differences between home and school in behavioral expectations of children, which sometimes led children to be inappropriately labeled as slow, indifferent, or difficult, or even as retarded; and sudden changes in children's behavior, often resulting from family crises of which the school knew nothing, for example desertion or death of a parent. Visiting teachers, like their movement, eventually proved too independent (and neighborhood-minded) in spirit and practice for local school systems, and were forced under bureaucratic control. (Much the same happened with visiting nurses and the medical establishment; see Melosh 1984).

For a time there was discussion of each school in every poor neighborhood housing a social service department, which would serve as a base for visiting teachers, and would sponsor a variety of community organizing and community betterment activities. Like settlements, schools proved hospitable to recreational activities, clubs, classes, and the like. But schools were even less suited than settlements to organizing the residents of poor neighborhoods to address basic social and economic concerns. They were perceived as far less rooted in their neighborhoods than were settlements. In fact, they were in the process of becoming more centralized in governance rather than less (Butts 1989:99). Given their essentially conservative mandate, to socialize immigrant children into the mores and norms of American society and to prepare all children for the demands of the emergent industrial culture, they were not perceived by most as vehicles for social reform. Indeed, schools were themselves increasingly an additional object of reformers led by John Dewey.

One revealing effort to use the school as a base for social reform was that initiated by the People's Institute of New York City (Fisher 1977). The institute was an innovative organization on Manhattan's Lower East Side founded by Charles Smith in 1897. Its original purpose was to address "the prevalence of class segregation and class conflict; the large numbers of impoverished, unassimilated immigrants; the climate of materialist values; and . . . the threat of revolutionary socialism" (Fisher 1977:475). In its early years the institute provided lectures and forums at Cooper Union, organized clubs, and supported legislative reform. One of its many early activities was a "People's Club" for immigrant workers, envisioned to provide a place for both leisure and educational activities. (The club apparently disintegrated soon after it was established, due to conflict between participants and staff, and among participants from different social class and ethnic groups, over control of the club's activities.)

In 1911, under new leadership due to the death of Charles Smith, the People's Institute established what was envisioned to be a self-governing, truly neighborhood-based "Social Center" at P.S. 63 on the Lower East Side. A community meeting was organized, and those neighborhood residents present elected a group of peers, the "Neighborhood Group," to govern the activities of the center. The Neighborhood Group proceeded to elect Clinton Childs, the social worker sent by the institute to work with the experiment, as the director of the experiment. Under Childs, it did go on to sponsor a variety of activities, such as a neighborhood information bureau and community discussions of important neighborhood concerns. It also achieved the goal of freeing the Social Center from financial dependence on the Board of Education, which freedom was supposed to lead to autonomy and self direction. But the institute's leadership and school authorities successfully discouraged the center from pursuing "direct social action by neighborhood residents" (Fisher 1977:477). The purpose of discussion and debate was the adjustment of neighborhood residents, not their political mobilization. Further, over time more and more of the center's activities became professionally sponsored and run. The tension between neighborhood and professional control in neighborhood organizations would emerge decades later as a central challenge to human services in poor neighborhoods.

Decline and Fragmentation of Reform Sentiment: 1910–1930

Settlements, school social centers, and other neighborhood innovations were not proving to be the transformative social institution earlier imagined. The basic conditions of life in poor neighborhoods were changing little. As would be the case again in the 1960s, attention to poverty at home was diverted to other concerns. Domestic social reform became entangled in international events. When the United States entered World War I in 1917, neighborhood institutions in poor neighborhoods volunteered or were drafted into the general war mobilization effort. Newly created local Councils of National Defense used neighborhood organizations as a vehicle for mobilizing and directing the domestic war effort (Fisher 1977).

What remained of the Progressive spirit was overwhelmed in the early postwar years by surprising feelings of anger and anxiety in the American people. (Some of this was related to management-labor turmoil; four million workers were involved in strikes and lockouts in 1919 alone; Dawley 1991:234). President Wilson had anticipated that, having been mobilized psychologically for war, Americans might turn those feelings inward, after the war was over, in search of enemies at home. Once led into war, he told a friend, the American people will "forget there ever was such a thing as tolerance. To fight you must be brutal and ruthless, and the spirit of ruthless brutality will enter into the very fibre of our national life, infecting Congress, the courts, the policeman on the beat, the man on the street" (W. Miller 1991:6–7).

The Progressive reform agenda indeed became entangled in the postwar intolerance and hysteria about the spread of Bolshevism to the United States. Poor immigrant neighborhoods, already perceived as the breeding ground for dependence and immorality, came to be perceived also as the breeding ground for radicals and Bolsheviks. Social activists among the Progressive leadership felt pressure to prove their loyalty with patriotic rhetoric. Neighborhood organizations in poor neighborhoods were asked to watch for un-American behavior in neighborhood residents. Longstanding efforts to expand public commitment to maternal and child health care were labeled as creeping socialism.

The fear of Bolshevism provided an excuse to rein in African American activism as well. African American leaders were accused of radicalism and sedition (W. Miller 1991:143). The number of lynchings increased, rising to seventy in the first year after the war; many of those lynched were soldiers, some still in uniform (Kerner Commission 1968:102) Respect for African Americans' economic contributions at home and courage on the battlefield was quickly transformed into suspicion of "the returning Negro veteran . . . who had learned to bayonet white men" (W. Miller 1991:140). African Americans were indeed more likely to resist racist language and actions after the war, angry that they had proved themselves once again as Americans, with little to show for it. The migration of large numbers of African Americans from the South to eastern and midwestern cities to meet the labor demands of the war contributed to growing racial conflict and violence in many poor, overcrowded urban neighborhoods. Settlements found their strategy of promoting good will among neighbors of little use in mediating the heightened racial conflict. Their failure to confront racial discrimination in the prewar years came back to haunt them, exacerbating their inability to address postwar race conflict (Dawley 1991:240).

The events surrounding World War I hastened, but did not cause, the decline in reform spirit that occurred after the war. Progressive analyses, theories, and approaches were too constrained and to some degree self-contradictory to alter the social conditions and individual difficulties they sought to address. Many Progressive reformers themselves were feeling disillusioned by the continued stubborn presence of sweatshops and child labor, starvation wages and long working hours (Schlesinger 1957). Some were coming to believe that their preoccupations with community renewal and with strengthening local democracy were of little interest either to the larger society or to poor families themselves. Some Progressives concluded that poor families preferred living in filthy, overcrowded conditions, and cared little about playgrounds and parks for their children. They failed to grasp that under conditions of extreme resource scarcity families could ill afford to actively support a reform agenda that furthered an abstract community. Thus as in one case involving the Northwestern University Settlement, when settlement staff succeeded in having a row of particularly horrendous tenements condemned, to be replaced by a pocket park, they were bewildered by displaced families' sudden display of intense attachment to those tenements (Philpott 1978:96).

As America entered the 1920s the sense of uncertainty about the course of society that had stimulated reform movements around the turn of the century was replaced by optimism that society's problems would fade away in the wash of prosperity and technological progress.

Confidence in the American way of life, by which was meant capitalism, was generally high. Settlement and other neighborhood work was becoming driven less by a holistic preoccupation with poverty and social relations and more by an interest in finding a niche and fighting for a share of resources in the rapidly developing and professionalizing human services. Conceived "as a process," neighborhood work "nevertheless succumbed to institutionalization" (Borris 1992:216). Settlements in particular struggled with the challenge of defining and articulating their distinct methods in terms that might "legitimate settlement work as a sphere of activity" within the emerging social problem-solving "marketplace" (Wenocur and Reisch 1989:41). For the most part settlements chose to adopt the techniques and structures of social service provision, especially casework and specialization.

Settlements, as well as other neighborhood agencies, were increasingly composed of numerous departments staffed by paid specialists defining their own sphere: child guidance, adult education, physical and mental hygiene, recreation (Chambers 1963:121). Residual societal concern about poverty, having been appropriated by the newly authoritative helping professions, was itself fragmented into specialized problems, such as infant mortality, juvenile delinquency, and single motherhood. Specialists redefined the focus of services to poor families from multifaceted support to treatment of specific adjustment problems exhibited by individuals. A growing proportion of poor individuals and families that had contact with neighborhood agencies became "cases," with case records, and caseloads suddenly began to grow. (The passage of legislation creating mothers' pensions in many states also created "cases," since continued receipt of assistance was conditioned on acceptance of monthly, or at least periodic, visits by social workers to check family status and provide various instructions.) The new professionals identified more with their community of peers than with the communities they worked in. They focused their organizational energies on carving out an area of helping that they could justify as their prerogative and defend against encroachment by others.

If the neighborhood had been the organizing concept for Progressives' efforts to understand and address poverty, and to reconstruct society, the individual and the small group became that locus in the 1920s. The notion of problem solving as a shared enterprise of the whole community—a function largely of good relations between settlement staff and neighborhood residents—was replaced gradually by the idea that it required specialized training and knowledge to understand the many variables that contributed to problems, particularly at the individual level. The "instinctive relationship" between settlement worker and neighborhood resident, to use Graham Taylor's phrase (Chambers 1963:115), was replaced by technique and procedure. The staff of neighborhood agencies continued to respond to immediate manifestations of poverty and hardship—negotiating with a landlord threatening to evict a family for failing to pay rent, bringing a bag of groceries to a family that had run out of food, trying to locate a husband who had deserted the family, seeking medical care for a sick child. But they were encouraged to view specific requests for assistance as an opportunity for broader and deeper entrée into the interior a family's life.

Progressive-era social reformers had used the concepts and language of community to forge their approach to addressing poverty in part because it fit, in part because it was all they had. Casework gave social workers what appeared to be more refined concepts and language for interpreting and addressing poverty. Casework was a direct descendant of nineteenth-century charity work. Proponents tried to distinguish casework from charity work by criticizing the superficial interviews and observations made by earlier nonprofessional charity workers, with the resulting sweeping generalizations. Mary Richmond, in *Social Diagnosis*, used the following exchange to demonstrate the inadequate interview technique of an untrained charity worker: "Assistance asked? `Coal and groceries.' Cause of need? `Out of work.' Any relatives able to assist? `No.' " (Richmond 1917:107). Richmond called this a "stupid compiling of misleading items," and went on to argue that a major "snare for the feet of the beginner is the pressure brought by the interviewed for premature action or for definite promises of action" (130). Tice (1992:63) cites another, perhaps more self-evident, example of the charity workers' approach of which the new caseworkers were so critical:

W. P. and his wife reported sick. Called and found home if it can be called such in such a state of extreme want, filth, and squalor—fruit boxes used for furniture—swarms of flies—a bed so dirty you couldn't tell the print of cloth—told them when they cleaned up help would be given. Called two days later and was refused admittance.

The emergent approach to casework gave new meaning to the nineteenth-century charity workers' commitment to investigation. It included (in ideal form) one or more home visits, interviews with relatives, collection of data from social, medical, and educational agencies family members had had contact with in the past, an employment history, and a search through municipal and other government records (Richmond 1917). It was only then that the caseworker should try to define the real nature and causes of a family's difficulties, develop a plan of action to address those difficulties, and work with the family over time to implement the plan. In practice few social workers had small enough caseloads to allow time for collecting so much information on individual families. Gordon (1988:295) points out that the intervention of the new helping professionals in families' lives often was initiated by family members themselves, particularly women. Still, few families could or would stand still to wait for a lengthy data collection process to conclude, let alone listen to a diagnosis and participate in whatever plan was proposed. Families were "engaged in their own processes of decision-making and problem-solving" on behalf of family survival (Stadum 1990:93).

Many of the questions caseworkers were trained to ask were still driven by an effort to distinguish the deserving from the undeserving poor:

What prospect does there seem to be that this family will retain or regain economic independence? That they will make a satisfactory social adjustment in this country? If the prospects are slight, would it be possible or desirable to deport them? (Richmond 1917:393)

The new techniques were intended mainly to provide a more detailed and individualized basis for labeling and sorting poor people.

Caseworkers, like their forebears in charity work, continued to seek solutions to economic problems that did not create dependence. Financial assistance was always a last resort. For example, the emerging social work establishment resisted the idea of mothers' pensions, partly in the traditional vein of concern about creating paupers, partly because they viewed marriage or employment to be the preferred solution to mothers' economic problems. Nonetheless, single mothers (the majority widowed, separated, or abandoned) often did not want husbands. They were "embittered and exhausted from the efforts of holding together a two-parent family" (Gordon 1988:105). Many were already employed, but in jobs that did not pay them enough to support their children.

Ironically, what had begun in the last decade of the nineteenth century as a search for a humane response to the damaging effects of industrial capitalism was coming more and more to reflect capitalism's principles and strategies. Even as social work educators were trying to make helping less haphazard, more systematic, and more efficient, even as they refined their "product" to make it more attractive to investors, such as the Community Chest, even as neighborhood services in poor neighborhoods were becoming more specialized and bureaucratic, some were worrying about the effects of these trends. By the mid-1920s some involved in neighborhood work were already worried about the growing social distance between professionals and poor people. Hyman Kaplan, the head of Cincinnati's Jewish social agencies, argued for the need for "generalists" who could "act as a buffer between client and technician" (Kirschner 1986:84). The organizational locus of family services and supports was also shifting during this period, with truly neighborhood-based and locally shaped programs gradually becoming replaced by "outposts . . . of specialized bureaucracies" (Kahn 1976:27). A few social service leaders worried about the loss of "feel for neighborhood" resulting from administrative centralization; they argued for decentralization of services as a means of renewing their communitarian spirit (Kirschner 1986:84).

It seemed that only those few who had begun their careers before the turn of the century worried about the shift from a commitment to studying and addressing poverty-related problems to a focus on individual and family adjustment in neighborhood work with poor families. Nonetheless millions of families were not benefiting from the economic growth of the 1920s. Wealth was increasingly concentrated in a few hands. Although wages increased 1 percent annually during the 1920s, profits (little of which went to workers) increased 9 percent (Dawley 1991:337). By 1929 2 percent of the population had two-thirds of the nation's savings. Wages for the majority of workers were actually eroding in real dollar terms, and remained below even conservative estimates of minimum family "health and decency budgets" (Schlesinger 1957:67, 111).

By 1928 and 1929 mothers and fathers were showing up in increasing numbers at settlements and other neighborhood agencies seeking financial assistance, food, clothing, and shelter. In much the same way they had addressed tenement conditions and child labor a generation earlier, settlements first observed and then began to document the extent and effects of growing unemployment in their neighborhoods. National and local Federation of Settlement reports, which included case studies from numerous individual settlements, were one of the few sources of data providing a warning of growing unemployment and hardship, pointing out its structural sources and likely long-term nature. Settlement leaders went to local, state, and federal officials to warn of a growing national crisis. But elected and unelected civic leaders, not to mention business leaders, did not want to listen. Helen Hall, then with the University Settlement in Philadelphia, recalls one of the largest employers in the city telling her that "anyone who really wanted a job could get one, while at the same time he was discharging several hundred men a day" (Hall 1971:13).

The primary early response to growing unemployment was modest private relief from local charities—sometimes provided under threat of violence by desperate household heads—and community-initiated make-work schemes, for example sending unemployed men out into the neighborhood to shovel snow and then canvassing other local households to donate a few pennies to them (Piven and Cloward 1971:49 and 61). One plan, "block aid," called for residents on each block in small or large cities to take care of the unemployed on their block. Food generally remained the preferred form of relief among the private charities, followed by work relief, and only then by money. Helen Hall, by then director of the Henry Street Settlement, noted that reluctant and overwhelmed local public relief agencies employed "all sorts of cruel devices . . . to make the money go around. In New York, for instance, one was called `Skip the Feed,' by which to save money the monthly food order of every tenth family was arbitrarily skipped by the Home Relief Bureau of the Department of Welfare" (Hall 1971:12).

During the previous three decades the schools, like the settlements, had assumed for themselves the role of helping integrate poor children and adults into an increasingly complicated economy and society (Janowitz 1978:455). Now, like the settlements and other neighborhood institutions, they were also being forced to struggle with the human costs of a decade of unparalleled "prosperity." Teachers observed growing evidence of family hardship, and struggled to respond. Detroit teachers "collected shoes so that pupils could come to class; New York teachers learned that a fifth of the school children were malnourished and contributed funds for school lunches from their own diminishing salaries" (Tyack, Lowe, and Hansot 1984:24). In a nursery school in Philadelphia children "invented a new game—eviction. They collected all the old doll furniture in one corner, then moved it to another. `We ain't got no money for the rent, so we's moved into a new house,' one of them said to the teacher" (Tyack, Lowe, and Hansot 1984:92). The educational community, like their social work colleagues and indeed many Americans, struggled to make sense of the pervasive hardship of able-bodied men spending months and then years of their life unemployed. Few blamed capitalism per se. Again, as in the 1880s and 1890s, it was the excessiveness, greed, and corruption of a few bad men that was perceived to be the cause of a whole society's problems. A handful of educational leaders (mostly university-based) viewed the Depression in similar terms as earlier Progressives had viewed the turmoil of the 1890s: as a societal crisis that required basic social and institutional reform (Tyack, Lowe, and Hansot 1984). As had the Progressives with the neighborhood, they proposed an enlarged role for local school systems in social reconstruction. This role would not come to pass. Local school systems were run almost exclusively by socially conservative men with close ties to the local business community and church establishment.

New Threads in Neighborhood Initiative

The magnitude of unemployment in the 1930s contributed to lack of attention to particular marginal groups and local communities. Nonetheless at this time a growing interest in neighborhood among urban sociologists, particularly in Chicago, provided a new impetus for neighborhood initiative. These sociologists focused their attention on the effects of industrialism and urban life on family and local group functioning. They focused especially on the structure, dynamics, and life cycles of poor immigrant neighborhoods: for example, on intergenerational patterns in mutual support and social control. They found that over time the authority of family and primary social group "disintegrated as secondary groups, based on common interests, replaced primary groups in which customary and traditional sanctions prevailed" (Lasch 1977:34). The "Chicago" school of sociologists also trained the first generation of professional community organizers, heirs to the early settlement workers. Two very different (but tangentially connected) initiatives of that era, the Chicago Area Project and the Back of the Yards Neighborhood Council, also in Chicago, illustrated new threads of neighborhood work that would eventually find their way right into the major poverty-related social experiments of the 1960s.

Chicago Area Project

The Chicago Area Project (CAP), conceived by Clifford Shaw at the Illinois Institute for Juvenile Research (IJR) and Ernest Burgess of the University of Chicago, was envisioned primarily as a social experiment in neighborhood-based juvenile delinquency prevention. As would be the case again in the late 1950s, the problem of juvenile delinquency was receiving growing attention, both in its own right and as a proxy for a broader array of interrelated social problems, themselves linked to the debilitating effects of poverty and social marginality. Shaw in particular recognized that the "neighborhoods of Chicago which had the highest delinquency rates also had the highest rates of tuberculosis and infant mortality; the greatest physical deterioration; populations that seemed demoralized" (Horwitt 1989:48). The clustering of problems seemed at once to reflect and to create the distinctive milieu of many poor neighborhoods.

Field researchers sent out by IJR to poor neighborhoods observed that antisocial, delinquent behavior was more the norm than the exception among neighborhood children and youth. They also noted a loss of allegiance among community youth to the traditional mores of their families and group, especially in second and third generation immigrant families. These observations strengthened Shaw's doubts about then prevailing psychological causal theories, and led to a focus on the social environment. He attributed youths' loss of attachment to traditional mores to a breakdown in informal and indigenous institutional social controls, which breakdown itself was attributed to feelings of marginality, anomie, and powerlessness among community adults. In effect juvenile delinquency was one result of a breakdown in neighborhood structure, and more generally of some immigrant groups' failure to adapt their social mores and institutions to "the urban industrial order" (Kobrin 1959:21.). It was also (implicitly) a result of the lack of attachment of some local communities to the larger society. Like their predecessors, CAP's formulators did not continue with their causal logic, asking why so many youth in the community saw no reason to follow the rules, why so many adults felt powerless and apathetic, and why a particular community was deteriorated and isolated. Horwitt (1989:49) suggests that Shaw was not oblivious to basic causes of many neighborhood problems, including inadequate and unreliable wages, exploitive landlords, and neglect by municipal government. He recognized that the enormous energy many adults had to expend simply to assure family survival often precluded "active participation in strengthening institutions, whether one's own family or communal institutions." But Shaw was "a practical man by nature," and wanted to do something immediately helpful.

The Chicago Area Project was an initiative in community building, using local institutional innovation as a basis for drawing the socially marginal community into an active role in solving what were perceived to be its own local problems, under professional guidance. It extended the settlement vision by relying on community members to play active helping roles, and over time key leadership roles, in its delinquency prevention and community-organizing activity. It was also more sensitive to the importance of indigenous community organizations, notably the church, in meeting the social and economic needs of community residents.

Three low-income neighborhoods were involved initially in CAP, the first and most successful of which was Russell Square (Schlossman and Sedlak 1983). This neighborhood on Chicago's South Side was located near the steel mills, where most neighborhood men worked intermittently, as the effects of the Depression reached different mills at different times. Housing was old, dilapidated, and overcrowded, with few sanitary facilities. Absentee landlords, combined with redlining by banks, contributed to the severely deteriorated condition of the housing stock. Smoke and grime from the steel mills covered everything. The community had few conventional businesses, except for a multitude of saloons, which served not only as social centers but as moneylenders, employment bureaus, and so forth. Russell Square was also geographically isolated, and this contributed to a strong (if ambivalent) sense of territorial identity and ethnic cohesion, critical to Shaw's theoretical assumptions about community self-renewal.

Russell Square also had one of the highest rates of juvenile delinquency in Chicago. Much of that delinquency involved petty theft and property destruction within the community. Youth gangs especially liked "to break into schools and desecrate them. . . . They threw ink on the walls and ceilings, smashed furniture, carved desk tops, broke windows, tore books apart and emptied desks" (Schlossman and Sedlak 1983:30). Shaw and colleagues struggled to understand why youth devoted so much energy to destroying their own community. Young people reportedly told them that they felt ashamed of their neighborhood "and the stigma attached to living there" (Schlossman and Sedlak 1983:22).

The project in Russell Square operated through the Russell Square Community Committee, directed by a board composed of the more financially secure community residents. The committee included a small paid program staff and a large number of volunteers, critical to the spirit of CAP. Most of the funds for ongoing project activities were raised locally. Early on Clifford Shaw enlisted the aid of the local Catholic church and its priest, to which community residents had a strong allegiance. He helped raise money and provide the staff for a Boy's Club in the basement of the church, at once linking CAP to the church in community residents' minds and creating a foundation for the more innovative activities he envisioned as the heart of the project. The central innovation of CAP was "curbstone counseling" with the members of youth gangs. Ideally the curbstone counselor was either a young adult from the community who "had somehow internalized and acted upon conventional values," despite a poor upbringing, or, even better, a former delinquent who had straightened out (Schlossman and Sedlak 1983:61). In practice some of the curbstone counselors, especially early on, were paid staff, young men with social work or sociology backgrounds from local universities. Part of their role was to identify young men from the community who could be recruited as indigenous curbstone counselors.

Curbstone counselors' central role was to embody and provide the social control—caring, feedback, guidance, and monitoring—that presumably had dissipated in the community. They were to hang out with the street gangs, develop the trust of their members, and gradually exert their healthy influence (i.e., communicating norms and expectations) through trusting, nonjudgmental personal relationships. (They were advised to focus especially on gang leaders, the inverted version of the community's natural leaders.) Like settlements workers, curbstone counselors were also to act as mediators and interpreters, in this case between delinquent youth and various authorities and institutions, including the schools and the probation department of the juvenile court. They tried to convince younger children and youth to return to or stick with school, and they tried to find older ones jobs, sometimes with CAP itself.

The Russell Square Community Committee also focused its organizational energies on general community improvement, especially physical improvement. For example, it organized the community block by block to use garbage cans, and developed an educational campaign to discourage residents from dumping garbage in alleys and vacant lots (Schlossman and Sedlak 1983:48). It also mounted a large shrub-planting campaign. Shaw hoped to use these discrete campaigns to enhance neighborhood residents' sense of control over their lives. But lack of garbage cans or shrubs were not what underlay neighborhood residents' feelings of powerlessness. Among the things the committee did not do was pressure the city for better services, seeming to accept the idea that community residents were themselves responsible for the deteriorated condition of their community. Nor did it address neglect by landlords, redlining by banks, and related causes of community dispirit.

Back of the Yards Neighborhood Council

One of the Chicago Area Project's curbstone counselors was Saul Alinsky, at the time a graduate student at the University of Chicago. In 1938 Shaw sent Alinsky into the Back of the Yards, located next to the stockyards and packinghouses, and considered one of Chicago's worst slum neighborhoods, with the intention of having him initiate a CAP delinquency prevention project there. Like Russell Square, Back of the Yards was a stigmatized community. Unlike Russell Square, it was ethnically heterogeneous, with a good deal of antagonism between different groups.

Alinsky, like his teachers and colleagues, viewed most poor neighborhoods as composed primarily of numerous small, segmented groups, formed for mutual aid, protection, and support. Uniquely, through, he was also beginning to view such neighborhoods in an explicitly political light. He was coming to believe that more important than the segmented quality of poor neighborhoods was their overall exploitation and neglect by outside institutions, and that in this common experience lay the seeds of an approach to addressing community problems.

Alinsky's nascent instincts about organizing poor communities were reinforced by his early experiences in the Back of the Yards community, in particular by his contacts with local union organizers for the Congress of Industrial Organizations, who were trying to organize the packinghouse workers. The ethnic fragmentation in Back of the Yards, and the social conservatism of primary institutions such as the Catholic church and ethnic associations, had hampered efforts to organize the packinghouse workers for decades. By the late 1930s social and economic conditions in the neighborhood had become so bad that a new generation of labor organizers had a more receptive audience (Horwitt 1989:62). The labor organizers' clear, specific goals and systematic approach to building a local organization provided Alinsky a strategic prototype for his own future organizing work. At the same time their conflict with the church and local ethnic associations reinforced for him the importance of enlisting the support of key indigenous institutions.

In the fall of 1938 Alinsky met Joseph Meegan, a park director and community leader in Back of the Yards who was becoming increasingly outraged by living conditions in the neighborhood. A series of discussions between the two men led to the idea of a community-wide reform organization, an umbrella organization that would provide a forum for mobilizing all the discrete constituencies of the community around common priority problems identified through democratic processes of discussion, deliberation, and voting (Slayton 1986). Thus was born the Back of the Yards Neighborhood Council (BYNC), a new form of neighborhood organization that would be replicated and adapted in hundreds of low-income neighborhoods in coming decades. The genius of Alinsky's and Meegan's strategy

lay in its simultaneous acceptance of segmented and naturalistic separations and its development of a way to overcome the restrictions of those systems. . . . Meegan assumed that the Poles would still resent the Lithuanians, that the Slovaks would still detest the Bohemians . . . what [BYNC] provided was a place where, once a month, everyone in the neighborhood could join together to try to wrest from outside authorities the resources they all needed. (Slayton 1986:205)

Alinsky's and Meegan's vision, though more militant than that of the settlement leaders at the turn of the century, was in many respects just as pragmatic and optimistic. Those earlier reformers had assumed that most Americans, regardless of class and group difference, shared the same ultimate interests, and just needed to be helped to see so. Alinsky and

Meegan assumed that people wanted a setting where they could temporarily set aside their narrow interests in the service of common interests, to be democratically defined. Alinsky was also reviving and refining the Progressive assumption that the most likely approach to addressing poverty and its correlates was to strengthen local democracy.

The Back of the Yards Neighborhood Council was initiated with an enormous community meeting in early summer 1939, attended by 350 people and dozens of organizations, including various churches, local business organizations, organized labor, ethnic mutual aid associations, athletic and social clubs (Horwitt 1989:69–72, Slayton 1986:203). The participants separated into four committees, health, child welfare and delinquency, housing, and unemployment, which were to meet regularly in coming weeks and months and report back to the larger group, offering recommendations for action to be voted upon by the entire group. Priorities set through voting provided the basis for the overall BYNC agenda.

The council's office was established in Davis Square Park, which Meegan still directed. Alinsky and Meegan focused on trying to assure a number of concrete accomplishments during the first year, in part to establish the council's reputation for "getting things done for the neighborhood residents." An Infant Welfare Station was established in Davis Square Park, as was a free lunch program for children. Plans were made for a recreation center. The council gathered complaints about municipal services, forwarded them to municipal authorities, and followed up with pressure from local leaders. It sponsored job fairs, pushed for more national Youth Administration jobs, and pressured local businesses to hire neighborhood residents in exchange for supporting a "Buy Local" campaign (Horwitt 1989:84). A Neighborhood Youth Committee, including the police captain, the high school principal, parish priests, parents, and business representatives, was set up to resolve specific complaints and find ways to divert delinquent youth from the juvenile justice system. The council eventually went on to open up a credit union.

Alinsky made sure that early BYNC achievements were viewed as battles won, and that victories were celebrated and publicized, giving participants a sense of validation for their efforts and communicating a sense of the council's efficacy (losing battles were also analyzed for tactical mistakes). The relative militancy of BYNC tactics in attempting to make City Hall more responsive to the community (e.g., holding sit-ins, using the media to publicize problems), as well as its efforts to become the primary source of allegiance and support for neighborhood residents, angered local ward leaders and City Hall. The mayor (Edward Kelly) tried unsuccessfully to ban BYNC meetings, by having the park district deny the use of Davis Square Park to BYNC (Horwitt 1989:148). Alinsky, in what would become a trademark, redefined that challenge to the organization as a threat to the community, and used it to increase support for BYNC.

Over time Alinsky withdrew from the leadership of BYNC, leaving it to Joseph Meegan and a handful of local priests who had come to play an active leadership role. Although BYNC continued to be an effective neighborhood reform organization, and was instrumental in a number of discrete campaigns to improve the quality of life in Back of the Yards, it failed to build bridges to other social reform and social service organizations. (Alinsky actually tried to drive the University of Chicago Settlement House out of the community.) The council also had relatively little influence on broader social processes and changes swirling around the neighborhood, including loss of jobs, due to decline in the local meat-packing industry, and growing racial conflict, as a growing African American population encroached on the eastern and southern borders of the neighborhood. By the mid-1950s BYNC actually had become an organizational vehicle for defending the neighborhood against that encroachment. Alinsky had been successful in getting the Back of the Yards community to internalize his tactics (Katznelson 1990). But he had been much less successful in communicating a vision of how newly acquired power might be used to create an authentic, inclusive community.

URBAN RENEWAL AND PUBLIC HOUSING

A DECADE OF MISTAKES

The return of prosperity and the emergence of an external enemy in 1940s encouraged once again the notion that "America was a classless, consensual society" (Patterson 1986:84). The belief that poverty would somehow disappear of its own accord reemerged in academic and popular literature, and the profound preoccupation with unemployment receded. At the same time the 1940s and 1950s were a period of major social and economic change; as in the past poor families and poor neighborhoods would bear the brunt of the dislocation resulting from such change. Even before World War II advances in transportation and changes in production technology had begun contributing to the dispersal of factories from inner-city neighborhoods, reducing what remained of the interpenetration between work and neighborhood life. This trend accelerated after the war. As workplaces dispersed so did the fluid, segmented, yet cohesive ethnic communities that had populated inner-city neighborhoods—haltingly at first, then with accelerating speed after World War II as efforts to hold the color line failed.

The mechanization of farming in the early 1940s, combined with the demand for labor during World War II, stimulated a second, massive wave of African American migration from the South to inner-city neighborhoods of the Northeast and Midwest. This migration would continue through the 1960s, long after the temporary war-related demand for new workers in the older cities ceased. It would result by the late 1950s in a growing discrepancy between the size and skills of the urban workforce and the demands of the urban labor market. Immediately it provided a new basis for identity and solidarity in traditional immigrant neighborhoods— the fragile solidarity found in efforts to exclude others. Local governments joined neighborhood residents, developers and real estate interests in an effort to control the process of neighborhood change. Nonetheless efforts to defend neighborhood boundaries, and then individual blocks, against the incursion of African Americans could not withstand the pressure of the enormous numbers of people involved, some four million between 1940 and 1970.

New and what would prove to be enduring boundaries of greatly expanded African American ghettos in Chicago, Detroit, Philadelphia, New York, Cleveland, and other cities took shape during these years. Deindustrialization, government focus on downtown economic renewal, and a highway construction program that often cut poor, minority neighborhoods off from the rest of the city, contributed to growing economic marginality and social isolation in these expanded ghettos. Public housing, which had originated in the 1930s as both an employment program and a constructive response to poor families' need for decent housing, was used in the 1950s as a kind of "anchor," locating, solidifying, and holding minority ghettos in place as one after another of the major institutions of society deserted them. At the same time efforts to counter slum clearance and public housing construction plans, made with no input from neighborhood residents, provided a new basis for community organizing (and a foundation for future efforts at local economic renewal) in minority neighborhoods. In the coming decades neighborhood-based strategies for addressing poverty would be increasingly shaped by the fact and the consequences of urban African Americans' physical, social, and economic exclusion from the life of the larger society.

Prelude: Expansion and Solidification of the Ghetto

Lemann (1991) argues that the twentieth-century migration of African Americans out of the South and into the North changed America. It is more accurate to argue that it eventually forced white urban Americans to deal with issues that they preferred not to recognize and deal with. When African Americans began migrating north in the early part of the century, in flight from from sharecropping and Jim Crow, from terrible schools and housing, from malnutrition and grinding poverty—"from all the inequities of a system that reduced them to serfs" (Groh 1972:2)—they believed at first that they had indeed reached the promised land. As one man wrote to family members still in the South, "I should have been here twenty years ago. I just begin to feel like a man. It's a great deal of pleasure knowing that you have got some privilege" (Groh 1972:2, 52–53).

Over time, African Americans' actual experiences in the North proved much more ambiguous than the promise of that experience. For example, African Americans found their employment options restricted to occupations—porters, waiters, janitors, laundresses—that "were not desirable enough to be contested by whites" (Spear 1967:31). The only opportunity they had to enter most trades was as strikebreakers, an activity that served to increase racial hostility. (Some African Americans actually were recruited north as strikebreakers, brought from the South on special trains sent by factory owners; Massey and Denton 1993:28.) Still African Americans kept coming, in part because the myth of greater freedom in the North outlived the reality, in part because they had no choice. Mechanization of farming during the 1940s and 1950s, first with tractors and later with the mechanical cotton picker and tobacco harvester, greatly reduced the demand for agricultural labor. (Jones [1992a] points out that while as many whites as blacks were caught up in these trends, northern industry was much more hospitable to white migrants than to African Americans.)

As migration accelerated in the 1940s and 1950s it significantly redefined the character of poverty in the United States. The population living in poverty was still heterogeneous, but it was increasingly less likely to be composed of second or third generation immigrants and rural agricultural workers and more likely to be composed of urban minorities. From 1950 to 1966 virtually 100 percent of the 6.5 million increase in the African American population in the United States occurred in the cities, and of this increase 86 percent was in the central cities (Kerner Commission 1968). By the late 1950s close to a majority of poor Americans lived in inner-city neighborhoods, and the majority of inner-city poor were first-generation African American migrants and their children (Groh 1972:113). Economic inequality between whites and African Americans also grew during the 1950s, with whites benefiting far more than blacks from the economic growth of the period. The relative position of African American men declined the most during the 1950s. With each recession the gap in unemployment rates between black and white men grew larger, reaching 112 percent by the early 1960s. In 1949 the median income of African American men was 53 percent of that of white men. By 1959 it had fallen to 49 percent of that of white men (Marris and Rein 1973:11).

The change in the composition of the poverty population coincided with concerted efforts to renew individualistic theories about the cause of poverty. Many Americans reinterpreted the depression of the 1930s as an aberration, or as a natural part of the business cycle. This freed them once again to view poverty as an exception, a local problem belonging to the people and the neighborhoods in which it was found. Policy makers, journalists, and academics "too often only saw evidence of degradation, rather than determination, in the weary faces of people who moved north" (Jones 1992a:206). They argued that African American had brought their poverty-causing behavior with them from the South, much as observers such as Jacob Riis had argued fifty years earlier with respect to European immigrants. By the late 1950s a self-destructive urban culture of poverty would be described, a culture transplanted whole cloth from the South into the northern ghettos, but far more toxic because the behaviors involved were no longer functional adaptations to oppression. Among the attributes noted of this culture were the female-headed family, a sense of passivity and fatality, a present- rather than future-orientation, and a distrust of the outside world. Perhaps what social observers were noting (without being aware of it) were the early returns on the social isolation of the ghettos and the economic marginality of their residents.

Factors in individual migrants' backgrounds, including education and family history, unquestionably affected their adjustment in the North. Some were unprepared for the difficulty they would face in keeping their family together and making a life for themselves. As always, some people who had had difficult lives made more than their share of bad decisions—a residue of such lives. But personal factors were far less influential than systematic discrimination and, later on, accelerating deindustrialization in the cities. African American migrants struggled just as hard as earlier immigrant groups to find a place for themselves in the urban economy (Whitman 1991). They were just as willing as earlier immigrants to take the jobs that no one else wanted. They simply did not have enough time to succeed, barely a decade. They were caught at the wrong end of the process of urban industrialization. African American migrants also had much less residential mobility than white migrants, and were unable to follow manufacturing jobs out of the central city in the 1950s and 1960s. By the early 1960s even the number of poorly paying, dead-end service jobs in the city began a steady, secular decline.

African Americans frequently found themselves excluded from the better blue-collar jobs, especially in industries where unions controlled the labor market (Mollenkopf 1983:82). Even during the war racial discrimination proved more powerful than the urgent need for labor. A survey by the United Auto Workers in April 1943 found that only 74 out of 280 manufacturing enterprises employing women were willing to hire black women (Anderson 1982:xxx). One major aviation company on the West Coast declared openly that African Americans would only be hired in janitorial positions, "regardless of their training as aircraft workers" (Kerner Commission 1968:104). Only a threatened march on Washington by hundreds of thousands of black workers opened up defense industries to African Americans. Those companies that felt compelled to hire blacks during the war found ways to release them after, even when their skills were still needed. The Ford Motor Company "reduced employment at its River Rouge plant, which had over 30 percent black workers, from 85,000 in 1945 to 30,000 in 1960," even though the Rouge grounds offered more than enough room for retooling and rebuilding (Sugrue 1993:103). In the jobs African Americans found during and after the war they were treated in ways surprisingly similar to their treatment in the South. Perhaps most painful was the extension of the color line, with its dynamic "of fear and avoidance and constant threat," into what was supposed to have been a less racist region of the country (Anderson and Pickering 1986:387).

Changing Neighborhoods and Growing Racial Conflict

By the 1950s the core of the African American ghettos in the major cities was already established. In New York, for example, the Harlem ghetto had really taken shape during the 1920s. Between 1920 and 1930 87,000 African Americans arrived in Harlem and 118,000 whites left it. By 1930 some 70 percent of New York's African American population lived in Harlem (Osofsky 1964:129). In 1910 two thirds of Chicago's 44,000 African Americans lived in small pockets of predominately white census tracts. By 1930 two-thirds of some 233,000 African Americans lived in census tracts that were over 90 percent African American (Anderson and Pickering 1986:53). Two key factors in the early formation of the ghetto were skyrocketing rents and lack of access to other neighborhoods (through means discussed earlier, notably restrictive covenants, threats, violence, and simple refusal to rent to African Americans). Since African Americans were denied the residential mobility open to white immigrants, they could not respond to rent-gouging by moving. So they doubled and tripled up, putting enormous strain on often already dilapidated housing stock.

As after World War I African Americans in the post-World War II period expected that their contribution to the war effort would ease their struggle for social and economic inclusion. This expectation was laid to rest by a renewed wave of violence against African Americans, much of it at the edge of the steadily expanding ghetto. (Intimations of a continuing struggle were evident even during the war, with conflicts over jobs and housing leading to race riots in Detroit, Harlem, and other cities.) The emerging Civil Rights movement was focused on historic injustice in the South, and would not turn to urban issues until the 1960s. In 1949 the Supreme Court outlawed the use of racially motivated restrictive covenants. But that seemed only to worsen the fears of whites about the process and effects of neighborhood change. Working-class whites especially saw not only their life savings (invested in their homes) but the communities they had worked hard to build—social clubs, job networks, churches, schools—at risk of being unraveled by integration.

Efforts to deliberately integrate white neighborhoods, or even efforts by individual African American families simply to move into decent housing that happened to be in a white neighborhood, were met with astonishing resistance. When one African American family moved into an all-white housing project on Chicago's far South Side, it provoked a riot, followed by nine months of constant intimidation until the family moved out (Lemann 1991:74). It is interesting to note that white resistance to black encroachment on all-white neighborhoods paralleled much the same process that had occurred in the South in the decades after the Civil War. Southern lynchings were most likely to occur in predominantly white counties experiencing an influx of blacks.

At the same time that racial transition at the edges of existing all black neighborhoods was resisted by whites, it sometimes was deliberately provoked by white and African American real estate speculators who scared whites into selling at a low price even before African Americans moved onto a block, telling home owners that if they waited their property value would plummet. The speculators would then turn around and sell or rent those dwellings to African American families at a higher price, often jamming two or three families into a house that previously housed one family. They also would use the presence of those minority families to scare out and then buy out the remaining whites (Milgram 1979:105). When the new owners were not neighborhood residents, as was often the case, they would not make the investment needed to maintain a property, worsening the condition of already old housing stock stressed by overcrowding.

Working-class African Americans were in a bind of their own. They were blocked from access to the new suburbs by racial steering, deliberate misinformation from realtors (saying a property was sold when it wasn't), discrimination in mortgage loans, and other techniques (Massey and Denton 1993:50–51). This meant that they had to carve out a new niche for themselves in the cities or remain in deteriorating neighborhoods. Equally important it meant that they were not able to participate in and benefit from the enormous appreciation in the value of suburban homes during the following decades. (This alone accounts for a good part of the discrepancy in wealth between middle-class white and black families.)

As whites fled urban neighborhoods they could not defend against black encroachment, the political relationship of those neighborhoods to municipal government changed dramatically. Community leaders and residents found that the allocation of public services and private resources, set through a long historical negotiation process among the different ethnic and political constituencies, no longer held (Mollenkopf 1983). Constricting urban resources exacerbated the effects of a changing relationship between poor minority neighborhoods and city governments. Efforts by African American community leaders to negotiate a fair share of contracting urban resources for their neighborhoods usually proved fruitless. Education, fire, police, sanitation, and other services deteriorated (Lemann 1991:82). The political machines, which retained their hold over racially changing neighborhoods, refused to share the increasingly scarce patronage jobs with the new residents of those neighborhoods (Kerner Commission 1968:144).

Neighborhood Initiative in the 1950s: Urban Renewal and Public Housing

Urban Renewal as Poverty Policy

Efforts to address poverty during the 1950s centered around two strategies. The first was the careful administration of public relief. The second was urban renewal, which quickly came to mean the clearance, rebuilding, and reviving of central city business districts, and the building of massive public housing projects in poor and working-class African American (and to a lesser extent Hispanic) neighborhoods. Limiting the availability, amount, and duration of relief was thought to be the best way to force people to seek and hold on to jobs. The reality was that the majority of poor women with children were already working, and sought relief because of inadequate wages and cyclical or seasonal unemployment (Piven and Cloward 1971:128; these authors have argued that, far from addressing poverty, relief practices complemented and enforced low-wage work by ensuring an adequate low-wage labor force). In the event, less than one in five poor families received public aid during the 1950s, and those who did "were not to be envied. Of households on AFDC [Aid to Families with Dependent Children], 28 percent in 1960 lacked flush toilets and hot water, and 17 percent did without running water at all" (Patterson 1986:86; undoubtedly some of these families lived in rural areas).

Urban renewal, a term evocative of the Progressives' "municipal housekeeping," also proved to be a deceptive poverty-fighting strategy. In ideal terms it meant reinvesting in the slums: "schools, hospitals, slum clearance . . . sanitation, parks, playgrounds, police, and a thousand other things" that improve the quality of neighborhood life (Galbraith 1958:249). To those who actually had the political power and economic influence to define and implement it, urban renewal meant reviving downtown areas as centers for the rapidly expanding white-collar professions (e.g., advertising, marketing, product development, middle management), the development of luxury housing, slum clearance at the edge of the downtown area, and construction of public housing in minority ghettos.

The end of World War II brought both an employment crisis and a housing crisis to poor neighborhoods, and, as noted earlier, reignited overt racial conflict. These conditions, combined with widespread fears of a renewed depression, and the acquired habit of government intervention into many areas of American life, contributed to a new round of federal government intervention in the cities. The Federal Housing Act of 1949 authorized "the elimination of substandard and other inadequate housing through the clearance of slums and blighted areas, and the realization as soon as feasible of the goal of a decent home and a suitable living environment for every American family, thus contributing to the development and redevelopment of communities" (section 2 of the act). The act authorized the production of eight hundred thousand new units of public housing over five years. It also stipulated that local government should plan and determine how federal funds were used to create a generally orderly and harmonious urban environment (Greer 1965:5–6). In response to a stream of criticism, and very weak implementation, the act was amended in 1954 to include more explicit provision for relocating families displaced by clearance and a more active role by the private sector in urban renewal.

Three very different constituencies—mayors, private developers, and low-income housing advocates—shaped the 1949 Housing Act, and more especially its subsequent revision. Mayors needed an urban renewal program that helped them replace the loss of manufacturing enterprises, and that would be visible enough to be claimed as a tangible benefit for the city. (In the 1950s mayors could make if not break their careers on the success of downtown renewal projects; see Fox 1986:100). Urban real estate interests "wanted federal policies and programs similar to those benefiting other forms of capital: minerals and natural resources, agriculture, heavy industry and transportation" (Fox 1986:90). Low-income housing advocates wanted both a critical mass of units built and the cause of low-income housing to drive the urban renewal program. For their part federal officials wanted to address the interests of all three groups. They also had two objectives of their own: first to assure social (if not economic) stability in neighborhoods, which implicitly meant keeping them racially homogeneous (Funye and Shiffman 1972:203), and second to "avoid the crystallization of conservative, doctrinaire business opposition" against public housing per se (Mollenkopf 1983:80). The result of efforts to accommodate different interests and cross-pressures was a law with multiple purposes, framed in vague language that left abundant room for interpretation by federal and local authorities. In turn the strategy adopted by local authorities was to make urban renewal an economic revitalization program focused on central business districts and to separate it from public housing. The political benefits of separating the two was reinforced by the prevailing urban planning model of "separation of uses," which prevented the development of mixed use projects (Fox 1986:102).

The particular way in which urban renewal was interpreted and carried out in the 1950s belied the federal government's benign intents, such as they were. In most cities urban renewal and public housing became complementary strategies for achieving two closely related ends: to buffer city centers and their commercial and cultural institutions from the tide of African American migration, and at the same time to reinforce territorial segregation through zoning, and carefully coordinated location of schools, transportation routes, and public housing (Fainstein and Fainstein 1983). In other words the principal thrust of local interpretations of federal policy was to separate and protect the program of economic revitalization from the processes occurring in older, racially changing neighborhoods, leaving the former to the private interests of private developers and viewing the latter as a problem of containment.

By the 1950s older inner-city neighborhoods were viewed as obsolete, as sources of urban blight. An obsolete and blighted neighborhood was ancient and decaying, belonging in function and mood to the nineteenth century, not the modern city (Mollenkopf 1983:152). The idea of blight carried additional emotional resonance, evoking something almost alive, a disease that could spread from one building and one block to another. Blighted areas were seen to require major surgery. As one observer noted, "We must cut out the whole cancer and not leave any diseased tissue" (Gillette 1983:437). From a manufacturing perspective the label of obsolescence, at least, made sense. The new patterns of assembly line production, requiring long, low industrial plants, had "cut short the useful life of [the] cramped multistory factories" characteristic of older cities (Frieden and Sagalyn 1989:44). The few urban efforts mounted to clear land for new manufacturing enterprise proved costly and difficult to mount (Frieden and Sagalyn 1989:44).

City officials argued that they had little choice but to pursue the construction of office buildings for the emergent service industry, and to support luxury housing, as means for reviving the central city. Nonetheless, inner-city neighborhoods were not obsolete in the eyes of people who made their lives there. Residents knew better than anyone the problems of their neighborhoods. As Herbert Gans's West Enders responded when asked about how they felt (1962:289): "What's so good about the West End? We're used to it." To West Enders, like those in other older neighborhoods, the central fact was that their neighborhood was their home and their world. Furthermore, if a neighborhood was blighted it was because of exploitive landlords and neglectful city governments. (In reality tenement landlords themselves felt "squeezed by the declining fortune of the cities, with increased taxes and maintenance costs occurring just as tenants' incomes were declining; Bartlet 1993:139).

The constituency that benefited the most from the view of older neighborhoods as obsolete was downtown developers. The housing acts not only provided private developers federal subsidies and tax breaks for their land purchases and development activities, but gave them unprecedented powers of eminent domain, powers that the Supreme Court had denied the federal government itself in the 1930s. Only 20 percent of housing in a neighborhood had to be classified as blighted to allow City Hall and business interests to declare eminent domain and force residents out. This gave those interests a wide variety of neighborhoods to choose for their purposes, and as a result many viable and vital low-income neighborhoods were destroyed for no good reason. (The housing acts also prohibited clearing old factories and warehouses for urban renewal purposes. Only housing could be cleared.) Half of the land that was cleared by urban renewal was never developed or built on, serving only as a tax write-off for the purchaser and leaving that part of the affected neighborhood permanently disfigured (Haar 1975:21). Little low-income housing of any sort was built on cleared land, and almost no public housing.

The eventual effect of urban renewal from a housing perspective was the destruction of four units of low-income housing for each one built, with a net decrease in low-income housing stock of 90 percent during the 1950s (Greer 1965:56). Detroit, for example, built 758 low-income housing units over a fifteen-year period, while demolishing 8,000. New Haven built 951 while demolishing 6,500. Newark built 3,760, but demolished 12,000 (Frieden and Sagalyn 1989:52). Between 1950 and 1970 Cincinnati's urban renewal program destroyed 15 to 20,000 dwellings, displaced fifty thousand people (mostly blacks), and produced 1,000 units (Davis 1991:131). Urban renewal also caused the destruction of hundreds of viable (if nor always stable) neighborhoods with their webs of relationships, institutions, and social support built up over decades. In destroying neighborhoods it also destroyed thousands of small businesses. Davis (1991:137) notes that "when Kenyon-Barr, Cincinnati's oldest black neighborhood, home to 10,000 black families, was destroyed, 500 shops, churches, and other non-residential facilities, and 300 commercial and manufacturing establishments were also destroyed." Close to 70 percent of the people displaced by urban renewal were African American or Hispanic, exacerbating the overcrowding that already existed in minority neighborhoods due to migration from the South, Puerto Rico, and Mexico (Willhelm and Powell 1975:119). Only half of all people displaced from their homes and neighborhoods received any relocation payment at all, and for those who did the average payment was 69 dollars per family.

Urban renewal planners, and at least some residents of poor neighborhoods, viewed the prospect of relocation as redemptive. As one resident on Washington, D.C.'s Southwest Side—the site of a major urban renewal effort in the late 1950s—noted, it provided a chance for her and her family to "be born again and start a new life" (District of Columbia Redevelopment Land Agency 1964:39). Nonetheless for most of those who lived, worked, and owned property in affected neighborhoods, urban renewal signaled devaluation and abandonment rather than renewal. The act of or even the declared need for slum clearance communicated to people that their neighborhood was worth little, and therefore indirectly that they themselves were. Urban renewal plans for a neighborhood could be approved as much as five years before any activity occurred. The threat of urban renewal hanging over a neighborhood, or plans to raze only a few discrete blocks, were almost as effective in undermining older neighborhoods as the physical act of slum clearance. In many neighborhoods such a threat led many of the most stable families to leave. This was the case on the Lower East Side of Manhattan. In anticipation of urban renewal many landlords abandoned ordinary property maintenance. Uncertainty about a neighborhood's future undermined financial support for neighborhood agencies, weakening them just when they were most needed (District of Columbia Redevelopment Land Agency 1964:25). In some cases social agencies were forced to abandon neighborhoods that were still living, viable communities of people.

The effects of all these processes were exacerbated by the fact that urban renewal tended to displace the most vulnerable families in a neighborhood, who then had to struggle with little support to build a new life for themselves. Hall (1971:236) describes such families moving "from one tenement to another as they were pulled down, just a few steps ahead of the bulldozer, until some were moved six or seven times. Meanwhile, many lived in buildings unfit for the rats that infested them, wrecked by vandalism, and sometimes without heat or light." As noted, the most resourceful families in the older and economically marginal neighborhoods that were likely targets for urban renewal often left the neighborhood even before any slum clearance began. Remaining families had little economic or political clout, and their dependence on public assistance often made them reluctant to assert rights embodied in federal law and local program regulations. Relocation authorities often only informed people of their rights when explicitly asked.

The disruptiveness and trauma of urban renewal was exacerbated by the federal highway program, which displaced almost as many people as urban renewal itself. As with urban renewal planners, highway planners "had a knack for picking low-income neighborhoods where low-income residents had deep attachments to friends, relatives, neighbors, churches, schools, and local businesses" (Frieden and Sagalyn 1989:33). As with urban renewal, African American and Hispanic neighborhoods were particularly susceptible to the highway program. In Los Angeles five highways were pushed through the main Mexican American neighborhood, Boyle Heights. Frieden and Sagalyn (1989:29) argue that the practice of running highway routes through minority neighborhoods, or between minority neighborhoods and others, was hardly incidental:

Very few blacks lived in Minnesota, but the road-builders found them. . . . [As one participant in the Minnesota program noted,] "We went through the black section between Minneapolis and St. Paul, about four blocks wide, and we took out the home of every black man in that city. And woman and child. In both those cities practically. It ain't there anymore, is it?"

In spite of accumulating evidence on the ground, most government officials, media observers, and urban planners somehow managed to ignore or distort the real stories of urban renewal and the highway program well into the 1960s. Planning documents in Cincinnati suggested that only twelve hundred people would be displaced by urban renewal, barely 3 percent of the actual number (Davis 1991:131). Federal government data, compiled from local urban renewal agency reports, suggested that most relocated families were living in good housing. A 1957 article in Harper's magazine, in noting the displacement and relocation of 881 New Haven families so that a new spur could be added to the Connecticut turnpike, reported that "if federal funds hold out, New Haven may be the first slumless city" (cited in Powledge 1970:37). Planners, intent on demonstrating that neighborhoods targeted for renewal had outlived their usefulness, ignored evidence of community life. Often they seemed not even to realize that neighborhoods were complex, ineffable things, made up of thousands of relationships, interactions, and interconnections that took decades to build, and that when housing and small businesses were bulldozed these less tangible things were destroyed as well.

In the 1950s citizen participation, though mandated in federal law, was a nascent idea. Neighborhood organizations in poor, minority neighborhoods fought to influence urban renewal programs, but with little success. For example, the Neighborhood Planning Conference in South Philadelphia and a like planning effort in North Philadelphia developed their own neighborhood renewal plans and presented them to the city planning commission. In both cases the plans were dismissed by the city

(Hallman 1984:116–117). By the mid-1960s residents and business own-ers in poor, minority neighborhoods would be much better organized to stop the wholesale destruction associated with urban renewal and the highway program. (Better organized neighborhoods were in some respects a by-product or urban renewal, as poor neighborhoods often organized in order to protect their survival. That was the case, for example, in Chicago's Woodlawn neighborhood and on Boston's South Side.) At any rate it hardly mattered. By the mid-1960s the strategy of urban renewal itself was becoming obsolete and blighted.

Public Housing as Neighborhood Initiative

Public housing first emerged in poor neighborhoods in the 1930s. For proponents it held promise of forever altering the character of those neighborhoods, and therefore of their residents. The idea of public hous-ing for the poor had existed for decades. Until the Great Depression pro-ponents had never managed to overcome the opposition of real estate and banking interests, who feared a loss of business and profit, and who worried that the federal government would become involved in the reg-ulation of private housing as well. Growing inequality in the years lead-ing up to the Depression had created a latent constituency for govern-ment intervention, a generation of people "malnourished on the congestion of our cities and abuses of industrialism" (Mollenkopf 1983:56). The depth and breadth of the Great Depression in a sense provided the excuse, if not the basic reason, for an activist as opposed to mediating federal gov-ernment role in the economy and in social life. In this climate, and with-in a framework stressing the jobs created in housing construction, pub-lic housing managed finally to gain a foothold.

The rationale for public housing derived in part from the longstand-ing view of tenements and slum districts as malignant entities breeding disease, immorality, and despair. Progressive reformers had long argued that slums damaged the people who lived there, particularly children. The "new housers," as proponents were sometimes described, also argued that slums were a social threat to and an economic burden on society. A mid-1930s assessment of one poor neighborhood in Cleveland found that while it contained 2.47 percent of the city's population, it pro-vided only .75 percent of the city's property tax revenue. Meanwhile that neighborhood consumed 4.47 percent of the city's police budget, 7.3 percent of public health funds, and 14.4 percent of fire department expenditures (Teaford 1993:86).

The rationale for public housing derived also from earlier utopian ideas and experiments with "new communities" and their potential for comprehensive physical and social reconstruction (Janowitz 1978). To proponents public housing offered the same potential. It would address definitively the problems created by the physical and social environment of the slums by incorporating all at once what architects, urban planners, and sociologists were sure they knew about how to create healthy, planned, and controlled environments. Public housing would reduce prostitution, illegitimacy, juvenile delinquency, and infant mortality. It would shape parents' and children's behavior and daily lives and long-term aspirations. For example, attractive, well-defined play areas would keep children off the streets. Units "were laid out so that each family could learn responsibility and self-reliance by maintaining an assigned area" (Bauman 1987:52). At the same time public housing, like the slum it was intended to replace, was envisioned as a temporary community, a way station, for families in the early stages of achieving the American dream. Small and spartan apartments were designed to remind any families with tendencies toward dependency that public housing was not intended as a place to settle into for a long time (Wright 1981:219).

The first urban public housing was undertaken by the Public Works Administration (PWA) in the mid-1930s, in collaboration with unions and other nonprofit organizations (Wright 1981:224). In 1937 the stage was set for the massive expansion of public housing for low-income families in the 1950s, with the passage of the Wagner-Steagall Housing Act. Housing built under the act was targeted at the poorest families, those with little income or resources. Each apartment built had to have its counterpart in a tenement apartment torn down, shifting the balance of the act somewhat from housing production to slum clearance (Wright 1981:229). Strict income restrictions required that if people's income improved they had to move out of public housing. While these requirements did not push out the working poor completely, they created a dilemma for many families who did become ineligible, since there was a big rental gap between public housing and minimally decent private rental housing.

The early housing projects completed with Wagner-Steagall funding (actually low-cost loans to local and state government) remained mod-

est in scale, usually small clusters of architecturally attractive and socially sensible low-rise units, and for the most part were well maintained.
By 1942 there were 175,000 public housing units in 290 communities;
by 1946 another 195,000 units had been built, many near wartime factories (Atlas and Dreier 1992:76). During this period public housing
was not yet a stigmatized program (in part because African Americans
and other minorities still constituted less than half the population served).
In other words, public housing worked fairly well as a social program
during the pre- and postwar period, although the number of units built
never came anywhere near meeting the demand. In fact, to the present
day the bulk of public housing works at some level for some of the populations served, most notably the elderly (37 percent of all residents) and
the disabled (11 percent).

Nonetheless even in the early years of public housing tensions were
emerging that would continue to influence the program in future decades.
For one thing, a tension existed in both legislation and management of
public housing between the objective of providing housing for the poorest, most dependent families, and that of using it to create model environments for the working poor. Speaking of the early years of the
Philadelphia housing authority, Bauman (1987:52) notes that "since the
authority intended to rehabilitate the city socially and economically, selecting worthy tenants for the new [public] housing was crucial." In practice this meant that former residents of slums razed to make room for
new housing had no priority in gaining access to new housing built on
the site of their former homes. People with no jobs, people in ill health,
single mothers and their children, and other categories of the dependent
poor were actually ineligible for some early public housing, which was
designated for the working poor.

There was tension also over the federal government's authority to
impose its intentions on local communities and the private housing market. In the mid-1930s, for example, slum landlords took the federal government to court, arguing successfully in the case of U.S. v Certain
Lands in City of Louisville that the federal government had no right to
condemn private land. This led the federal government to help create,
and subsequently work through, local and state housing authorities,
since local and state government did have this right in law.

Still the federal government in the 1930s and 1940s retained significant influence over the approach to and uses of public housing, and it proved unwilling to use public housing as a tool to address residential segregation or to promote integration, rather just the opposite. If "a neighborhood was white, no blacks would be admitted into the public housing" (Wright 1981:225). This latter policy corresponded with the federal government's longstanding role in reinforcing and even promoting residential segregation in private housing. For example, throughout the 1930s Federal Housing Authority administrators advised and sometimes required "developers of residential projects to draw up restrictive covenants against nonwhites as a condition of obtaining FHA-insured financing" (Judd 1991:740).

Public Housing in the 1950s

The renewed construction of public housing after World War II continued to be constrained by historic factors. For example, real estate interests, worried that the government was usurping the private market, used their influence to assure that most new public housing was targeted at the poorest families. This eventually would contribute to the political unpopularity of public housing, and thus to increasing financial neglect (Atlas and Dreier 1992:77). Renewed construction was shaped also by emerging social concerns, particularly the pressure to house growing minority populations in many cities (in addition to those displaced by urban renewal), and by the desire among whites to control the process of neighborhood change.

Site selection for new housing was controlled by municipal planning agencies dominated by private real estate interests. It was influenced by pressure from "a white working class that cherished its insularity, and feared the power of government to engineer racial change, destroy local property values, and alter an established way of life" (Bauman 1987:160). The result was housing located either in the heart of minority ghettos, or, if at the edge, bounded by such physical barriers as highways, railroad tracks, and rivers. A few housing reformers, such as Dorothy Montgomery in Philadelphia and Robert Taylor in Chicago, tried to maintain the earlier vision of public housing as a social reform program, and to add to it the purpose of promoting residential integration. They were thwarted not only by whites but occasionally by black leaders fearful of losing their voting base. In his battles with the Chicago City Council to have new public housing built outside the ghetto, Robert Taylor "received virtually no support from the head of the black political machine, Congressman William Dawson" (Massey and Denton 1993:214).

The majority of projects built in the large cities in the 1950s and early 1960s were so called "elevator" high rises, dense collections of multi-story buildings, often arranged around large courtyards, empty but for a few pieces of playground equipment. At least early on the housing reformer Elizabeth Wood believed that the new "vertical neighborhoods" would "compete with the suburbs for social desirability, especially for families with children" (Marciniak 1986:73). As initially conceived and planned the high rise projects were deemed "a visible expression of economic efficiency and social order" (Wright 1981:236). Higher density was seen to be needed to reduce land costs. In fact the per unit costs for high rises were not cheaper than for low rises, since the costs figured for the latter were based on unrealistic land values. (In 1956 Congress, angry at the higher than expected costs of the units in high rise buildings, cut federal housing allowances for low-income people in general.) It was believed that projects had to be large if they were to alter the character of the surrounding slum neighborhood for the better, small projects would be "beaten down" and overwhelmed by the blight and disorder of the larger physical and social environment (Wright 1981:234).

Efficiency and social order took on curious architectural and procedural meanings in many projects. For example, in many projects elevators were designed to stop on every other floor, to save money. This decision obviously created great inconvenience for a mother with young children carrying a load of groceries or laundry up to her apartment on a nonelevator floor. Incinerator chutes had tiny openings. In the process of forcing a bag of garbage through the opening the bag might burst, leaving garbage all over the floor. (Incinerator chutes, like elevators, were sometimes also located on every other floor, and even on the floor that had no elevator. In retrospect it appears as if such decisions were deliberately designed to make peoples' lives more difficult.) The few common areas in most projects were alienating in appearance and feeling. There were no small, defined, and protected areas where mothers with children might sit and get to know each other. A project for ten thousand people might have one or two play areas. As one resident of a Chicago project told a visiting researcher: "The people who built this place certainly did-n't know nothing about human beings, especially children. When they drew the plans for these projects, seems like they didn't expect no children to live in it. But it's 7,000 of them here, and one playground and two tot lots" (Moore 1969:12). In some projects no space was created or allocated for human service and recreational agencies.

In 1952, unsure of how much of its public housing allotment from the federal government should be used for high-rise units, the Philadelphia Public Housing Authority commissioned a study of an existing high-rise project in New York City called the Jacob Riis Homes. The study was conducted by Anthony Wallace, an anthropologist from the University of Pennsylvania. According to Bauman (1987:132), Wallace found the Riis homes to be "an inhumane, hostile world characterized by fear, `fear of children falling out of windows, fear of death in crossing a superhighway to get to a playground.' " Wallace also noted a mood of despair, which he attributed to limited contact between mothers and children, and the lack of roles for men in community life (not just as providers).

In spite of their inherently unsocial qualities, demand for apartments in the new projects was great, and would remain so until the early 1960s. Because they were public, project buildings and apartments invariably met minimal building code requirements, at least in their early years. Most poor African Americans had never lived in such buildings or apartments. (Later, as expenses outpaced income, housing authorities cut back on maintenance, repairs, and services.) There is abundant anecdotal evidence of families' joy and excitement with the improvements of life in the project. Former or long-term residents remember being struck by the newness, the cleanliness, and the light, by their own or their children's first bath in a bathtub, by adequate heat and hot water (Hall 1971:243, Marciniak 1986:88–89).

Although the lives of public housing residents were filled with rules and regulations—from unannounced inspections, to limits on the time house guests could remain, to instructions on how to clean the apartment—these rules were disembedded from any rooted social organization. For one thing, project designers and managers retained for at least a few years the residual notion of the project as a temporary home for its residents, a way station for poor working families who were not going to remain poor for long (Marciniak 1986:64). As artificially constructed communities, public housing projects lacked the intergenerational time needed for social structure, social controls, and leadership to emerge. (By the time such structure and leadership did emerge, with tenant committees and the like, it was often too late—gangs had filled the vacuum.) No one was in charge, in any real sense. The local housing authority was an external bureaucracy whose agents were always available to collect rent, but (at least from residents' perspectives) were all too rarely available to assure needed repairs. Over time, as the common areas in many projects—particularly the courtyards—became more dangerous, whatever tentative sense of community had begun to emerge through common use of those areas began to atrophy; feelings of community stopped at one's apartment door.

Temporal limitations aside, public housing projects lacked many of the ingredients that underlie community, however it is defined. Site selection practices assured that public housing would be located in areas with little or no job base, and often little or no commercial base. Thus housing projects and their environs lacked the mixed economic activity that might create some basis for interdependence and exchange. Lack of conventional economic activity made projects particularly susceptible to becoming bases for the drug trade. The pressure to house growing numbers of young, female-headed families also undermined the heterogeneity in life stage and life situation that might have helped the development of community. By the mid-1950s efforts to use careful screening to seek two-parent working families were overwhelmed by the numbers of economically and socially marginal families being displaced by urban renewal, as well as those continuing to arrive from the South. Few if any apartments were set aside for older people who might have served as sources of authority and stability. Housing authorities deliberately conformed to the requirements of the federal government to fill projects according to the ethnic or racial balance in a neighborhood. Since projects were located in all-black neighborhoods, this "required" them to be filled solely with African Americans. (In the mid-1950s, by which time most high-rise projects or project sites were located far from white neighborhoods, a number of states passed laws prohibiting the allocation of units by race in a public housing project. In 1962 the federal government followed suit.)

Settlements and other social agencies tried to establish a presence in as many projects as possible. For example, by 1959 various social agencies were operating sixty-nine community centers in New York City's public housing projects (Trolander 1987:83). As they had half a century earlier, the settlements and other agencies defined their mission as assisting project residents in their assimilation and adjustment to the new culture of the urban housing project. As before, they not only battled project gangs for the allegiance of children and youth, but furnished model apartments, in which they taught good housekeeping (Trolander 1987: 82). A very few social agencies also attempted some building and community organizing, in an effort to deliberately create a sense of common responsibility for the community among tenants. For example, the Henry Street Settlement developed an outreach program in the La Guardia Homes in Manhattan, a predominantly Puerto Rican project (Hall 1971:240). Tenant "organizers," first social work students and later tenant home visitors, attempted to get tenants to work together within their buildings on building problems, and to attract tenants to various committees focused on one or another aspect of community life.

In their work social agencies were sometimes constrained by the reluctance of the local housing authority to have other sources of authority in a project. (Public housing authorities in a number of cities developed their own social service departments, staffed by social workers, which competed as well as cooperated with private agencies.) Social agencies were sometimes constrained by their status as outsiders. More fundamentally, the achievements of social agencies—a tenant committee, a nursery school, a parent aide program, a community center for recreation activities and dances, cooperatively purchased equipment such as a mimeograph machine, cleaning equipment, and so forth—were dwarfed by the numbers of people and, increasingly, by the magnitude of the problems in some projects.

By the early 1960s public housing was no longer a way station on the way to a better life for most tenants; rather it had become a new kind of poorhouse. The great majority of recorded tenants, if not actual residents, were single mothers with young children. Only a tiny percentage of tenants worked. (New York City was and continues to be an exception to this pattern, having a higher percentage of working poor in its projects.) As control over tenant selection broke down under the pressure of numbers needing housing and court suits by civil liberties groups, public housing became a refuge for the poorest and most troubled families. The emergence of tenants' rights laws made it increasingly difficult for project management to evict disruptive families (Lemann 1991:233). The density of the projects, combined with the lack of economic opportunity and absence of communal social controls, contributed to high crime rates. Describing a public housing project in which he lived as a participant observer for nine months during that time, Moore (1969:4) noted a paradox: "Here were slums without rats, filth without alleys, and halls and stairways soiled by human waste where there was adequate plumbing." Under these conditions the reform and renewal spirit that underlay earlier visions of public housing gave way to a preoccupation with security and moral breakdown.

As was inevitable the social stigma increasingly attached to the projects became internalized in children and adults. Referring to the Cabrini Green project on Chicago's near North Side, Marciniak (1986:39) notes that "ever since the 1950s, the press, radio, and television have not hesitated to remind Cabrini Green residents that the place they call home is a slum. . . . The mass media has shaped the image of the Cabrini Green neighborhood as much as the residents themselves." By the early 1960s residents of the projects were belittling themselves, referring to their own communities as warehouses and reservations. Projects had become permanent homes for families who nonetheless saw almost no reason to invest themselves in the community. As one resident noted: "There is little point in sinking roots here. Nobody cares about anything. If you sweep the steps, somebody else or their children just mess them up again. The only people who live here anyway is them that can't do no better" (Moore 1969:33). In a recent interview (Scheer 1992:62) the rap star Sister Souljah describes her experience of growing up in a public housing project this way:

I was surrounded all the time by fear and lack of understanding—fear of being victimized and a lack of understanding of how it came to pass that we all ended up there. . . . Do you understand what I'm saying? You're constantly surrounded by debauchery. You can't understand why it's like that, and you have this fear of ending up that way yourself. When you grow up in that environment and you don't know any history, you develop a self-hatred. Everything is so negative that you naturally blame it on the people in the environment.

Negative perceptions of the projects by the media and residents were echoed by the public at large, and eventually by Congress, undermining the already tenuous financial commitment to the projects of local and federal government.

Perhaps the most damaging aspects of the high-rise projects were their profound social isolation from the larger urban community of which they were theoretically a part; and what would later be called their "concentration effects"—the effects of enormous numbers of vulnerable and marginal people living close together in a context that was also characterized by a lack of most institutional social resource, from churches to after-school programs. Resource scarcity had a damaging effect on social support networks, thinning them out and leaving only a residue of mutual assistance. Schools for project children, when needed, were built at the edge of projects, solidifying the narrow boundaries of children's social world.

When John Kennedy came into office he appointed an experienced public housing administrator, Marie McGuire, to head the federal Public Housing Administration. McGuire tried to turn the problems generated by the deliberate creation of socially isolated and economically marginal communities into opportunity. Public housing projects would be reconceived as "bases for the rehabilitation and generation of desires, hopes, and energies of people to help themselves" (cited in Bauman 1987:186). But by then public housing had become one of the most politically unpopular federal programs. The money for turning public housing projects into giant "social welfare centers" (Bauman 1987:183) was never provided. In fact the 1960s inaugurated a period of severe federal and local neglect and underfunding for public housing maintenance that continues to the present day. (The original "financing formula" for public housing called for the federal government to pay capital costs, and for local housing authorities to use tenant rents, limited to 30 percent of adjusted gross income, to pay operating costs. Because the "income" of tenants in public housing—usually public assistance—has declined steadily over the years, the necessary local housing authority subsidy has grown, to $1,000 per unit annually; Hartman 1993:9). One recent estimate places "modernization" costs of public housing at $31 billion (Newman 1993:21).

By the late 1960s no more high-rise projects were being built in inner-city neighborhoods. Since then conditions in high-rise public housing projects have worsened, and the lessons of their failure have been extensively debated. Many observers have noted that public housing began to decline when it stopped screening potential residents, when it began serving as a place to house poorest families, instead of the working poor, and when management lost the authority to sanction and evict residents who broke community rules. To others the idea of publicly owned housing is inherently misguided: when a piece of property is owned by everyone it is really owned by no one. The costs of neglecting it weigh lightly on any individual resident. To still others the lessons of public housing reside in what it reflects about American society's racism, and its continuing unwillingness to confront issues of inequality and exclusion. Public housing only served to remove social problems from view, and to concentrate them geographically. It did not address their sources.

Public housing never created vertical neighborhoods, as its early proponents hoped it would. One cannot administratively create communities, with their subtle patterns of exchange, social control, and social nurturance. The vacuum in governance and social organization of community life in public housing projects ironically and tragically has been filled by gangs. Perhaps for the first time in the history of any community, adults have abdicated community leadership to youth. Gangs control and "protect" (in only the most superficial sense) particular buildings and their residents. They also try to protect and nurture their younger members, in exchange for total obedience in the performance of a variety of illegal and often dangerous errands. Some gangs in the projects on Chicago's South Side now require their younger members to stay in school, and fine them for getting poor grades. They also have funds that can be drawn on for school supplies by young gang members as well as by residents of the buildings they control. Some gangs assign members or building residents to keeping hallways and public areas in front of building clean.

The roles of gangs in providing social organization and drugs in providing an economic base for neighborhood life in housing projects create a dilemma for adults and children alike. Community residents, including gang members themselves, "decry the existence of a predominantly drug-oriented economic structure, and work toward its eradication, but at the same time, [feel they] have no choice but to participate in it" (Venkatesh 1993:11). Those who refuse to have anything to do with drugs still rely on the gang associated with their building for protection and loans.

It is possible that if adult residents of public housing projects had public resources to draw on for the development and maintenance of community life they would not be so dependent on gangs for this purpose.

Over the past two decades the federal government has focused its low-income housing policies, such as they were, on promoting the production and subsidizing the rental of privately owned housing. The major program that emerged, Section 8, had two parts. One provided rent subsidies, or guarantees, to developers, who then selected their own tenants. The other provided vouchers to low-income people (equivalent to the difference between the rent and 30 percent of their adjusted gross income), to help them gain access to the private rental market (Newman 1993:22–23). While more effective in preventing social isolation than public housing, both programs, particularly the former, have had their own limitations. These include a tendency for developers to select more socially desirable tenants, especially elderly people, at the expense of young, minority families, poor-quality construction of low-income units built, and difficulties for certificate recipients in finding housing for which to use their certificates (Hartman 1993:11). There has also been a good deal of favoritism in the selection of developers to receive tax breaks for these programs.

In the late 1980s the idea of selling public housing units to their residents emerged within HUD, with the rationale that ownership would instill pride of residence and would provide poor families an important financial asset. This idea, which came to be embodied in a federal program called Project HOPE, ignored most of the realities of project existence, including the basic fact that the land and property residents would own has lost its worth in the marketplace. It is land and property that has been demeaned by the market, just as its potential owners have been abandoned by the larger society of which they are a part. This may explain in part the disappointing results of an HUD demonstration designed to sell thirteen hundred units in seventeen relatively more attractive public housing projects (Rohe and Stegman 1992). The local housing authorities involved were only able to sell one in four units, in large part because of lack of tenant means and interest.

NEIGHBORHOOD
INITIATIVES
OF THE 1960s

James Morone (1990:250) has noted Americans' tendency to use broad, ill-defined but resonant ideas, "potent myths," to fuel periodic efforts to address problems of social and economic inequality. In the 1960s the idea of neighborhood initiative, combined with education and training, served that role. Indeed it became a kind of canvas upon which was projected all the anxieties, frustrations, wishes, and expectations of a fragmenting society. As in the Progressive era, neighborhood initiative in the 1960s was viewed as a vehicle for assimilating socially and economically marginal people into the larger society. Far more than in that earlier era, it became a vehicle through which disenfranchised Americans struggled to identify and communicate the causes of their disenfranchisement, and through which they finally demanded a response to their political, social, and economic exclusion.

One core problem with neighborhood initiative in the 1960s, clear only in retrospect, was the rapidly weakening economic and social connections between the minority poor in inner-city neighborhoods and the larger world outside those neighborhoods. Even as professional reformers were developing innovative education programs to prepare the children and youth of southern migrants for the demands of a changing economy, that economy was receding from their lives. Even as inner-city residents were learning to organize to make demands on the larger society, it was becoming less and less clear what their objectives should and could be. The focus on integration at the beginning of the decade gradually shifted to a focus on self-reliance, separate development, and community control of public institutions. This shift, driven simultaneously by feelings of abandonment and an effort to assert pride and dignity in a distinct identity, only seemed to worsen the exclusion to which it was a response.

It was difficult to find the right meaning, purpose, and focus for community control. Was it to be about access to and control over an equitable share of public resources—the traditional urban battle—or about deeper issues such as racial and economic injustice and residential discrimination? If the latter, how could community control be used to stimulate basic social change throughout society, and in all its institutions, and to reverse a deteriorating urban job market? Did community control imply recreating complete social systems, or just controlling local branches of societal institutions? What could community control mean when the institutions involved—schools, housing, welfare—were those that were supposed to be manifestations of society's interest in supporting the community and preparing its residents for entry into the mainstream?

The dilemma of forging a constructive response to exclusion was heightened by the very real damage that such exclusion was causing inside the excluded communities, to individual community members and to the community as whole. As noted in the previous chapter, a variety of factors were conspiring to damage inner-city neighborhoods as communities. What was true of the public housing projects in an absolute sense was also becoming true of the neighborhoods surrounding them. The structures and ingredients of community—from mutual aid associations, to church social programs, to school-based activities, to small businesses—were gradually dissipating with the loss of the economic and tax base.

Informal social control and support systems were weakening. Youth not only ignored and avoided community elders but now mocked those elders' commitment to a society that did not reward them for their efforts. The local political machine, which historically had provided access to a share of public resources, practical assistance with problems, and an "interpretive link" to the new urban world for immigrants, no longer provided that function in many inner-city communities (Ohlin 1960:8). Neighborhood residents could not help but internalize in their outlook and behavior the social neglect, depredation, and disorganization of their community. The inherently fragile logic of local development, and later separate development, was weakened by the difficulty of pursuing such strategies in depleted communities.

The problems to which neighborhood initiative would be responding in the 1960s had become entangled in ways that made very different causal analyses valid, and a coherent, helpful program of local reform difficult. It is possible that neighborhood initiative in inner-city neighborhoods would have found a way to respond to the challenges it faced if it had been able to remain as it began the decade, a set of modest local enterprises. But neighborhood initiative in the 1960s was pulled into larger national events in a way that had never happened before. It was asked to bear the weight of a President's public commitment to eradicating poverty. It was asked also to bear the weight of addressing the accumulated consequences of Americans' chronic denial of the costs inherent in their choices most notably in their effort to maintain the color line at all costs (Anderson and Pickering 1986).

Between the Decades

Descriptions of the poverty-fighting initiatives of the 1960s often begin with the events of that decade, "as if American society emerged in 1964 from a state of nature" (Reed and Bond 1991:735). The 1960s themselves often appear to have sprung up out of the earth whole cloth. In reality the 1960s were more an intensification of than a departure from the previous decade. Unemployment and underemployment in the ghetto already had become impervious to broader economic conditions by the mid-1950s. Loss of local businesses in the inner-city began in the 1950s as well, stimulated by urban renewal and racial turnover. It then accelerated through the 1960s and 1970s (see Wacquant and Wilson 1989).

Urban renewal plans continued to flow from planners, consultants, and developers who did not bother to speak to the residents of the neighborhoods involved (in part because it was expected that those residents would still be living in the same neighborhood; Fainstein 1990:223). Most city governments, preoccupied with downtown decline and eroding tax bases, ignored the implications of changes taking place in poor neighborhoods, until something forced them to pay attention. The earliest visible expressions of frustration in the inner-city often came from youth. In Chicago and Oakland, for example, violent conflict between white and African American students in racially changing high schools forced city government to take stock of what was happening in the neighborhoods surrounding those high schools. In retrospect these small (though violent) disturbances, combining racial fears and anger and frustration over lack of economic opportunity, were precursors to the far larger ghetto riots of the mid-1960s. Immediately they focused attention on youth as both social barometers and a logical focus of reform efforts.

The Civil Rights movement "turned north" to find that de facto segregation was just as serious a problem as the de jure variety. In fact segregation in the North was in certain respects more insidious, because of the prevailing myth that it was not deliberate, rather a by-product of whites' efforts to protect their economic interests, something any group was entitled to do (Reed 1992:635). As it turned north the Civil Rights movement began raising expectations with respect to social reform in the northern ghettos. Its legalistic orientation made it better suited to address individual exclusion than community exclusion. Nonetheless, its constituent elements, particularly the NAACP and the Congress on Racial Equality, became involved in northern school integration efforts, efforts to pressure companies to hire more minorities, and, to an extent, general community organizing (sometimes competing with each other in the process.)

The Civil Rights movement provided a vehicle for urban African Americans to reveal both "the extent of their hurt" and their growing strength (Clark 1968:73). If whites could accept these feelings and realities, this presumably would provide a foundation for eliminating the ghetto. The movement also stimulated the renewal of nonviolent "direct action" to express demands. The tools of direct action—sit-ins, boycotts, rent strikes, marches, street demonstrations—were not totally new to the northern and midwestern cities. In the 1930s, to cite just one example, a group of women in Harlem called the Harlem Housewives League (supported by Marcus Garvey's Universal Negro Improvement Association) organized a boycott of chain stores that refused to hire African Americans (Greenberg 1992:403). Now they were used again to try to open up jobs to inner-city residents in local institutions such as banks and supermarkets, or to improve access to whole categories of jobs, such as the building trades. They were used also to protest segregated, deteriorating schools and housing, to block urban renewal plans made without neighborhood involvement, and to protest rent increases in deteriorated, rat-infested apartments (Kerner Commission 1968:109). For example, New York City experienced a wave of rent strikes in the winter of 1963–1964, in Harlem, the Lower East Side, and Brooklyn. Organizers "took out" some five hundred buildings, putting rent money in escrow accounts, and tried to force landlords to make repairs on deteriorated properties (Cloward and Piven 1972:xxx).

The emergence of direct action strategies coincided with a renewed interest in community development (Ohlin 1960), and contributed generally to optimism about neighborhood and community politics among professional reformers. Armed "with little more than Saul Alinsky's view of a world divided between `haves' and `have-nots,' they embraced a politics of local action convinced, as Alinsky was, that the community could overcome the malaise of the Eisenhower years and the sterility of the labor movement" (Katznelson 1981:193). Ghandian nonviolence combined with Alinsky's protest strategies appeared to be a potent mixture. In 1960 in the Woodlawn neighborhood of Chicago Nicholas von Hoffman, an Alinsky protégé, worked with three local ministers to turn The Woodlawn Organization (TWO) into a direct action machine (Silberman 1964:54–57). TWO investigated local merchants accused of price gouging and doctoring their produce scales, developed a business ethics code, and used a street demonstration of a thousand neighborhood residents to suggest that suspected merchants comply with the code. It organized rent strikes. It addressed overcrowding in local segregated schools by sending "truth squads" into nearby all-white schools to photograph half-empty classes, and then sent members to Board of Education meetings to get TWO demands on the agenda.

TWO also blocked a University of Chicago urban renewal plan, insisting that low-income housing be built on vacant land before any existing buildings were torn down. In reviewing the first four years of the TWO experience, Silberman (1964:58) concluded that while Woodlawn obviously "remains a slum . . . still largely sunk in poverty and crime . . . it is a slum with hope—one that is developing the means of raising itself `by its own bootstraps.'"

In a pattern that would be repeated throughout the decade, the enormous energy that went into local direct action efforts in the early 1960s usually had modest positive results—a few jobs, a promise of more funding for local schools, a more responsive bureaucracy, or modest improvements in an apartment building. In the New York City rent strikes noted above the main result for tenants was a number of evictions. Landlords had little interest in and often little financial ability to invest in their buildings. Schools and housing became no more, indeed perhaps less, integrated as the decade wore on. Moreover, the tendency to combine the objective of integration with other objectives, whether more jobs, services, or housing, caused whites to be more reluctant to support those other objectives. For example, the effort to use public housing as a mechanism to integrate the housing market contributed to the dramatic decline in construction of public housing in many cities (Cloward and Piven 1972:175).

By the middle of the decade it was becoming apparent to residents of inner-city neighborhoods that the modest effects of direct action only masked larger social trends and deeply rooted institutional practices. Immediate official responses to the riots in Watts and other cities ignored the accumulation of social and economic grievances that underpinned them, focusing instead on outsiders, professional agitators, and unruly migrants from the South, presumed to have organized and fueled them. (In fact without exception the riots in different cities were sparked by idiosyncratic incidents, and contrary to assumptions 75 percent of rioters were born in the North; Kerner Commission 1968:chap. 1, p. 74). Responses to the riots suggested to African Americans that whites simply had been waiting for an excuse to abandon their commitment to social reform. Looking back it seemed clear that the language of fear and division had been labeling African Americans as different from earlier migrants as soon as they arrived from the South (Whitman 1991b:117).

The realization that little had really changed in whites' attitudes toward African Americans was an important ingredient in the ascendance of more militant, separatist approaches to neighborhood improvement as the decade wore on.

Institutional Responses: From Outside and From Within

Two major neighborhood-based initiatives provided both prototypes and impetus for the major federal efforts to address poverty in the 1960s. The first, the Ford Foundation's Gray Areas program, was conceived in 1959, began operation in 1961, and by 1965 had spent $26.5 million in Boston, Oakland, New Haven, Philadelphia, and Washington, D.C. (Ford Foundation 1964, 1967). The second, Mobilization for Youth (MFY), originating at the Henry Street Settlement in New York, was launched in May 1962 with a ceremony in the White House Rose Garden. Focused on one neighborhood, Manhattan's Lower East Side, it had an initial three-year budget of $12.5 million, with funding coming from the National Institute of Mental Health and other federal agencies, the Ford Foundation, and the City of New York (Moynihan 1969:58).

Gray Areas

The Gray Areas program was conceived and managed by the Ford Foundation's Public Affairs division, and in particular by Paul Ylvisaker. Ylvisaker and colleagues were frustrated by the unresponsiveness of predominant social institutions, notably schools, social welfare bureaucracies, and municipal governments as a whole, to the support needs of growing numbers of minority migrants to the cities (Ford Foundation 1964). They recognized, albeit dimly, that there was growing anger in the inner-city about the process and fruits of urban renewal (Ylvisaker 1973:19, 23). Like others at the time, they were concerned about the growing potential for social disorder—in particular the potential for the chronic low-level violence of alienated inner-city youth to escalate. Such fears were captured by James Conant's description of unemployed African American youth as "social dynamite" (cited in Sherraden and Adamek 1984:933).

In the 1950s the Ford Foundation's strategy for addressing urban problems had focused on research and some technical assistance with administrative reform of metropolitan government and support for urban renewal efforts. This emphasis, like the institutions and officials it was targeting, virtually ignored the growing isolation and marginalization of inner-city neighborhoods. There is some evidence that Ylvisaker and colleagues were aware that racial discrimination was partly responsible for unemployment, poor schools, and related problems in the inner-city. But, as Ylvisaker relates in a 1973 interview, Milton Katz, one of his colleagues at Ford, warned him that race was "Verboten territory—the first time I'd heard anybody talk this explicitly. And he [Katz] said, we can't obviously deal with race, that's out, that's Verboten" (Ylvisaker 1973:20). The apparent prohibition against dealing directly with race was addressed by focusing instead on "place," the "gray areas" between central city and suburb. Discrimination and segregation as causes of urban African Americans' problems were by-passed by a causal analysis that focused on the very real stresses and dislocations caused by migration (O'Conner 1993:17).

Paul Ylvisaker's writings and speeches at the time suggest that he himself was ambivalent about the obstacles to assimilation facing inner-city residents, and about the causes of community decline. Ylvisaker and colleagues, like their Progressive-era predecessors, had no inclination to question the basic tenets of the social and economic system that had created and sustained the Ford Foundation. They believed that America's values, economic, and social system essentially were sound, and just periodically needed rebalancing (Aaron and Hahn 1991:3). They believed that different groups in society ultimately had the same interests but were frustrated by not knowing how to combine their energies in a constructive process. (The tendency to deny the reality of fundamental differences in interests among social classes, economic, and related groups, and the ways in which that tendency constrains problem solving, is explored in depth by Harrington 1986.) At the same time Ylvisaker implicitly acknowledged the validity and depth of inner-city grievances (Ylvisaker 1973:23). As communities gray areas were "a crushing burden on the people who live there and a burden of conscience as well as economic cost to the larger affluent society" (Ford Foundation 1967:4).

Paul Ylvisaker described urban society as a "benevolent anarchy" whose social institutions had become so bureaucratized that they had forgotten their purpose of mitigating the harshness of the marketplace (Marris and Rein 1973:52). But he also feared that simply encouraging these institutions to reform themselves by providing funding for innovation would not work. For one thing the money was likely to be used primarily to buffer the chronic budget crises experienced by urban school systems and other public bureaucracies (Ylvisaker 1973:24–25). Moreover, as a group services in poor neighborhoods were incoherent and too often at cross-purposes with each other: some trying to nurture poor people, some trying to control and punish them, some fostering independence and self-help, others fostering dependence on government. The possibility of genuine conflict of interests between the poor and dominant institutions was not considered in most analyses underlying Gray Areas. Such a consideration might have led Ford to a different explanation of the irrelevance and unresponsiveness of services to poor families and communities; for example, that the large education and social service bureaucracies were doing generally what they were supposed to be doing—serving the interests of those holding economic and political power (Marris and Rein 1973:45).

There was at the time a beginning recognition that for many residents inner-city neighborhoods were no longer stopping places on the way to the mainstream. Lloyd Ohlin, in a prophetic paper written in 1960 for the Ford Foundation, suggested that the key question facing Ford and others was "What types and patterns of institutional arrangements should be developed to meet both the assimilation and maintenance needs of residents in deprived urban areas most effectively?" (Ohlin 1960:4–5). This emergent line of thought suggested a dual emphasis on strengthening inner-city neighborhoods as communities where people made their lives and on creating and strengthening pathways out of the inner-city. The two emphases would be linked throughout the decade by the principle of guided self-help, or "resident participation in community affairs" (Ohlin 1960:5). The act or process of participation was envisioned to strengthen both the local community and the participant, and could serve as a new kind of route into the mainstream. When embodied in a larger "social movement" it also could create pressure for the accommodation of indigenous demands by mainstream institutions.

Ylvisaker and colleagues' analysis, combined with the ideological constraints of working within the Ford Foundation context, in fact yielded a program with a dual focus. The first objective of Gray Areas was "to speed the transition of the urban in-migrant and slum resident" from a person with inadequate education and work skills to one prepared to compete for jobs in the urban economy (Ford Foundation 1964:1). As interpreted by Ford Foundation staff and the local Gray Areas projects this objective would be achieved by by-passing "unprepared" adults, and focusing on their children and youth. The explanation for this interpretation does not appear in planning documents or subsequent reports. It may have been influenced by a growing focus in academic research on the intergenerational transmission of poverty. It may be derived also from the fact that Gray Areas grew in part out of an earlier education initiative called Great Cities Schools. The focus on youth was partly explained by the prevailing academic and policy interest in juvenile delinquency, a problem seen to encapsulate the range of negative forces at work in inner-city neighborhoods.

The other objective of Gray Areas was to strengthen the capacity and commitment of mainstream institutions that were supposed to be serving the inner-city, including schools, employment services, the police, and the criminal justice system (Cunningham 1970:253). The problems with prevailing services suggested the need for one coherent, comprehensive vision and plan for poor neighborhoods—not likely to be achieved by independently funding separate bureaucracies to deal with inner-city problems—and for one neutral (and ideally new) local institution that, through the lure of modest funds and good intentions, could bring all the institutions and constituencies in a neighborhood together to act in concert. Thus was reborn the neighborhood coordinating agency for addressing poverty, in a more difficult context than earlier reincarnations because of the greater complexity in the human service system, and a much greater social distance between that system and its clients. As originally envisioned the Gray Areas program did not include an emphasis on resident participation in shaping and defining the program as a whole or specific services. Within a few years Gray Areas' omission of both a clear conceptualization of the purposes of resident participation (e.g., individual improvement, leadership development, community organization) and specific means for residents of poor communities to exert the social and political pressure envisioned by Ohlin in his background paper would create problems in all five communities funded by Ford.

In each city a private nonprofit corporation was formed to be the primary vehicle through which the Gray Areas grant was channeled. This agency would avoid the trap of becoming just another agency fighting for its prerogatives "by repudiating any claim to permanence or direct control" (Marris and Rein 1973:284). It was responsible for developing a plan for the target neighborhood (or neighborhoods), with input from city government, the schools, social agencies, and neighborhood leaders. It was then to use that plan, combined with a core of Ford Foundation money, to leverage financial commitments from other public and private, local and national agencies. For example, most of the Gray Areas programs secured some to considerable federal funding from the Department of Labor (for youth employment and training) and/or the President's Council on Juvenile Delinquency (to be described later).

The five Gray Areas projects selected for funding were among a larger group that had already been involved in Ford's urban school reform initiative. Ford Foundation staff went out to prospective cities, brought political leaders, community leaders, and public bureaucracy heads together, and asked, "What would you do if you had money to work on these problems [i.e., the problems of urban minorities and inadequacies of prevailing institutions designed to serve them]?" (Ylvisaker 1973:27). The question seemed intended primarily to stimulate contact and dialogue among various constituencies in each city rather than to encourage locally rooted strategies. Under Ford's guidance the central focus of all the projects would be nudged toward innovative education programs (including preschool), recreation, youth development, and youth employment programs. Each local program nonetheless developed differently, had a distinct set of corollary emphases, and yielded somewhat distinct lessons.

The New Haven Gray Areas project, under the auspices of Community Progress Inc. (CPI), was perhaps the best known and most widely publicized of the Gray Areas programs. It emerged, as would Boston's program, from a locally perceived necessity to develop services to complement urban renewal. A Ford Foundation review (1967:13) quotes former mayor Richard Lee as recalling that "as relocation workers interviewed tenants to prepare for moving them, they discovered awesome depths of disease and disability, sullenness and hostility, ignorance and aimlessness. The physical relocation of these inner-city dwellers merely relocated their problems." (This view in fact was similar to the prevailing view within the Ford Foundation that inner-city residents and their communities were inert and passive.) Mayor Lee tried with little success to encourage private social welfare agencies to respond to the human problems being uncovered by urban renewal (Murphy 1971:23). So Howard Hallman, who worked for New Haven's redevelopment authority, pieced together a proposal to Ford from various discrete reform ideas floating around locally and nationally. Presumably the leverage of Ford Foundation funding would help induce the local human service community, including the schools, to be more responsive to New Haven's poor families and communities.

After a number of rounds of negotiation with Ford, funding was approved, and a nonprofit corporation, Community Progress Inc. (CPI) was established to manage the program. Mitchell Sviridoff, a local labor leader and former president of the Board of Education, with close ties to Mayor Lee as well as to a variety of national organizations including the Ford Foundation, was hired to be the director. Sviridoff was strongly committed to local institutional reform, but wary of both the local school and social welfare leadership and of the potential for any reform initiative to become politicized by the leaders of New Haven's minority communities. Perhaps for these reasons his leadership team consisted of a small, tightly knit group of reform-minded professionals (Powledge 1970).

In 1962 CPI obtained a $2.5 million grant from Ford to develop programs in seven of New Haven's poorest neighborhoods, with a population of about ninety thousand people. Within five years some ten times that amount would be attracted from other sources, principally through the federal government's delinquency and manpower programs, and later through the community action program of the War on Poverty (Ford Foundation 1967:14). None of the specific programs proposed by CPI was new. The innovation was in reinventing them as a collectivity, and at a time when they desperately needed to be reinvented.

Among the components of the New Haven program were preschool education, remedial reading, combined education and job training for youth, lay teacher aides, home school coordinators, after-school programs, summer camping, and neighborhood libraries. A Helping Teacher program used experienced master teachers to provide support and guidance to their peers, including curricular ideas, help in figuring out how to work with children with special needs, and with families (Marris and Rein 1973:60). One school in each of the seven neighborhoods was turned into a community school, hosting an array of educational, recreational, cultural, and caregiving activities open to all community residents till late in the evening. Activities included play groups for young children and their mothers, lounges for teens, dance classes, and adult education. Local health and welfare agencies put staff in the schools part time, as did legal services (Ford Foundation 1967:15).

CPI established neighborhood service teams to serve as a two-way information bridge between CPI and neighborhood residents, and to try to stimulate self-help activities. It established neighborhood employment centers to refer youth and young adults to job training programs and, when possible, actual jobs. It started a skill center for training in job skills identified by local employers as relevant to their needs. It also developed a program of paid community work experience for older teens, who worked in crews on various public works and community service jobs around the city. Foremen for each crew were picked from among slightly older community residents with relevant work experience. Sviridoff used his labor and business connections to try to get more minorities into union apprenticeship programs and to try to convince local employers to hire those enrolled in the various CPI employment and training activities. He had modest success in both these endeavors.

Community Progress Inc.'s closely held approach to proposal development carried over into the management of the program. CPI's leadership tried to create a constituency-free basis for addressing persistent problems in New Haven, one rooted instead in expertise and innovative service strategies. This is exactly what Progressive reformers had tried but failed to accomplish decades earlier in a much less bureaucratic and mistrustful social context. Seymour Sarason, a Yale professor actively involved in local institutional reform, noted that CPI's leadership team viewed the local schools, social service and health departments as partly responsible for the problems in New Haven's inner-city neighborhoods, and therefore excluded their leadership from policy setting in the Gray Areas program (Sarason 1978:838). CPI's directors also seemed not to have faith in poor people themselves. Howard Hallman, by then CPI's deputy director, wrote that "for the vast majority of the poor, poverty is a disability that precludes meaningful participation in planning" (Hallman mimeo cited in Murphy 1971:50). CPI's concern with New Haven's inner-city community was described by Murphy, a participant observer

in the initiative, as "largely anticipatory and defensive, a strategic posture rooted in the fear that the antipoverty project would become
embroiled" in the politics and emotions of inner-city grievances and fail
to accomplish its purpose (Murphy 1971:119).

Sviridoff's executive-centered management approach eventually
became a target of growing inner-city anger, even though there were far
more justifiable targets for such anger. Sviridoff's particular nemesis was
the Hill Neighborhood Union, a militant group whose demands for participation in program governance he viewed as an opportunistic power
play rather than an expression of community interest. Nonetheless by 1964
Ford Foundation staff were warning each other and Sviridoff that New
Haven's Gray Areas program seemed cast more in the mode of doing for
than doing with poor people. (CPI formed a Resident Advisory Committee
in 1965, but by then the agency had lost control of the processes of neighborhood renewal in a number of target neighborhoods.) In part due to
its resistance to community participation in program governance, CPI's
efforts became linked in the minds of the community's minority leadership to New Haven's urban renewal program, whose public image had
begun deteriorating locally, if not yet nationally. One report at the time
noted that "black leaders in New Haven indicate that they doubt that white
people in any of our cities have been as kind to black people." At the
same time, that kindness did not include providing blacks key roles in
redevelopment planning and management (Wright 1968:73).

William Ryan, a psychologist recently arrived in New Haven, and
involved in a citizen's group trying to address living conditions in poor
communities, noted an "Alice-in-Wonderland" quality to local urban
renewal and poverty-fighting efforts (cited in Powledge 1970:189). The
optimistic rhetoric of city officials and professional reformers associated with CPI bore little resemblance to what could be easily observed by
anyone spending even a modest amount of time in poor neighborhoods.
But negative assessments of CPI's helpfulness seemed due more to the
larger climate of anger and disillusionment in the African American
community than to concrete evidence of lack of accomplishments on the
part of CPI. Indeed, in spite of the expenditure of millions of dollars, and
the presence of dozens of new educational and social services, community
leaders in the target neighborhoods "frequently maintained that nothing
had been done" (Powledge 1970:282). Conditions were in fact actually

worsening during the 1960s in most of the neighborhoods targeted by CPI, in terms of employment, housing, and residents' sense of alienation and exclusion.

CPI and its staff actually were squeezed from many sides. Although CPI's efforts to improve the education of poor children involved innovations largely at the margin of the school system, indeed innovations such as preschool education that eventually would make classroom teachers' work easier, such efforts nonetheless implied that prevailing practice and attitudes were inadequate. As such they were met with suspicion and resistance, particularly at the classroom level. Individual schools and their staff did buy into CPI's vision of teachers reaching harder to understand the lives and situation of poor minority children, of schools as linchpins of community renewal and self-help. But the overall quality of inner-city education changed little. The modest pattern of effects from what seemed to be a considerable investment were very sobering for CPI's leaders, who just a few years earlier had been touting the program as "a pioneering effort, aiming at kind of a comprehensive social plan that has never before been prepared" (Murphy 1971:68).

The other four Gray Areas projects experienced a variety of difficulties getting started, although two of the four evolved into viable initiatives. Oakland's project grew out of the efforts of the police chief to bring some coherence to public agency responses to escalating gang violence and the broader problems of juvenile delinquency, particularly in the neighborhood surrounding Castlemont High School. At a preliminary stage he pulled together staff from the police, the schools, recreation, probation, and public health to share information on "potential trouble spots," and begin discussing ways of reducing conflict. That itself proved helpful:

The police began to change their views of probation officers as "a bunch of bleeding hearts." Probation people, sitting across the table from police, had to stop thinking of them as "skull-cracking cops." Recreation officials no longer thought dogmatically, "If I had hold of that kid first, he wouldn't have gotten into trouble." (FORD FOUNDATION 1967:7)

Discussion among these agencies also made clear that just preventing gang conflict from flaring up was not enough. Efforts had to be made to address the social conditions underlying the conflict, including alienation from the process of schooling and lack of economic opportunity. The

Castlemont High neighborhood, with a population of seventy thousand, was truly a "Gray Area." It was in transition from a predominantly white to an ethnically diverse neighborhood. It was not the poorest area of Oakland, but it contained a growing percentage of struggling and vulnerable families. Together with the local Urban League and the Council of Social Agencies, the city formed the Oakland Interagency Project. A proposal was prepared outlining a number of "action programs" by different city and county departments and the two private groups, with delinquency prevention as a kind of thematic emphasis. The Ford Foundation made a $2 million grant to the city of Oakland in 1961.

The project started to unravel practically as soon as it was funded. What had been presented to Ford as one project was really little more than a collection of independent proposals from entities that had made no commitment to giving up any of their autonomy to a common enterprise. Oakland's city manager, who was coordinating the proposal development effort, had not been able to work through the relationships of the various parts to each other, or to the whole, or to clarify where authority lay (Marris and Rein 1973:129). Conflict emerged, especially between public and private agencies, and evolved into a power struggle over project leadership. Public departments also yielded little ground to each other. Although a coherent project with interrelated pieces never emerged, interagency and interdepartmental conflict eventually subsided, allowing for concentration on substantive activities for children and youth. These included Youth Study Centers in the schools, where younger children and youth were given homework help by older peer tutors as well as adult volunteers, an innovative educational and social support program for teen mothers that helped them continue their school careers, and a variety of other education and training programs similar to those in New Haven.

Like the New Haven program, the Boston Gray Areas program grew in part out of concern by the mayor and his urban renewal administrator that the human side of urban renewal could no longer be neglected. The urban renewal administrator, Edward Logue, had helped the Ford Foundation shape the Gray Areas program, and was also deeply committed to urban renewal as a social reform strategy. He created a new agency, called Action for Boston Community Development (ABCD), to plan and coordinate efforts in neighborhoods designated for renewal. The program began in September 1962 with a $1.9 million grant from the Ford

Foundation. The Ford grant was soon supplemented by funding from the President's Council on Juvenile Delinquency, the Department of Labor, and other sources.

As originally envisioned ABCD was to employ a network of community organizers who would work with and through community-based social service agencies, particularly settlements, to develop a neighborhood renewal plan. As in other cities the Boston Gray Areas project proposed a variety of educational innovations, youth employment activities, legal services, and delinquency prevention activities. The specific programs stimulated by ABCD generally had modest success. Inadequate involvement of school-level staff in planning and preparing school-based innovations contributed to a good deal of resistance to proposed educational programs. The various innovations were perceived as new requirements thrust upon local schools by outsiders. As in New Haven, the Youth Employment Centers attracted and enrolled hundreds of young men and women, but did not have much to offer them in the way of job opportunities (Marris and Rein 1973:71). As a result they concentrated on general job preparation activities and referral to other training programs.

Action for Boston Community Development (indeed Boston's project as a whole) also struggled to find an identity linked to but distinct from its various constituencies. Edward Logue was determined that the project would be rooted in and integrated with Boston's urban renewal program. But ABCD's community organizers quickly came to identify with the strong resistance to urban renewal in most target neighborhoods, and in many cases were responsible for organizing their community against Logue's own plans. The settlements and other community-based social service agencies, which had been losing hold of their changing neighborhoods for decades, saw the Gray Areas program as an opportunity for self-renewal, and tried to place themselves at the heart of the program. When ABCD had trouble fielding its own planning and organizing staff in some neighborhoods, it turned to these agencies to do so, further strengthening their hand in the project. The local social service agency networks in fact became the core of the Boston project, and ABCD itself would evolve into a large social service agency under the community action program.

In discussing the Gray Areas experience Paul Ylvisaker (1973:28) noted that "we had that beautiful running time of two or three years . . . when the world wanted to solve the problems, when the Ford Foundation was golden, when Kennedy was in office and you could talk about the experimental programs that would go into governmental programs." By 1964 the ideas underlying Gray Areas, and to some extent the projects themselves, were in fact becoming absorbed into the emergent federal War on Poverty. Many of the innovative educational, health, social, and legal services funded by the federal government in the 1960s first emerged or reemerged in Gray Areas. The War on Poverty's community action program adopted the Ford Foundation's objective of trying to bring established bureaucratic institutions together to work in a common reform project. It also adopted the idea of creating a new agency to shape and coordinate neighborhood-based poverty alleviation efforts.

In contrast, the actual experience of the Gray Areas projects was hardly attended to in planning the federal antipoverty effort (perhaps because this experience was ongoing, thus too close to be analyzed and digested.) Marris and Rein (1973:209) argue that those shaping the War on Poverty took the assumptions and strategies of the Gray Areas program for granted. Yet many of these assumptions and strategies already were proving problematic in practice. Even the more successful Gray Areas projects were experiencing a variety fundamental and practical tensions: between means and ends (they made a virtue of necessity, doing what they could rather than what they had to do), between their professed neutrality and their commitment to alleviating poverty and inequality, and between their desire to maintain control over the reform process and their commitment to community initiative. The promise of new resources in resource-scarce contexts did not lead as hoped to new forms of collaboration. Rather it heightened wariness and competition among human service providers and between providers and neighborhood groups. The difficulties the Gray Areas coordinating agencies experienced in establishing legitimacy and exerting influence demonstrated the enormous power of public bureaucracies to resist idealistic appeals to their better nature (even appeals accompanied by funds) and the limitations of a neutral stance in addressing problems of inequality and exclusion. The projects' difficulties also signaled the end of a long era of acquiescence among inner-city neighborhoods to externally initiated reform and illustrated the growing social distance between the inner-city poor and the larger society surrounding them.

Katznelson (1989:202) notes that the experts shaping the War on Poverty "sought to enhance economic opportunity at the interface of structure and behavior." They were interested in making a basically sound opportunity system work the way it was supposed to, and in making sure people had the capacity to take advantage of available opportunity. In this formulation the War on Poverty planners surely were influenced by Paul Ylvisaker and others involved with Gray Areas. The Ford Foundation's effort to respond to the growing marginalization of the inner city and its residents was timely and prescient. Nonetheless its limited causal analyses and localized focus helped set all the causal analyses and interventions that were to follow in too limited a framework. As early as 1964 there was evidence that enriched human services could play only a modest role in altering people's life situation and prospects, and that the roots of many of the problems addressed by the Gray Areas projects were located outside the target neighborhoods—in a receding labor market, an eroding tax base for urban schools, housing policies that intensified ghetto isolation, and an historic pattern of racial discrimination that was not abating.

Mobilization for Youth

Mobilization for Youth (MFY) was a second initiative that had a key formative influence on the War on Poverty. It was initiated in 1962 and funded by the National Institute of Mental Health, the President's Council on Juvenile Delinquency, the Ford Foundation's Youth Program, and local foundations. Mobilization for Youth emerged from discussions among the board and staff of the Henry Street Settlement in New York about about how best to address the Lower East Side's growing gang problems. Helen Hall, Henry Street's director at the time, writes that the initial conception was to attack the multiple causes of delinquency by saturating the whole Lower East Side "with services enough to change its living conditions" (Hall 1971:272). Six settlement houses on the Lower East Side were to play a key role guiding the initiative and organizing neighborhood residents to help themselves. A proposal was submitted to the National Institute of Mental Health, the federal agency concerned with delinquency, which responded that it was not coherent and theoretically rooted enough, and needed a stronger research design.

Lloyd Ohlin and Richard Cloward of the Columbia University School of Social Work, who had already been involved as consultants, took on the role of preparing a revised proposal, drawing on their recently articulated theory of delinquency (Cloward and Ohlin 1960). Reacting in part to the abuse of psychoanalytic theory in prevailing formulations of delinquency, they argued that delinquent behavior such as stealing and gang affiliation was caused by exclusion from opportunity to employ socially approved means (education, part-time jobs, participation in organized extracurricular activities) to strive for and achieve socially approved goals. Lack of conventional opportunity alienated inner-city youth from societal norms and pushed them to adopt the norms of the street and the gang. The implication was that "we [society] must provide the social and psychological resources that make conformity possible" (revised Mobilization for Youth proposal, cited in Moynihan 1969:55).

The $12 million program that emerged in 1961 after four years of planning embodied many of the same assumptions and component activities as the Gray Area projects, with an added focus on street-corner social work and involvement of community adults reminiscent of the Chicago Area Project. The role of the settlements was downplayed and a new organization (i.e., Mobilization for Youth) was created to play a mediating role, bringing all parts of the community together in a common endeavor. One key focus, in the education domain, was to encourage teachers to become more sensitive and responsive to the needs and situation of the children they taught, and at the same time to develop more positive expectations of those children. The rationale for getting community adults involved in various project activities was to turn them into positive role models for youth and to increase their identification with the community and the larger social order. This in turn would encourage adults to reassert social control over their children and community life in general.

Within a year or two predilection and experience working with schools, other public bureaucracies, and landlords were leading MFY's directors and staff to redefine program assumptions, purposes, and strategies. Efforts to encourage curricular reforms, more outreach to families (including home visiting by teachers), and more sensitivity to individual children's strengths and vulnerabilities consistently met with resistance and occasionally "with near-hysterical resistance" (Marris and Rein 1973:49). Seemingly modest suggestions and requests yielded disproportionate turmoil. For example, MFY staff organized a group of Puerto

Rican mothers to present discrete requests to the principal of their children's school: scheduling parent-teacher conferences at times convenient for parents, providing books for children to take home, and so forth. The principal refused to meet with the parents until forced to by escalating pressure (Marris and Rein 1973:67). The meeting that finally took place was angry and worsened the situation. The mothers' group subsequently tried to get the principal fired. Other principals in the neighborhood responded in turn, demanding that George Brager, one of MFY's directors, be fired. In a telegram to Mayor Robert Wagner the principals argued that MFY's community workers were "becoming full-time paid agitators and organizers for extremist groups." The MFY program had become subverted "from its original plan to war against delinquency into a war against individual schools and their leaders, to what purpose we cannot at the present time divine" (telegram cited in Moynihan 1969:115).

Much the same dynamic occurred in many MFY social service activities. A storefront neighborhood service center on Stanton Street, initially conceived as an information, referral, and counseling center, quickly became a locus of organizing against the practices of the city welfare department. The bulk of the problems brought to the center by neighborhood residents involved their welfare grants (which included housing, food, utilities, clothing, and other allowances). The staff at the Stanton Street Center at first tried to act in a mediating role, sorting out whatever misunderstanding or miscommunication presumably was leading to specific problems with families' grants. They soon found (or at least felt) that this approach got them nowhere with the welfare office. Their own growing anger led in turn to a growing identification with the grievances of neighborhood residents, and a change in role from mediation to advocacy. The primary "force of such advocacy was in serving notice upon the low-level [welfare agency] employee that he would be held responsible for his actions to his supervisor and on up the line (Cloward and Elman 1973:122). One Stanton Street worker noted that "when I go to Welfare I don't wait around for the stall. If I don't get treated with respect I start hollering for the supervisor" (Cloward and Elman 1973:124). At the same time the Stanton Street staff reported becoming increasingly impatient with neighborhood residents themselves, "who had transferred some of their previous dependency on welfare to the storefront on Stanton Street" (Cloward and Elman 1973:129).

Already implicit in Cloward and Ohlin's delinquency theory was the idea that modest educational reforms and youth employment programs would not change the basic structure of educational and economic opportunity for marginal youth. Early program experience suggested to MFY staff that the problem they were dealing with was not benignly bureaucratic agencies and apathetic poor people but powerlessness in the face of deliberate efforts to exclude (Moynihan 1969:108). The practices of public bureaucracies seemed deliberately designed to further weaken poor people, and even to divide them from each other. (Gilbert [1970:4] writes that "dependency and fragmentation are reinforced through the use of isolative benefits," through the control of information, and by encouraging poor people to relate to the bureaucracy.) By implication MFY could not sustain its role as a neutral institution, mediating among different constituencies, trying to find common interests. Its community organizing efforts shifted from encouragement and persuasion to confrontation. Such confrontation eventually included rent strikes, protests in the offices of city officials, and legal action against the welfare department and the police.

Most of MFY's funds went into conventional services—preschool programs, after-school programs, youth employment, and training. Nonetheless MFY's early history of confrontation with public bureaucracies created a climate of anger and distrust. Further, in trying to mobilize neighborhood residents against prevailing social institutions, MFY staff did not pay enough attention to, or simply never figured out how to factor in, families' existing relationships with and dependence on those institutions. Poor families' lives were "woven into the fabric of community life"; however unsatisfactory families' relationships with schools, police, landlords, and social agencies may have been, those relationships did exist, and were critical to families (Hall 1971:274). MFY staff also did not consider the possibility that the insensitivity, indifference, and occasional punitiveness they were observing in frontline educators and welfare workers was primarily defensive, not so much a deliberate effort to control poor children and families as insecurity, frustration, and anger with impossible mandates and difficult working conditions. If teachers projected that anger onto their students, principals onto parents, and welfare workers onto their clients, then that was something that had to be recognized and addressed by MFY. For their part the leadership of public agencies spent far more energy being angry with and attacking MFY than they ever had attacking rent-gouging slumlords or trying to respond to the modest requests of community residents.

Helen Hall (1971:274) writes that the most important innovation of MFY was that "it broke the back of `littleness' in locally rooted efforts to address poverty-related problems. Mobilization for Youth was the first neighborhood initiative of that era to encourage minority residents of an inner-city neighborhood to define the initiative's agenda. It expanded the idea of community-based work for neighborhood residents beyond such limited roles as teacher aides, most notably creating paid jobs for neighborhood residents as organizers. Many of the men and women originally trained by MFY would go on to play key roles in the larger community control initiatives of the late 1960s as well as in specific battles over housing, neighborhood renewal, and so forth.

Mobilization for Youth was in some respects very different than the Gray Areas projects. It was more activist and confrontational in its efforts to bring about institutional change in schools, welfare departments, and housing authorities. It focused more fully on leadership development within the target community. Yet, as in Gray Areas, there was a tension in the MFY initiative between means and ends, and between the local focus and the external roots of problems being addressed. For example, there was not much the initiative could do to assure jobs for neighborhood youth (Currie 1993:5). Making the neighborhood the frame for an effort to address poverty and injustice complicated discrete issues that were already difficult enough to sort through—for example high rates of school failure among neighborhood children and youth—by loading them with social and political freight. Each issue seemed to evoke, and therefore came to stand for, all the problems of life on the Lower East Side. Discrete issues were in fact interconnected, and an important message from MFY was that a critical mass of issues has to be addressed in neighborhood initiative. For example children's school difficulties often stemmed from the interaction of worries and vulnerabilities brought to school from home, lack of effort or sensitivity on the part of schools themselves, budgetary strains, and absence of a social environment that gave meaning to trying hard in school. In some respects it was the balance—in focus, stance, scope of objectives—that proved so difficult to achieve in MFY, especially with strong emotions buffeting the whole initiative.

Community Action and the War on Poverty

Today for the first time in the history of the human race a great nation is able to make and is willing to make a commitment to eradicating poverty among its people.

—LYNDON JOHNSON, *on the signing of the Economic Opportunity Act, August 20, 1964*

Miller and Rein (1973) note that many of our social reform movements are stories of the compromises that have to be made to mobilize support for reform in the U.S. context. The War on Poverty, in which a structural analysis of poverty by senior government officials, focusing on unequal access to jobs, was converted into a primarily service-based reform initiative, was certainly one such story (Katz 1989:91). The conversion was driven by the enormous financial costs and political constraints to a major public sector job creation program. It was made to seem feasible by the availability of prototypes for a neighborhood-based strategy— that is, the Gray Areas programs, Mobilization for Youth, and the programs of the President's Council on Juvenile Delinquency. It was validated by a conviction among key Office of Economic Opportunity (OEO) planners that the neighborhood truly was the best place to tackle poverty and its correlates.

It has frequently been noted that the War on Poverty was one of the few great national programs that did not arise from public pressure or demand (see Moynihan 1969, Sundquist 1969). That view is not completely accurate. Poverty and inequality certainly were not major public issues. Nonetheless there was a growing undercurrent of public anxiety about what was happening in the cities, a prophetic fear of the "bursting of bounds—of segregation, deference, demarcated space" (Katznelson 1981:4), a feeling that simply "restating our individual and collective purposes" in a more convincing form was not going to suffice in the face of urban problems (Kenniston 1960:428). There was also a growing self-awareness of political powerlessness among African Americans. The Civil Rights movement had tapped into growing anger when it moved into the northern ghettos. The conditions in the ghettos also directed Civil Rights leaders' attention to poverty-related issues such as unemployment and job discrimination. By late 1963 and early 1964 both Civil Rights leaders and an emerging group of indigenous community leaders were beginning to channel the anger they found into the new political tools of direct action and protest focused on jobs, school conditions, and other social issues.

President Johnson was made aware by economic advisors that economic growth was likely to have little impact on unemployment and inadequate wages within the inner city and in marginal rural areas (Katz 1989:91). Yet along with many of those recruited to plan the War on Poverty he failed to perceive or perhaps to acknowledge the economic and social trends that had been undermining the urban economy for decades. He believed that poverty and inequality were transitory; that the obstacles to escaping poverty were located at the margins of and even outside the economy (Blum 1991:170). Sanford Kravitz, one of the planners, describes the thinking in OEO at the time (Kravitz and Kolodner 1969:33):

Any set of proposed solutions to the central problem of poverty must deal with the individual problems that are faced by the poor in their own communities—problems that are beyond the provision of direct financial assistance and beyond the provision of employment through the usual marketplace.

As in the Gray Areas program, OEO planners were preoccupied with institutional breakdown, particularly among institutions such as state and local governments and schools that were supposed to diffuse opportunity (Marris and Rein 1973:1). They were concerned with the lack of coordination among existing agencies serving the poor. Not least they believed in the symbolic if not actual power of collective community action, and at the same time believed that poor people lacked the will and organizational capacity to use this power to help themselves (Katz 1989:99).

As laid out in the Economic Opportunity Act of 1964, the War on Poverty had two major objectives: enhancing opportunity and preparing poor children, youth, and to a lesser extent adults to take advantage of new opportunities. In addition the War on Poverty was designed to be fought primarily within the boundaries of low-income communities themselves, and within a conceptual framework called community action. A new institution, the community action agency (CAA), was created to embody the federal government's assumptions, intentions, and specific programs. Preparing children and youth to take advantage of new opportunities was the job of a variety of specific service programs funded under the Economic Opportunity Act. There services were viewed loosely as a package, and by a few within OEO as the first coherent program to address poverty in the nation's history. (The discrete service programs of the War on Poverty are discussed in chapter 6).

Community action agencies served as the fiscal agent for (although usually did not directly administer) two types of programs: local initiative and national emphasis programs. The former, which received about 40 percent of community action funds, could include almost anything in the areas of neighborhood services, education, health, manpower, housing, social services, and economic development. National emphasis programs, which received about 50 percent of community action funds, included Head Start, Upward Bound, community health centers, family planning, and legal aid, among others. (The Job Corps and Neighborhood Youth Corps programs were administered by the Department of Labor, programs under Title I of the Elementary and Secondary Education Act by the Office of Education in Health, Education, and Welfare). Community action agencies directly administered only 20 percent of the programs funded under their auspices, "delegating" the rest to other agencies and organizations (Rose 1972:131)

Although 90 percent of community action funds went to direct services, at its heart the program was still conceived as part institutional reform and part community empowerment. The community action agency would provide a structure for poor communities to mobilize their own resources on behalf of their residents and a platform for giving poor people more of a voice in the bureaucratic institutions that shaped their lives. These two objectives would be accomplished through two strategies. First, established institutions and the newly created OEO service programs would come together in a reform coalition that would adopt a common, locally formulated strategy for improving community members' well-being. Second, community members would take a significant role in determining the priorities, resource deployment, and activities of the local "War on Poverty." This latter, reminiscent of MFY, was referred to as the principle of maximum feasible participation.

Maximum feasible participation was a broad idea that resonated strongly with basic American beliefs. Those beliefs hold that problems are best addressed by the people themselves rather than by government, by local citizens putting aside their narrow interests and coming together to determine the common good (Morone 1990:5). Moreover the process of participation in civic affairs itself can transform people and social issues—"private into public, conflict into cooperation, bondage into citizenship" (Morone 1990:5). At the same time participation is a relatively broad and ill-defined term. There were few extant models for citizen governance of civic affairs other than New England town meetings. Especially within the framework of isolated and depleted urban neighborhoods and massive public bureaucracies it was not clear what participation should and could mean. It probably was intended to mean advisement by community residents in local planning and decision-making coalitions, some role in administration of local OEO programs, and employment of neighborhood residents in helping roles vis-à-vis their neighbors and peers. There was an assumption that participation was inherently good for poor people themselves, for public and private social welfare institutions, and for society. It would improve poor people's mental health by countering their sense of alienation, it would increase mainstream institutions' cultural and neighborhood sensitivity, and it would strengthen democracy. It certainly was not viewed in the early OEO discussions (at least explicitly) as a vehicle that poor people and their self-appointed representatives would use to grasp political power, to attack government agencies, and even to try to create separate, self-governing local communities. But that is what it became.

The great majority of CAAs funded in 1964 through 1966 were private, nongovernmental agencies. Their authority and leverage in the community consisted of control over the grants for some of the new OEO direct service programs, and the influence embodied in their boards, which were supposed to include representatives of different segments of the community. The CAA boards, as well as their general organizational structure, quickly became one locus of efforts to clarify (and in effect control) the meaning of participation, and thereby the federal funds that flowed through the CAA. From the perspective of community action administrators in Washington the composition of local boards was intended to reflect the elements and interests that they believed made up poor neighborhoods: "the local principal, the minister, the settlement house director, the head of the tenant's union, the articulate welfare mother, the bright ex-convict who is a neighborhood leader" (Wofford 1969:101). Thus composed, boards were supposed to agree upon local community action priorities. Nonetheless regional community action administrators, mayors, major human service bureaucracies, private social service providers, Civil Rights groups, local religious leaders, independent community leaders, and local CAA directors each had their own view of the selection procedures, composition, and role of the board.

Between late 1964 and 1967 there were ongoing struggles over board composition and representation. Since local city halls and major human service providers were responsible for establishing 80 percent of CAAs (Rose 1972:131), they were in a strong position initially to assert control, which they usually did. According to Berry, Portney, and Thomson (1993:27), this was not what Congress had intended. They argue that contrary to conventional wisdom Congress was not ambivalent in its intentions regarding maximum feasible participation. They note that a year after the initial legislation was passed the House Labor and Public Welfare Committee "chided [OEO] for not going far enough" in its interpretation of participation, and directed OEO to make sure that participation of the poor extended to "all levels and stages of planning and administration." In its 1966 ammendments to the Economic Opportunity Act, Congress passed legislation requiring that one-third of each CAA board be made up of representatives of the poor.

Nonetheless as more neighborhood representatives joined CAA boards it became clear that a personal history of hardship and exploitation did not incline a person to be community-minded, in fact often the opposite was true. Community residents on CAA boards also did not necessarily represent the most disenfranchised segments of a community. Indeed they often represented a fairly narrow set of interests, notably that of family, friends, and allies. Moynihan (1969:138) argues that "patronage, which was the source of stability in the original ethnic neighborhood political organization, became a source of instability in the contrived organization created to fill the gap left by the real thing." Lack of clarity about the purpose of community action boards complicated struggles over representation and provided an entrée for abuse by board members.

Civil rights organizations and a growing group of black power advocates also fought for places on CAA boards. They viewed the financial and organizational resources provided by community action as a potential base of political power for African Americans. Both white political leaders and the federal community action administrators were ambivalent about the more explicitly racial and political vision of the community action program. On the one hand community action was one of the few available vehicles for absorbing and containing minority militancy. It could serve to institutionalize minority demands "as a constituent component of the urban political regime" (Greenstone and Peterson 1973:7). In this way the fundamental challenge of black militants—that U.S. society live up to its ideals—could be transformed, and made to fit the traditional rules and boundaries of urban politics, which emphasized different groups (with basically equal claims) negotiating for their share of goods and services (Katznelson 1981:2, 177). On the other hand it was feared that opening the community action program to increasingly militant minority leaders could lead to a complete loss of control over the program by Washington, and the use of the program to attack prevailing social institutions.

For a brief period CAA boards, as well as the larger agencies themselves, did get opened up to minority political interests. By 1966 Congress and national and regional community action administrators were already backing away from that opening and attempting to regain control. Representative Edith Green of Oregon proposed an amendment to the federal authorizing legislation for community action that put its funding under the authority of state or local government. In the debate over the amendment Representative Sam Gibbons of Florida noted that he did not think "you should turn over the whole War on Poverty to the poor any more than you should turn the hospitals over to the sick" (Altshuler 1970:111). Other critics of the way participation was evolving argued that "what the poor need are jobs, not organizing into trouble-making groups" (Cahn and Cahn 1971:16). By 1966 and 1967 struggles over control were shifting to other institutions, particularly the education system. Moreover the racial and political meanings of community control were becoming smothered by a general movement to decentralize services (Katznelson 1981:177).

OEO direct service programs under the community action umbrella—including Head Start, neighborhood service centers, and community health centers—also struggled with the meaning of participation, in particular the role of neighborhood residents in goal setting, governance, and service provision. Since these programs also had specific substantive objectives such as improved child development or improved maternal and child health, the struggles were in part about identity. Was the touchstone for decision making quality of child health or development services, creating new careers for adults, greater voice for consumers of services, mobilizing community residents to address community problems, or community control of services? Were these different objectives inherently linked or inherently contradictory under the prevailing conditions of most inner-city neighborhoods? Such struggles also reflected the ambivalence about the causes and most appropriate responses to poverty embedded in the basic design of the War on Poverty. Not least such struggles reflected the practical problem of having to do so much, of trying to fulfill so many social functions too quickly.

In Head Start there was conflict from the outset about the most appropriate roles for parents and community representatives. Head Start was motivated in part by presumptions of community residents' inadequacy as parents. This presumption clashed with an alternative view of parents as the group that knew their children and community best, and the group with the most at stake, therefore a group that should play a key role in staff selection, financial management, and even curricular design. Still a third view held that Head Start was as much a community development as a child development program. As such it should serve as a base for organizing parents to act on community problems (Valentine and Stark 1979:308). Early Head Start experience, notably resistance to parent governance from professionals (especially in the Head Start programs run by the schools), confusion and disorder in the daily lives of some parent-governed programs (see Payne, Mercer, Payne, and Davison 1973:part 1) also shaped evolving views of participation. By the late 1960s Head Start administration in Washington had settled on three meanings for parent participation: parent education, participation as volunteers as paid aides, and advisement in policy setting.

In the case of neighborhood service centers lack of clarity of mandate contributed to difficulty in creating a useful framework for participation. Neighborhood service centers initially were envisioned in part as a vehicle for neighborhood residents to reshape the larger human service environment. Residents would implicitly define the problems with prevailing services and create a reform agenda through their particular requests for assistance. They also would have a voice by assuming board and staff positions. This initial vision was constrained by a host of social, economic, and institutional realities. Neighborhood service centers had little leverage for shaping either other providers' policies and practices or basic social conditions in their neighborhoods. Defining key neighborhood service problems did not induce other providers to alter their existing approaches. When neighborhood residents said that what they needed was jobs or better housing there was little the neighborhood service center staff could do about such requests. It proved difficult to find neighborhood residents with the energy and focus to play active, consistent roles on center boards. Over time, rather than shaping the external social and institutional environment, most neighborhood service centers found themselves increasingly shaped by that environment to behave in ways that resembled prevailing institutions: foregoing outreach both to the community and to other service providers, worrying about caseloads, restricting eligibility, specializing in particular kinds of counseling, and so forth (Perlman 1975).

In all the OEO programs there was little effort to prepare community residents for decision making and governance roles. For example many community action agencies that operated across a number of neighborhoods tried to create structures for the expression of neighborhood interests. These efforts had mixed success, and often were constrained by lack of support for and guidance of those who assumed leadership roles. Trenton's CAA developed three autonomous neighborhood councils, outside the agency, which were intended to propose and even run local programs and to provide an organized voice for neighborhood residents. It was even envisioned that these local councils would pressure the CAA itself to respond to neighborhood concerns. According to the CAA director, "It didn't work." The councils' elected officers had little understanding of their responsibilities, seemed "unwilling to pursue" specific programmatic ideas, and some seemed not to trust the community residents they were supposed to be representing. The CAA director noted that it was a trying experience "to be locked into a system of community participation that gave formal recognition to a few self-seeking persons as the official spokesmen for and representatives of the poor" (Farrell 1969:146–147)

At some point most CAAs resolved organizational issues, and moved on to face equally difficult questions about purpose, role, authority, and legitimacy in the local community. One putative task of the CAAs was coordination of the general poverty-fighting effort in a community. OEO, like the Ford Foundation before it, assumed that a new agency, starting fresh and free of existing antagonisms, would be in the best position to bring different institutions together in common purpose. In this they were hampered not only by relatively limited resources but by the fact that they were a new, externally created institution. For example, the CAAs were never really able to gain a role in community economic development, an indigenous movement that was becoming a principal engine of development in inner-city communities. (The reasons for this are not clear in the historical record.) The CAAs struggled particularly with issues of authority and role in the area of human service coordination and reform.

As private agencies CAAs had no authority, and only such legitimacy as resided in their boards, to take the lead in coordinating community services, especially publicly funded ones such as schools, public aid, public health, and housing. With respect to reform there was a tendency to try to have it both ways—to ask established institutions to work with them and simultaneously to pressure them to reform. Community action agencies often found themselves organizing community residents to demand reform of schools, welfare departments, and housing authorities—the very institutions they were simultaneously trying to work with collaboratively to develop a community plan for fighting poverty. In some cases the attempt to embrace both cooperation and confrontation proved untenable. A particular incident or event, for example a putative wrong done to a community, denied by an established agency, or differing interpretations of a problematic school or housing situation, forced a community action agency to decide who its constituency was and whose interests it represented.

Over time most community action agencies settled on a cooperative rather than confrontational stance, scaled down their ambitions, and began seeking a defensible niche in their communities. In this they were helped along by the Office of Economic Opportunity, which, responding to the lack of clarity in CAA purposes and to growing pressure from established urban power holders for OEO to reign in the handful of militant CAAs, began seeking greater control over CAA activities. It did so by earmarking an increasing proportion of community action funds for the so-called national emphasis programs. This converted many CAAs primarily into delegate agencies and grantees for human service programs, with guidelines that left little room for local discretion. In these new roles community action agencies increasingly dealt with City Hall and its various departments "through bureaucratic channels rather than through citizen action" (Fainstein 1990:226).

The Results of Community Action

Community action was a small program, relative to the total body of Great Society legislation (which included Social Security reforms, Medicare, Medicaid, and Food Stamps), and even in the context of the War on Poverty programs of the Office of Economic Opportunity. The principal strategies in that war, and the principal routes out of poverty envisioned for inner-city children and youth, were education and preparation for employment, supported by social services. But community action also evoked and eventually became entangled in the basic social issues facing U.S. society in the 1960s. Those issues had to do with the distribution of economic progress and political power, the persistence of racial discrimination in housing and jobs, and the continued viability of American ideals.

On its own terms community action had a modest positive influence on the lives of poor families and the conditions of inner-city life. It provided resources for a host of new neighborhood based services and supports for helping families cope with poverty-related hardships. Although there often was not much to decide about, the participation requirement in community action programs established the principle of poor people's right and ability to decide in matters concerning their own and their community's life. By affording community residents an opportunity to assume key staff and advisory roles in its programs, community action created a modest number of jobs and planted the seed for the eventual emergence of a black municipal bureaucracy in many cities. Community action brought people together who would not normally have come together, leading to dialogue, new relationships, and occasionally to coalition building.

Community action created or fostered scores of new local affiliations and organizations—single-issue coalitions, tenant organizations, legal services, public interest law firms, various rights organizations. These organizations did what they could to improve community life, gave poor people critical support in coping with poverty-related stresses, and a voice in at least some of the issues shaping their lives. Thus in East Harlem's Puerto Rican community a group of residents (calling itself the "Real Great Society") built vest pocket parks out of vacant lots, with homemade playground equipment for children (Cahn and Cahn 1971:18). The new organizations came to play a critical role in securing and protecting the rights of poor children and families against the unchecked discretion of the human service service and public assistance bureaucracies. In the South Bronx welfare recipients organized to pressure the welfare department to release money for winter clothes that they were entitled to but had never received (Cahn and Cahn 1971:21). Neighborhood organizations in scores of poor neighborhoods helped block urban renewal plans that had been developed with little attention to their effects on the lives of the people involved.

The accumulation of small achievements in community action was no small thing to those affected. At the same time it was fragile. Many individual and community effects dissipated or fell apart before they could become consolidated. Organizing and other self-help efforts were undermined by lack of support from both municipal authorities and OEO itself. Macler Shepherd describes the results of one such effort in an inner-city neighborhood in St. Louis (Tax 1967:426):

We found ourselves with absentee landlords, absentee representatives, absentee school teachers, and others coming in eight hours a day to tell us what was good for us. We decided that the only way to get help was to help ourselves, and we became an organization called Nineteenth Ward Improvement Organization. The political powers got scared at first. . . . Then they decided we were only a small group and that there was no need to worry about us.

When residents of poor communities finally began to take the federal government up on its offer, and attempted to set local priorities, the federal government began backing away from its commitments to them. The first director of Trenton, New Jersey's community action program recalls going to the regional OEO office to negotiate for the funding of two clear, hard-won community priorities—community schools and reading programs—and being told that these were not OEO priorities. He responded, "The hell it isn't. . . . Who does the OEO think it is to tell us what our priorities are?" (Farrell 1969:133). When the poor in a particular neighborhood managed to achieve a tactical victory on a key local issue, or even wrest control of the community action program from established interests, they received little support from OEO in building on such achievement to develop a constructive program of local action. The large public bureaucracies found little resistance from OEO in their persistent efforts to transform community action's focus on institutional change and client rights to a focus on individual rehabilitation (Rose 1972:148).

It proved more difficult than expected in most instances to build, or even to locate, the common good around which to pull together diverse segments of local communities, let alone to foster support from outside those communities. The representatives of institutions rooted outside disenfranchised communities and people from inside rarely were willing to take the risks necessary to gain each others' trust. Those who came to the negotiating table already controlling decisions, access, and resources often remained unconvinced of the wisdom of relinquishing prerogatives or resources to those who claimed they represented disenfranchised community members. Clearly there was a strong measure of self-interest in their reluctance. But there also were questions about whether the representatives of the powerless really had the common interests of the community in mind. Those who came to the table to fight for the interests of neighborhood residents also often came with a good deal of mistrust regarding the intentions of established interests. The mistrust was often enforced by ensuing events.

Most important of all, community action was unable to articulate reasons for and had little leverage to attract private investment back into inner-city communities. It faced an inherent dilemma in its strategic focus within the boundaries of poor neighborhoods themselves. By the 1960s "conditions for indigenous local organization [in poor neighborhoods] were far less propitious than they had been at the turn of the century" (Polsky 1991:174). There were thinner informal and formal social networks, less community structure, fewer locally rooted institutions; services were more bureaucratically entrenched. There were few jobs, other than those created by community action itself, to contend for. The new institutions and forms of participation fostered by community action were minorities' only path into the mainstream, an exceedingly narrow path. (Even some of these institutions and sources of participation "were set aside after they had deflected the black movement from its radical, holistic, and redistributive possibilities"; Katznelson 1981:186). While often helpful to individual families and communities, the discrete benefits and reforms associated with community action programs were pushing against social and economic forces far more powerful they were. This problem is captured by Jerome Carlin, a leading figure in San Fransisco's legal aid program, who noted that "we undoubtedly brought some solace and relief to many individual tenants by delaying an eviction or forcing a landlord to make some repairs. Nevertheless in those same three years the housing situation in San Fransisco became a great deal worse" (Carlin 1973:146).

Model Cities

The various forms and expressions of local mobilization in inner-city communities in the mid-1960s never became unified into a national movement. But "they were sufficiently threatening or persuasive to precipitate a [new] national urban policy" (Fainstein 1987:328). That policy was embodied initially in Model Cities, the first program of the new federal Department of Housing and Urban Development (HUD). Model Cities was to be implemented through the very political structures—city governments—that community action had been designed to by-pass. It brought reform strategy full circle, back to the assumptions and objectives of Gray Areas. Model Cities was intended to strengthen local governments' commitment and ability to rehabilitate inner-city neighborhoods through careful professional planning, coordination of federal and local programs, concentration of resources, and innovation. Model Cities was to be community development decoupled from community action, or more specifically from community action's presumed tendency to engender conflict and disaffection (see Lemann 1991:198).

Nonetheless the social and political climate for neighborhood-based initiative was profoundly different than it had been just a few years earlier. Inner-city residents and black Civil Rights leaders were disillusioned by the inability of any reform strategy—use of the courts, nonviolent direct action, or a federally declared War on Poverty—to compel white America to respond to their exclusion. There was a growing sense of unfulfilled promises and betrayal within the inner city. The experiences of urban renewal and community action had confirmed inner-city residents' doubts about whites rather than their hopes. They had learned that public and private resources for poor communities "come with a price tag that virtually never leaves local goals unchanged" (Perry 1985:16). Municipal authorities and public bureaucracies often acted as grudging rather than wholehearted partners. Playing by the rules, even when those rules seemed to evolve from month to month, did not pay off.

While the demands and grievances of minorities were channeled into the new institutions and participatory structures of the War on Poverty, the underlying social issues were not so easily contained. Not being local they "exploded the community boundaries" (Katznelson 1981:115), engulfed the cities, and negated what little remained of a sense of social progress. Ghetto riots occurred every summer from 1963 through 1968, peaking in 1967 (Kerner Commission 1968:65). Although the trail of racial injuries leading to the riots stretched back over three hundred years, most were precipitated by specific (often minor) incidents involving the police, who had become the immediate object of the diffuse anger and tension filling the air in many communities. (For a description of precipitating events in a number of cities see Kerner Commission 1968, chapter 1. Reading the report, one gets impression that local authorities had no idea how to respond to the anger being expressed, particularly by youth—no thoughts, no words or gestures—except to "meet force with force," as the mayor of Newark put it.)

The ghetto riots of the 1960s were at the time and continue to be interpreted in very different ways. A few saw a conspiracy, or at least a deliberate provocation by a small number of trained agitators, in the riots. President Johnson reportedly told David Ginsburg, the executive direc tor of the Kerner Commission, that "it was simply not possible to have so many outbreaks at the same time without someone orchestrating it" (Lemann 1991:190). The conspiracy theory was easily refuted by the idiosyncratic patterns of the riots (Kerner Commission 1968:67–74). Indirectly it was also refuted by the choice of targets. Mimicking the inward focus of community action, community residents turned their anger and frustration inward, focusing on whatever physical symbols of the larger society they could find as well as the few remaining local signs of economic and social life. When necessary, the police made sure that rioters' destruction was limited to their own already seriously injured communities.

A few, like Fox (1986:138), argued that violence had long played an important role in shaping the social and political structure of cities. Viewing the 1960s riots within that historical framework, Fox argued that they represented a purposeful effort to command respect, to alter the urban social structure. Nonetheless, Janowitz (1969:327) points out that no leadership emerged from the riots to express specific political demands. Many viewed the riots as spontaneous, or simply as one more cry for help for some form of racial justice. Clark (1965:17) argued that "the masses of Negroes do not `choose' tactics at all. They respond to the pressures of their lives and react spontaneously to incidents which trigger explosions or demonstrations." One woman noted after the 1965 Watts riots that "the only way we can get anyone to listen is to start a riot" (Haar 1975:9).

The riots did momentarily draw the federal government's renewed attention. After Watts, funding for the local community action program was increased and discussions in Washington about new urban programs picked up. But by then such gestures were interpreted as an attempt to buy off the black community. In 1967 President Johnson appointed a National Commission on Civil Disorders to investigate the causes of the riots. There was widespread expectation that the commission would locate those causes in the ghetto itself, in the "tangled pathologies" of ghetto life (Anderson and Pickering 1986:372). Instead the commission report looked outward, finding "that white society is deeply implicated in the ghetto" (Kerner Commission 1968:1). Still, for many white Americans, including some in Congress, the principal effect of the riots was to provide an excuse "to re-categorize poor blacks as undeserving, since they rioted in spite of new programs and passage of civil rights legislation" (Gans 1991:301). One of the tragedies of the riots was that corporations that had been planning to relocate a small portion of operations to the ghetto put those plans on hold, ostensibly until things settled down (Janowitz 1969:328).

The ghetto riots led to a modest debate on the meaning of inner-city poverty in Senate hearings on the proposed Model Cities legislation. On one side were those such as Attorney General Nicholas Katzenbach, who noted in a hearing on August 17, 1966, that "the riots were indeed fomented by agitators—agitators named disease and despair, joblessness and hopelessness, [and] rat-infested housing" (Haar 1975:80).

Katzenbach's view was echoed by Senator Mike Mansfield, who noted at a later hearing that disrespect for law was "symptomatic of a society that does not live up to its responsibilities" (Haar 1975:83). On the other side were a number of senators, especially southern senators, who believed that inner-city residents had no one to blame but themselves. The substantive result of the Senate hearings on Model Cities was a watered down program, unlikely to achieve HUD's objectives, even if circumstances had been more positive.

The original vision for Model Cities was for a heavily funded demonstration program in a small number of cities. Some of the funding would be new appropriations, the rest money redirected from other urban renewal programs. Model Cities not only was to provide for a concerted, coherent social service effort but for construction of racially and economically integrated housing that would help keep upwardly mobile blacks and whites tied to central city neighborhoods. The housing component of Model Cities was viewed as an important symbol of commitment to rebuild inner-city neighborhoods and an opportunity to redefine urban renewal. The legislation that was passed was weakened in both these areas. In response to pressure to spread program resources more widely, a small number of cities quickly became 75 cities, and within two years had become 150. (During that same period initial funding of about $500 million was reduced to about $300 million.) Senator John Sparkman of Alabama, chairman of the Housing Committee, insisted that provisions in the proposed legislation requiring local Model Cities projects to promote residential integration be dropped (Lemann 1989:56).

The focus of the Model Cities program was targeted, or "model" inner-city neighborhoods with populations of about fifty thousand residents. Cities interested in a Model Cities grant had to develop an elaborate plan, which included most or all existing human service agencies and programs serving the target neighborhood. The plan was to be developed by a newly created body called a City Demonstration Agency (CDA), composed of elected officials, representatives of major agencies (e.g., schools, housing authorities, health, welfare, employment), labor, and business leaders. The CDA was under the authority of the elected city council and the mayor, who had veto power over any plans developed. Funding for planning, and later for the program itself, flowed through local government.

In many respects Model Cities was set up to minimize rather than foster the participation of neighborhood residents in program planning and
governance. The guidelines developed by HUD interpreted the citizen
participation requirements in the legislation to mean only that neighborhood residents have an advisory role in the proposal development and
decision-making process (Warren 1969:246). In most cities plans were
prepared by City Hall before neighborhood residents could mobilize,
indeed before they were aware that a new program was being planned.
Nonetheless when they did learn of program plans many inner-city
neighborhoods were both disposed, because of their experiences with
community action, and already organized to react quickly to their exclusion from the planning process. When they did react they discovered that
they were able to tie up planning or program monies from HUD to a particular city, in turn providing further impetus for them to demand a role
in the program (Warren 1969:248).

In Philadelphia, to cite one example, community organizations from
the target neighborhood formed a coalition, the Area Wide Council
(AWC) that insisted on partnership with City Hall in approving the planning proposal and administering the planning grant to the city. The
coalition threatened to send a delegation to Washington if the mayor did
not include wording in the Model Cities proposal guaranteeing residents' "authority to determine basic goals and policies" of Philadelphia's
program (Arnstein 1972:380). The mayor agreed to a partnership, and
the AWC managed to forge what it thought was a good working relationship with the city in preparing the full proposal. That relationship
apparently existed only in AWC's eyes, and the city, with HUD's blessing, had little difficulty completely isolating the AWC from the funded
Model Cities program. In New Haven, rather than isolating the key
neighborhood organization from the program, the mayor decided to
isolate the program itself, thereby isolating those who wanted to control
it. When the Hill Neighborhood Union, Paul Ylvisaker's nemesis, heard
that the mayor and his colleagues were developing a planning grant proposal, they created an alternative planning structure and process (the Hill
Ad Hoc Model Cities Steering Committee) to act as a foil for the formal
process (Powledge 1970:288). The existence of the ad hoc committee
undermined the self-proclaimed legitimacy of the mayor's planning
group and blocked the flow of planning money from Washington. Rather

than joining in partnership with an organization that he in turn viewed as illegitimate, the mayor created the Hill Neighborhood Corporation to administer the program, with eleven of twenty-one board members from the target neighborhoods. (The corporation soon undid itself through poor fiscal and program management). Similar struggles over control of the program occurred in Boston, Detroit, Newark, and Oakland. In a few cities groups representing neighborhood residents turned to the courts to enforce citizen participation requirements.

Model Cities also ran into a variety of obstacles in its goal of becoming a vehicle for service innovation and coordination. The content of the Model Cities service strategy was shaped by established bureaucracies, who had little difficulty assuring that the local "problem" would be defined in a way that allowed them to continue operating much as they had been. Most cities "learned how to appear to be coordinating" (Gardner 1989:7), but almost none was able to seriously reduce the fragmentation and cross-purposes that characterized local service systems. Neither the leverage nor in many cases the political will existed to accomplish this aim. Model Cities did help give coherence to various HUD-funded efforts, which included the fourteen-city neighborhood center pilot program, designed to build on community action's neighborhood service center idea (March 1968). But local Model Cities leadership secured little or no cooperation even from other federal programs (Haar 1975:167). Community action agencies had little role in the program, either in governance or service provision. (Ironically in some cities they were rejected by neighborhood residents as vehicles for representing neighborhood interests on the grounds that they had "made their peace with city hall" [Warren 1969:249]).

Finally, Model Cities was only modestly successful as an effort to redefine urban renewal. In late 1966 Ralph Taylor, an assistant secretary of HUD, outlined what an alternative conceptualization of urban renewal might yield:

new techniques for . . . rehabilitation, experimental approaches to urban taxation, new building systems and materials and construction techniques, flexible building codes and trade practices, a new urban design which can revitalize a slum neighborhood without tearing it down. (Warren 1969:246)

This vision was not accompanied by a strategy for reforming the local

politics of urban renewal. Nonprofit housing and community development agencies that attempted to take advantage of HUD's interest found
little support from local urban renewal boards and commissions, which
still tended to be controlled by large real estate and construction interests and to be susceptible to pressure from wealthy neighborhoods.
Ideas such as scatter site housing and building code reform rarely made
it through local legislative and regulatory processes.

By 1969 President Nixon declared the urban crisis over, and converted the unsolved social problems embodied in that crisis into a problem of
law and order. Model Cities survived a few more years, but it was already
off the Nixon administration's social policy agenda. From inner-city residents' perspective the fate of Model Cities, if it mattered, was a kind of final
betrayal. It reconfirmed inner-city neighborhoods' marginality and, unlike
community action, left few helpful neighborhood programs in its wake.

Conclusions

The neighborhood-based initiatives of the 1960s were both shaped by
and themselves shaped the larger social movements of the era: the federal War on Poverty, the Civil Rights movement, and not least the growing sense of militancy among ghetto residents themselves. They were
shaped equally by social trends that had begun long before that decade,
notably residential abandonment of the inner-city by whites, the narrow
economic logic of moving manufacturing to the suburbs, and the resulting fiscal pressures on city governments that led to disinvestment through
budget cuts. From the perspective of the early 1960s there was a strong
appeal to the idea of renewing deteriorating neighborhoods and simultaneously opening up routes into the mainstream for the residents of those
neighborhoods. Nonetheless locating the urban strategies of the War on
Poverty almost exclusively in isolated and depleted neighborhoods was
a fatally flawed strategy, particularly in that time and place.

The locally and internally oriented strategies of community action and
Model Cities served in a modest way to further isolate and weaken the
already fragile ties between the residents of those neighborhoods and the
larger society, just the opposite of what was intended. The strong neighborhood focus fragmented both issues and the social movements underlying them into "community-sized components, thus separating com-

munity from community" (Katznelson 1981:180). To most residents of poor urban neighborhoods the participatory structures and processes created by community action yielded relatively little compared both to the promises made and the turmoil engendered. Within a few years of its initiation community action came to be identified, rightly or wrongly, with a larger social movement that repudiated mainstream society, and demanded a degree of local political hegemony that had never been demanded before. This allowed its modest aspirations and programs to become isolated and tainted, and therefore to be dismissed by a larger society all too ready to dismiss them. (The subsequent inability of community health centers, the Women, Infant and Children's (WIC) food program, and to a lesser extent Head Start to secure more than a modest proportion of the funds needed to serve those eligible may be related to their association with a tainted community action program.)

The federal government was not alone in its inability to forge a response to the situation in American's inner cities. Like the government, the Civil Rights movement did not have the means—even though it had the will—to address the already profound isolation of ghetto neighborhoods. As Anderson and Pickering (1986:371) argue, at the same time that the efforts of the Civil Rights movement were culminating in the passage of the 1964 Civil Rights Act and the 1965 Voting Rights Act the movement was becoming bogged down in the northern and midwestern ghettos. Mobilizing ghetto residents to fight for better schools or housing, or even more jobs among the businesses that remained in the cities, did not seem to get to the heart of the matter in the northern ghettos. At issue in poor minority neighborhoods in the 1960s was not simply an equitable share of the "divisible benefits of patronage and services" (Katznelson 1981:121) but questions of social and geographic exclusion and loss of economic roles. It proved enormously difficult in the cities to define and implement a vision of "life beyond the color line" (Anderson and Pickering 1986:376).

Finally inner-city residents themselves were driven to raise and struggle with issues of economic disinvestment, housing and job discrimination, educational neglect, punitive and arbitrary social welfare policy, and political disenfranchisement at the neighborhood level, for they had no other place to do so. Within poor neighborhoods the only readily available targets of anger and frustration were public bureaucracies, which in some ways had become a local substitute for the private economy. As Paul Ylvisaker of the Ford Foundation argued, these bureaucracies certainly were not playing the buffering and equalizing role that society had given them. The schools in particular were proving not to be the path out of the ghetto that the American myth had promised them to be. In some respects the schools and other public agencies were just as much victims of larger social and economic trends as were the neighborhoods in which they were situated. They were not the enemy, who anyway was difficult to define, but they were present in people's lives every day and therefore became a proxy for that enemy.

CHAPTER FOUR

COMMUNITY ECONOMIC DEVELOPMENT

Of all the neighborhood-based poverty-fighting strategies that have evolved in the United States, community economic development is the most direct and powerful. It is one of the few that was not imposed on poor neighborhoods but grew out of their own efforts to define their needs, control their fate, and create viable local communities. Community economic development, as embodied in community development corporations (CDCs), also has proven to be a relatively flexible and enduring strategy, adapting to changing public policies, and learning from its mistakes. At the same time though in most respects more productive than urban renewal, community action, and other neighborhood-based strategies, community economic development has been constrained by many of the same factors as these others. It has been able to attract investment capital back to inner-city neighborhoods, and to demonstrate how investment can address social as well as individual needs. It turned the problems of community neglect and racial exclusion inside out, and sought to make something constructive out of them. Yet it could not finally solve the riddle of how neighborhood initiative might undo the pervasive effects of these problems. As such its effects on the well-being of inner-city neighborhoods and the lives of their residents has been relatively modest (Carlson and Martinez 1988:292).

Underpinnings of Community Economic Development

The idea of community economic development has roots in nineteenth-century utopian and communitarian thought and in the efforts of early twentieth-century black leaders to find constructive responses to housing and employment discrimination. Nineteenth-century communitarian thinking already reflected the tensions of community-oriented development in poor communities. It tried to return the community to the center of economic life, and to link economic activity to such social objectives as fraternity and civic participation. At the same time this thinking was not so benign when it came to the poor. Robert Owen, following Charles Booth in England, suggested that the unemployable poor be placed in separate communities, given an initial capital grant and some training, and then be required to create their own local economy (see Himmelfarb 1991).

Within the black community there have long been separatist impulses. During the nineteenth century a small number of black leaders argued for a separate black state, either in Texas or Oklahoma (Alvarez 1971: 172). Booker T. Washington argued that neither whites nor blacks were ready for integration. In the interim he promoted black self-help and mutual assistance: "Let us in the future spend less time talking about the part of the city that we cannot live in, and more time making the part of the city that we live in beautiful and attractive" (cited in Philpot 1978: 209). Marcus Garvey's black nationalism in its own way also represented an effort to find a constructive response to exclusion. While Garvey's ultimate aim was the migration of African Americans back to Africa, he argued that in the interim they had to create their own self-sufficient communities, independent of white society. As Spear (1967:91) notes of

Chicago's early twentieth-century black leaders, they "chose" to create a separate, self-contained community—what he calls the institutional ghetto—in large part because they had no choice.

The specific strategy of community economic development reemerged in the mid-1960s out of a growing conviction among a subsequent generation of inner-city community leaders that the economic renewal of their communities was of little concern to the private sector or to government (Perry 1987). Black community leaders were beginning to see the goal of integration as a chimera, and the American ideals of social and geographic mobility and equal opportunity as irretrievably corrupted. The struggle to achieve integration in housing, schooling, and other domains not only had met great resistance, but had undermined other goals. For example, blacks' struggle to assure that public housing was located in white as well as black neighborhoods "had virtually halted the construction of public housing in many cities" (Cloward and Piven 1972:175). Inner-city neighborhoods increasingly were seen by their own residents as "economic backwaters," left behind and left out (Carlson and Martinez 1988:1). They no longer were even a battleground on which the traditional agencies of socialization, such as the schools and settlements, fought to link neighborhood residents to the larger society. Community economic development thus served at first as a concrete expression of renewed interest in an old idea in the African American community, that of separate development. This idea had many connotations, including the repudiation of integration as a social objective, an insistence on local control of as many social institutions as possible, an emphasis on self-reliance, and an affirmation of black identity. In a number of communities community economic development was also motivated by an immediate concern that the anger being expressed in urban riots—as often turned inward as outward—had to be redirected into constructive activity if inner-city communities were to survive.

As in earlier periods, separate development had different meanings to different people. To some in inner-city communities it was viewed as an end in itself. Strong communities would communicate self-reliance, strengthen their residents' pride of place and thereby their pride in themselves, and create a kind of parallel opportunity structure as well. To others separate development was viewed more strategically, as a necessary step in a circuitous journey toward inclusion. The idea was that poor

minority communities first had to be made stronger so they could negotiate entrance into the mainstream from a position of strength. Paths and
links to the mainstream had to be redeveloped. Echoing Booker T.
Washington, some in the black separatist movement also argued that
poor black families were unprepared economically and psychologically to live in white neighborhoods (Carlson and Martinez 1988:19). Some
viewed separate development as the most politically realistic expedient—
the most likely approach to securing modest gains in living conditions
in the ghetto without generating white opposition (see Cloward and
Piven 1972:188). Regardless of motive and intent there was no alternative to an effort by community members to take the economic and social
redevelopment of their communities into their own hands.

The problem was that while a strategy of separate development was
compelling, it seemed to avoid issues such as redlining by banks and insurance companies, loss of thousands of manufacturing jobs, outmigration
of middle-class blacks, and the resulting spatial concentration of poor
minorities with few skills. Inner-city neighborhoods were "financially strip-
mined . . . cash and profits exported, and only the debts left behind . . .
some debts visible in abandoned property, others invisible in the deterioration of institutional resources" (Perry 1987:145). Just as poor urban
neighborhoods were discovering the energizing effects of self-help, they
were losing the last of the resources needed to undergird self-help efforts.
Inner-city neighborhoods also lacked governance mechanisms to become
complete miniature social systems and a coherent set of positive norms
and beliefs to substitute for those of the larger society, however corrupt
the norms and beliefs of the latter might be. Moreover, to build a separate "community" within the larger one meant encouraging community
residents' primary identification with that community. Many inner-city
residents had by then come to view their own communities in a negative light, in part for good reason, in part because those communities had
been neglected and demeaned for so long by the larger society. The context of scarcity, and the difficulty of succeeding in that context, decreased
the likelihood that successful individuals would feel they had the luxury to invest the fruits of their success back in the community. Finally, as
some black leaders argued at the time, separatism played into the hands
of conservative whites. It was just what they wanted, and it mirrored their
own arguments that blacks were different (see Funnye and Shiffman

1972). As Whitney Young, Jr., argued, "All that comes from segregation is more segregation" (1972:214).

The renewed black separatist movement fueling early CDC development and other forms of local mobilization in the late 1960s and early 1970s eventually foundered on all these basic constraints as well as the destructive, exhausting effects of constant internal turmoil. Community economic development was one of the few impulses of this movement that would survive, in part by reinventing itself to seem responsive to the radically different social currents of the 1970s and then the 1980s. For example the CDCs proved adaptable to the Nixon administration's efforts to deemphasize the community and focus on individual entrepreneurs, "black capitalists," then to President Carter's neighborhood self-help and community development block grants, then to President Reagan's privatization. The CDCs drew on and incorporated the many positive and constructive messages and assumptions of the black separatist movement, reinterpreting them when necessary in socially sanctioned terms. For example, they argued that even the most excluded and depleted local communities were nonetheless communities, with a variety of resources that should be valued and viewed as potentially productive assets.

Community Development Corporations

Community development corporations, the principle vehicle for community economic development, were invented almost simultaneously in a number of cities in the latter half of the 1960s. Almost all the early CDCs were locally created, community-owned institutions. As a community activist involved with one CDC noted: "We will make plenty of mistakes on our own. We don't need anyone else to make them for us anymore" (Perry 1987:74). Some CDCs emerged from coalitions of local organizations that had been formed for other purposes, often as protest organizations. For example, The Woodlawn Organization (TWO) in Chicago, mentioned in the previous chapter, was first formed in 1959 as a federation of some one hundred community groups with a focus on fighting landlord-tenant battles, school deterioration, and corrupt merchants. By the end of the 1960s it had opened a supermarket, rehabilitated a number of brownstones, and developed a five hundred-unit apartment complex (Pearce and Steinbach 1987:21). In Philadelphia the Reverend Leon Sullivan originally formed an organization to boycott firms that refused to hire black youth who had been trained by his church. Eventually this organization would be transformed into the Opportunities Industrialization Center (OIC), a renowned CDC that trained and placed large numbers of minority workers as well as running its own manufacturing enterprises. Some CDCs emerged as a direct response to local riots. Newark's New Community Corporation emerged from an effort to find a constructive response to the despair and anger mobilized in the wake of Martin Luther King's assassination. A few, like Cleveland's Hough Area Development Corporation, emerged from long-standing local planning structures that had lost their energy but were reenergized by the idea of the community taking its fate into its own hands. In almost all cases sheer frustration, and a loss of patience with external institutions, played an important role in bringing community leaders and residents together to try to discover their own solutions to community problems. Put differently, while the CDCs emerged as a reaction to redlining, neglect, or encroachment, their agendas were not reactive, rather creative and positive.

The Office of Economic Opportunity became involved in the CDC movement in the late 1960s, through its responsibility for Title I-D of the Economic Opportunity Act, the Special Impact Program (SIP). This program, sponsored by Senators Jacob Javits and Robert Kennedy, was designed to spur business development in the inner city as well as to support local infrastructure renewal. The OEO had tried to pass this responsibility to the Department of Labor, but Senators Javits and Kennedy pressed the agency to take it back. Senator Kennedy was particularly committed to the idea of community economic development, having been both moved by a visit to the devastated Bedford-Stuyvesant community in early 1966 and "challenged by local black leaders to do something substantive about their problems" (Carlson and Martinez 1988:3). In 1972 Congress reauthorized and strengthened Title VII of the Economic Opportunity Act, creating community economic development as a separate program and making CDCs prime sponsors of various urban redevelopment programs. In 1975, with the demise of OEO, the new Community Services Administration took over the federal CDC program.

Between 1968 and 1974 the federal government spent $106 million on community economic development, a very small sum relative to the total need. A few CDCs received relatively large grants. For example the Bedford Stuyvesant Restoration Corporation received $33 million in federal funds during that period. The remaining thirty or so CDCs supported by the federal government received between $1 and $3 million (Kelly 1977). From the beginning of its involvement the federal government tried to assert control over CDC investment decisions, partly in reaction to the history of community action, partly due to a distrust of black separatist impulses. This meant that investment decisions often had to be approved by the government. In 1974 a "venture autonomy system" was introduced, permitting federally funded CDCs to make autonomous decisions for at least some investments (Kelly 1977:4). Federal funding for CDC activity remained at about $35 million per year until 1977, when it was increased to $47 million by the Carter administration. In the late 1960s the Ford Foundation became involved in supporting the development of CDCs, under the direction of Mitchell Sviridoff, who was then Ford's vice president for National Affairs. By the mid-1970s the Ford Foundation had become heavily involved in supporting CDC activity, weighing in with contributions that almost equalled those of the federal government.

The First Generation

The hundred fifty or so CDCs initiated in the 1960s and early 1970s tended to focus on the development and in many cases the management of large and small commercial projects, industrial parks (i.e., the physical infrastructure for business enterprises), or small to medium size manufacturing operations. CDCs developed shopping centers, for example developing a business plan, packaging financing, selecting, and developing the site, finding anchor tenants, and securing site improvements from the city (Pearce and Steinbach 1987). They financed small retail businesses such as dry cleaners, laundromats, food stores, and janitorial services. They financed small businesses designed to improve community living standards, such as dental and health clinics and child care centers. They set up factories that made everything from rail spikes to plastic and rubber molds to minority dolls to electronics assemblies. They ran job training programs. They made loans to, took equity stakes in, or purchased local businesses that otherwise would have closed down (Carlson and Martinez 1988, Faux 1971). Not least, CDCs were naturally and heavily involved in the development and rehabilitation of housing. They often purchased abandoned or tax-delinquent properties from city governments at nominal cost, using federal and private funds and a combination of contract and community resident labor to rehabilitate them.

The early CDCs tended to view their mission broadly as addressing not just market failures but a range of community problems, from deteriorated physical infrastructure, to lack of access to health care, to poor schools, to a decline in youth-serving organizations in the ghetto. CDCs pressed city governments to reinvest in and improve the quality of "public goods"—sidewalks, street lights, garbage collection, police protection (Bendick and Egan 1989:29). Many CDCs undertook advocacy on behalf of both individuals and communitywide issues. The majority provided at least some social services. A few CDCs sought to strengthen community control in different domains. Cincinnati's West End Development Corporation (WEDCO) imagined a self-governing community emerging from its efforts, with not only locally controlled institutions but a whole locally generated culture (Davis 1991).

CDCs evolved relatively complex structures, in part to embody their very different purposes of business development and community development, in part to manage very different types of projects. CDCs typically used a subsidiary structure that reflected their range of activities, with for-profit and nonprofit arms, and with functional divisions such as property management, construction, rehabilitation, social services, manpower, and venture capital. In many communities a nonprofit format was crucial for disarming resident mistrust and communicating the message that the CDC was operating for the benefit of the community (Perry 1987:96). The subsidiary structure helped limit the financial liability of the larger institution in the case of businesses or real estate developments that were forced to declare bankruptcy.

The early CDCs tended to operate on the principle that fewer, larger projects were more efficient and would have greater impact, both real and symbolic. They also tended to formulate ambitious plans that linked business development, housing, and commercial development in a vision of a renewed community (Garn, Tevis, and Snead 1975:398). Paradigmatic of the first generation CDCs was the Bedford Stuyvesant Restoration Corporation (BSRC) in New York City. During its early years BSRC "persuaded" IBM to establish a computer cable manufacturing facility in the neighborhood, creating three hundred jobs, undertook a large housing rehabilitation effort, built a mortgage loan pool, and made $3 million in small business loans (Carlson and Martinez 1988:7). IBM's commitment, though large by CDC standards, was hedged. It could have used a much larger manufacturing facility, but did not find the neighborhood attractive enough for one (Perry 1987:113). By the early 1970s BSRC was organizational host to a wide range of community development activities. It not only was a major lender and a manager of a good deal of rehabilitated rental property, it sponsored primary health care, social services, youth development, cultural affairs, and education activities.

Early (mid- to late-1970s) evaluations of CDCs provided a mixed picture (for a review see Carlson and Martinez 1988:41–49). The most notable positive finding of the early research was CDCs' viability as institutions, deriving in various degrees in different cases from strong community spirit and support, corporate support, and strong management (Garn, Tevis, and Snead 1975:406). Community Development Corporations were noted to provide minorities an unprecedented opportunity to control and manage investment capital (Carlson and Martinez 1988:49). They proved moderately adept at identifying, levering, pooling, and recycling investment capital (for specific strategies see Newman, Lynn, and Phillip 1986:74–90). They developed many innovative approaches to land use (e.g., land trusts), and to housing reinvestment. They also developed innovative training, compensation and ownership arrangements. For example, the Albina Corporation, located in Portland, Oregon, hired community residents who were considered hard-core unemployable to work in an ammunition container factory. The whole work force was considered to be in training the first few years, allowing the factory to use Department of Labor training funds to pay part of the salaries of workers. The Albina Corporation also created a unique mechanism, called a deferred compensation trust, for employees to become owners. The trust consisted of company shares that an employee became progressively more vested in with each year of employment. The Office of Economic Opportunity permitted its SIP funding to the Albina Corporation to be used to fund the trust until revenues from the factory were available to do so (Rothman 1971).

On the other side of the equation, the depleted state of many inner-city communities by the late 1960s and early 1970s, often compounded by destruction of businesses through looting and arson during the riots, strongly constrained the early CDC experience. The efforts of even the best capitalized and managed CDCs were dwarfed by the breadth and depth of neighborhood deterioration. CDCs had, as they continue to have, only modest success with job creation. Even the sizable manufacturing operations of the early CDCs typically provided from thirty to at most one hundred jobs in local communities in which thousands were unemployed or underemployed (Faux 1971:xx). Each job created required enormous financial and human effort. Creating one job could cost fifteen thousand dollars or more, not including training costs. Community residents who were hired usually required enormous support and ongoing training. Job retention frequently was a major problem. In general it proved difficult to achieve and sustain profitability in either commercial or manufacturing enterprises, even with a good deal of active and passive (e.g., tax) subsidy (Garn, Tevis, and Snead 1975:406). Many of the neighborhoods in which the first generation of CDCs were located had reached a point of depletion at which it was enormously difficult to attract investment and business back without extensive foundation and government subsidies, supports, and guarantees (Bendick and Egan 1989:22). It often was difficult to find or sustain a market for products. (Many manufacturing enterprises were begun in order to feed one or two particular artificial markets, as was the case with a Rochester CDC, which operated a small electronics factory for Xerox. When the needs of the host company changed there often was no market at all on the horizon.) The federal government did not make things any easier with its wariness of the use of government money to establish profit-making ventures. It insisted that fragile but healthy small businesses started with federal funds invest profits back into the community.

Even in housing, which was to become the principle CDC activity nationwide, there were many hard-won early lessons. CDCs learned that building or improving housing was fruitless if they did not also attend to ongoing arrangements and supports for maintaining that new or improved housing (Perry 1987:133). Thus, for example, the Greater Roxbury Development Corporation was eventually forced to declare bankruptcy on a 325-unit, tenant-managed housing development that had begun deteriorating almost from the time it was completed, because of inadequate planning and resources for maintenance. The Roxbury CDC realized belatedly that tenants needed extensive and ongoing technical assistance, and that there had to be relatively strict adherence to policies (Perry 1987:10). Even adequately supported housing developments proved vulnerable to the market dynamics and human factors that had undermined inner-city housing historically. Residents of a community-owned and managed development did not necessarily care for it better than if it had been owned by private landlords or the city.

An Evolving CDC Movement

The size and organizational complexity of the first generation CDCs, which in turn required large core operating budgets, reflected the urgent felt need to recreate almost all the elements of a local economy as well as the physical infrastructure, services, and social institutions that made up a community. At the same time, the large subsidy required to maintain CDC operations raised the stakes for the CDCs themselves. Given harsh community environments and an exaggerated legacy of mismanagement by community institutions associated with the War on Poverty, CDCs often felt that they had little margin for error In misjudging a market or the potential of an innovative investment idea. Franklin Thomas, reflecting on his tenure as head of the Bedford Stuyvesant Restoration Corporation, noted that "it is much tougher running a CDC than a bank or a regular corporation, where theft or bad loans are not make or break issues. In a CDC you worry about someone stealing fifty cents" (quoted in Carlson and Martinez 1988:296). The federal government and other CDC funders recognized the unusual situation of CDCs. Yet they still insisted on some appropriate criteria on which to evaluate individual CDCs' progress. CDCs argued that they were not businesses. Rather they were intermediary institutions and catalysts, trying to recreate marketplaces under very difficult conditions, and often trying to help others become profitable. Their operating philosophy was to make a virtue of necessity, taking on projects and activities that nobody else would. For these reasons it was (and to a great extent continues to be) inappropriate to evaluate CDCs primarily in terms of profitability, or, in the case of housing, in relation to returns expected by private developers. CDCs probably were most willing to be evaluated on the goal of staunching and reversing the outflow of capital from the local community, and as catalysts of institutional renewal. At the same time it seemed too much to expect CDCs to take sole responsibility for turning their communities around.

During the early 1970s the Nixon administration pushed CDCs to view themselves more as promoters of capitalism than as community developers. In Nixon's "black capitalism" there was an increased emphasis on individual progress, particularly the identification and nurturance of individual minority entrepreneurs, and a deemphasis on the community as a whole. The implicit thesis in this shift was that individual success would somehow spill over into the community at large. But it missed an important point about entrepreneurship: that it is extraordinarily difficult for an individual to act in an entrepreneurial manner without the support and validation of his or her community. Rather than the individual entrepreneur "being an individual who pulls his community up by the social ladder, he is a vehicle which the community uses to transport itself" (Sclar 1970:21). This support, evident historically in immigrant neighborhoods with their mutual assistance associations, was notably absent in the black ghettos of the 1970s. The resource depletion was so great that it created survival-oriented patterns of coping and relating. Often those who made the tremendous effort to get a small business off the ground, risking what little capital they had in the process, found suspicion and resentment rather than support (Perry 1987:15). In part this was because even when successful the ghetto entrepreneur was usually in a fragile position, and could ill-afford to be too community-minded. Some black community leaders actually saw the creation of a class of black capitalists as likely to undermine racial solidarity in the inner city, given capitalism's inherently fragmenting and divisive effects.

Many first generation CDCs eventually collapsed of their own weight and ambition. Over time both the surviving older CDCs and hundreds of newly emergent ones became smaller, more opportunistic, and more pragmatic. New projects were not always tied to the local community in which a CDC had its roots. For example, WEDCO, the CDC with the ambitious vision for Cincinnati's West End mentioned earlier, survived "by shifting its focus to more financially attractive and viable projects outside the West End" (Davis 1991:168). In many local communities CDCs continued to grow out of neighborhood organizing efforts that started for other purposes, such as tenant organizing, and the majority remained involved in advocacy and organizing. Nonetheless, individual CDC became less likely to take a confrontational stand on contentious issues such as bank lending or zoning practices and decisions (Pearce and

Steinbach 1987:32). Conversely they opted for a more cooperative, "businesslike" approach in their projects, appealing to the self-interest and latent social conscience of established institutions, and when possible bringing these institutions into projects as partners. CDCs also became more experienced in building on local community strengths and attending to community weaknesses in project design and management.

By the late 1970s CDCs were much less likely to start and manage their own businesses, and more likely to supply equity capital, loans, incubator space, planning, marketing, and accounting assistance (Pearce and Steinbach 1987:31). At one point in time, for instance, Bethel New Life in Chicago owned and operated a garment factory. This factory proved so draining in terms of financial resources and staff energy that it was spun off, although Bethel New Life retained an equity interest (Vidal 1992:73). CDCs were increasingly likely to think in terms of creating the lure, for example the financial and land packages, that would attract private investment to a community (Fainstein 1987:228) —in effect clearing the way for a business or residential project.

In their own continuing business development efforts CDCs found that the most promising strategy was to stay small and to seek out specialized market niches. Examples include a bakery specializing in gourmet cheesecake, a catering service, a roofing firm, and a small metal-casting enterprise (Bendick and Egan 1989:5). One limitation of this strategy was that it further minimized job creation. Nationally about 80 percent of minority-owned firms typical of those created by CDCs have no employees other than their proprietors. Another limitation was that it contributed only marginally to rebuilding a diverse local economy with a critical mass of activities that fed into each other. Moreover, even smaller businesses proved fragile: most lasted less than five years (Bendick and Egan 1989:5). CDCs also experimented with the purchase of franchises, especially in the fast food area. This linked them to the expertise and financial depth of large national corporations but also created few decent jobs. During the 1980s CDCs experienced a major decline in federal support for core operating expenses, which translated into reductions in staff size and an even greater tendency to play a brokerage role in various projects. At the same time the Ford Foundation was coming to recognize that its expectation that many CDCs would become self-sufficient through income and earnings was unrealistic (Carlson and Martinez 1988:346).

Ford thus recommitted itself to providing continuing subsidies for core operations to CDCs, including endowments in a few cases. Housing rehabilitation became the central activity of most CDCs (and the only activity of at least half of them), followed by commercial real estate development and business enterprise development (Vidal 1992). The focus on housing derived in part from the vacuum left by a dramatic decline in federal subsidies for housing production during the 1980s. In 1986–1987 CDCs produced more low-income housing than the Department of Housing and Urban Development (National Congress for Community Economic Development 1990:ii). It also made intrinsic sense. Domestic property—land and buildings used for shelter—is in some respects the "basic stuff" of which poor residential neighborhoods are made (Davis 1991:5). When that "stuff" is owned and maintained by people or institutions living outside the neighborhood, it follows that neighborhood residents will feel less ownership of it, and therefore of their neighborhood. Housing rehabilitation and production therefore were avenues for helping neighborhood residents become more invested in their neighborhood at many levels. Abandoned or neglected property was available at low or no cost, and could be rehabilitated at relatively modest expense (sometimes with "sweat equity"), keeping rental or ownership costs low. Housing rehabilitation was a good activity for building individual and institutional skills, from project planning, to management of contractors, to construction. It sometimes provided a natural lead into commercial revitalization, as was the case with Baltimore's Southeast Development, Inc. (Carlson and Martinez 1988:320). Not least, housing redevelopment was attractive to neighborhood residents. It was an accessible and visible way to control the process of neighborhood change and to stabilize a deteriorating neighborhood. When those who would live in the rehabilitated housing were involved in design decisions, for example where to locate play areas for children, the result was more livable and appropriate housing. Finally, housing was an area in which CDCs had always had relatively good success.

In recent years community economic development has come to encompass a variety of ideas and strategies that build on different aspects of the CDC experience. The use of passive tools like zoning exceptions, business and building code waivers, and tax breaks to stimulate ghetto investment is spreading. In Chicago, for example, Bethel New Life worked with other community groups to have a law passed in Cook County to wipe out back taxes for nonprofit groups taking ownership of deteriorated properties (National Congress for Community Economic Development 1990:2). Not all passive enabling strategies have proven equally useful. Regulatory relief has been very helpful. Tax relief has had more ambiguous effects, depending on the type of relief. Credits for hiring and training neighborhood residents appear modestly promising, as does accelerating depreciation for tangible investments. Capital gains exclusions are attractive only to someone selling a business, not someone considering creating a business. There has been a general tendency for incentives to attract existing businesses and their existing employees from one poor neighborhood to another, minimizing job creation effects (Drew 1992:80).

Community Development Corporations have sponsored or spawned a variety of new or alternative forms of financial organization. One example is Community Loan Funds (CLFs), also called revolving loan funds. These local, nonprofit organizations are lent money (capitalized) at very low rates by private individuals, church organizations, foundations, and the like. They then relend the money to carefully screened projects within a defined community area. Technical assistance is often provided with the loan. Existing community groups also have borrowed specific CDC strategies for leveraging outside capital or when feasible mobilizing local capital (such as the savings of neighborhood residents) for community investment purposes. As an example of the latter, a coalition of local black churches in the Brownsville section of Brooklyn, with assistance from Saul Alinsky's Industrial Areas Foundation, developed what it called the "Nehemiah Plan." This involved pooling together the savings and a portion of the income of working poor residents of a local housing project to finance their ownership of new, small single family homes in the neighborhood (Fainstein 1987:330). The coalition was also able to convince the federal government to become a partner in the project by providing mortgage interest subsidies. Another recent idea is that of "microenterprises"—one-person businesses—often based in the home. For example, in a Baltimore program called "BOSS" one woman was trained and provided capital to start a small business sewing school uniforms. A waiver of AFDC rules allowed her to earn income and keep profits from her business without losing eligibility for her grant and Medicaid benefits. Microenterprises pose some of the same job creation challenges as have all new business ventures in the inner city, requiring long-term, intensive support, and being expensive to create relative to the number of jobs created. They also require that individuals have a certain degree of initiative and confidence in their ability to defy the odds and make it on their own, a rare enough commodity anywhere.

CDCs as a Vehicle for Reinventing Capitalism

As discussed above, the depleted and unforgiving contexts in which CDCs operated historically forced them to struggle continuously with questions of strategy. Should they do a few narrow, focused things better or confront deeply rooted, intractable issues head on? How should they weigh the symbolic value of large projects such as shopping centers and the more concrete benefits of a small business? How should they work with institutions that had historically discriminated against their community? Yet it also led them to consider more philosophical questions about the relationship between community and economic life. Should they encourage people in inner-city neighborhoods to see their fates as somehow bound together? Should they try to be a model for a more humane way of managing economic life? Should land and property redeveloped by CDCs be viewed primarily as a commodity to be redeveloped for financial gain, or as a public good? Particularly in struggling to address these latter questions CDCs have become an important locus of efforts in the United States to redefine capitalism and its relationship to local communities. Community-based economic development represents one model for local communities to regain a measure of control over capital, and balance its use for private and public purposes.

In its early years the CDC movement struggled implicitly and at times explicitly with the question of whether it should develop as an ideological alternative to corporate capitalism. This struggle pervaded CDC policy and practice in almost every area: making loans, choosing projects, hiring contractors, managing residential properties, forming boards. The internal ideological struggles of CDCs were fueled by many factors. One was CDCs' wish to balance and integrate social goals with economic ones, consider the communitywide impact of investment decisions, and attend as much to the social fabric of the local community as to its economic life. CDCs sought to balance the narrow, more easily measurable objective of making a profit with the broader, more diffuse objective of supporting and strengthening community well-being and overall development. Thus, for example, the potential value of a shopping center was assessed in terms of the market for particular businesses, the jobs likely to be created, and the more intangible benefits to quality of community life. Bringing a particular block to life again with a mixed use commercial and residential project could make shopping more convenient, push out drug trafficking, and make it safer to walk in an area.

Gunn and Gunn (1991) point out that in practice balancing the profit motive and community development was often difficult. They describe the example of the CDC that develops a for-profit subsidiary. The subsidiary needs to be nimble. It needs to wear the clothing and speak the language of capitalism. The parent organization, on the other hand, wishes to build capacity and maintain a measure of community control through its broadly representative board, which feels empowered to question every move by the subsidiary to make sure it is in the community's best interest. The situation is further complicated by the financial dependence of the parent on the income of its for-profit child. But the problem was not just that business profit and community development were in some respects irreconcilable objectives. It was also that the latter was so ill-defined that it was hard to know what contributed to it (see Taub 1990:6). How widespread and enduring did the impact of a project have to be before it was considered to contribute to community development? What types of individual development and achievement counted as contributing to community development? What types did not?

In part CDCs' ideological and identity struggles represented an effort to negotiate a continuing series of cruel choices: should loans be made to those most likely to succeed or to those who would never get loans from conventional banks? Should jobs created go to community members, even if those community members lacked the skills to handle those jobs? At what point should a delinquent tenant in a CDC-owned building be evicted for nonpayment of rent? It also reflected an effort to control the terms on which external funders evaluated CDCs. If a top priority of a CDC was to make loans to small, struggling businesses, and more than half of these loans ultimately proved uncollectible, was that success or failure (Carlson and Martinez 1988:339)? To a certain extent, rather than reinterpreting capitalism, CDCs put themselves in the role of buffer and mediator between the marketplace and the local community. For example when a redevelopment effort required eviction of tenants from their homes, a CDC could manage the process more sensitively than an outside agency. A CDC could provide the technical support to help a minority contractor be successful in its first job. Or it could help institutions outside the community identify how they might be helpful to it.

Another factor fueling CDCs' internal struggles was their discovery that capitalism did not work by the principles that it proclaimed for itself. Most CDC businesses and to a lesser extent housing activities were premised on the notion that at a minimum they would be respected by the marketplace for their capitalist orientation. CDCs argued that they could be reliable, low-cost producers—all they asked was a chance to compete along with everyone else. But this premise was based on the notion that capitalism favors and promotes competition and diversity. The historical record suggests just the opposite: that capitalism is driven by the dynamics of monopolization (Gunn and Gunn 1991).

This reality underlay still another aspect of the CDCs' struggle to reinterpret capitalism. Community-based economic development embodied the somewhat utopian idea of trying to decentralize capitalism, of making communities once again stakeholders if not centers of economic activity. Much economic activity in the United States—especially production—long ago became rootless. Large corporations use local communities until they are depleted or inconvenient—with labor becoming too expensive, militant, or ill-prepared, or with location becoming inconvenient—and then move on. The result is an extraordinary vulnerability of local communities to economic decisions made by people who have nothing to do with those communities. Equally important, corporate capitalism organizes economic activity vertically rather than horizontally. In at least one respect then the long-term decline of inner-city communities has been driven by forces similar to those affecting many other types of local communities, that is, in the loss of a multifaceted and complex local economy that supports at least a measure of self-sufficiency and engenders a measure of local economic interdependence. Berry (1987:180) argues that it is the combination of self-sufficiency and interdependence that sustains a community. As he asks, "Can people be neighbors if they do not need each other or help each other?"

Community economic development thus was partly about the idea of trying to recreate the multifaceted, self-sufficient local economies that were destroyed long ago by corporate capitalism. In the same way that it tried to turn inner-city neighborhood neglect and racial exclusion on their heads, it tried to turn the complexity and scale of economic organization on its head. It argued that these broad economic patterns actually reinforced the value and necessity of locally based initiative (Newman, Lynn, and Phillip 1986:1). That is why community-based economic development is gaining attention in urban neighborhoods and local communities that are just now experiencing what inner-city neighborhoods began experiencing some forty years ago.

Conclusions

Community economic development has proven to be both a fragile and a vital strategy. It has not been able to reverse the basic process of economic decline in the most isolated and disadvantaged inner-city communities. This is illustrated by the enormous difficulty of creating even a few jobs and businesses in communities that have lost hundreds of thousands of jobs and thousands of businesses. It is illustrated by the difficulty of creating and sustaining private housing markets in the poorest and most isolated neighborhoods. After all it was only when the land and property of the inner-city was no longer attractive to those seeking private economic gain that it became available for public purposes. The CDC experience also suggests that a strategy of separate development does not provide the circuitous route to social integration that some expected. The idea that minorities could in effect force a change in basic patterns of relating with the white majority if their interactions were as business person to business person, capitalist to capitalist, rather than as client to provider, did not bear up. Views of minorities do not seem to be closely tied to their success (or even their failure) as capitalists.

Working in marginal neighborhoods with marginal populations, CDCs have themselves been called marginal (Pearce and Steinbach 1987:38). Especially in the poorest neighborhoods, CDCs have been able to do little to objectively alter the lives of most neighborhood residents. Yet the CDCs and their related innovations have provided means for inner-city communities to do something about their fate, even if only a little. Residents of Chicago's South Shore neighborhood, the focus of a major community redevelopment initiative in the early 1980s, acquired more positive expectations for the future of the neighborhood, which in turn had consequences for their investment in maintaining their homes (Taub 1990:9). Community development corporations have been a tremendously creative force in inner cities, stimulating both new institutions and economic redevelopment strategies. Fainstein (1987:330) notes that the enterprises operated by CDCs may not have offered great wages or career opportunities but at least they did not flee to the suburbs. Perry (1987:82) suggests that it is important to focus as much on the effort as on the outcome in considering the meaning of the CDC movement: "It is not the tool itself [the CDC] that is initially crucial, but the local commitment to finding, rediscovering or reinventing some such tool."

The CDC experience has served to illuminate the interconnectedness of different spheres of community life—the physical, economic, social, and educational. At the same time in its struggle with strategy it has illustrated how difficult it is to figure out what to do about interconnectedness. Whether CDCs have undertaken a few or a host of kinds of activities in different domains, it has proven difficult to find ways to have individual activities, for example social services, housing, and business development, reinforce each other in an additive fashion. On the other side the interconnectedness of things is partly what makes definitive change in a local community, particularly a depleted and neglected one, so difficult. The local community "is constructed out of networks of interlocking forces and institutions that maintain it, that keep it in its recognizable form as that particular community" (Perry 1987:33). In other words, the relationship among different aspects of community life is both what makes locally based initiative so attractive and what makes community development so difficult.

Issues for the Future in the CDC Movement

By one estimate there are now about two thousand CDCs in operation throughout the United States (Vidal 1992:29). Nonetheless at this point in time CDCs remain an inadequately supported and underutilized community development resource. Most CDCs have only modest institutional stability. Most also have quite modest visibility—especially in the private sector—although they enjoy strong support in their neighborhoods (Vidal 1992:14). The institutional and financial infrastructure embodied in CDCs remains very decentralized and diverse. In the absence of an identifiable federal program to support CDCs as institutions, intermediaries like the Ford Foundation's Local Initiatives Support Corporation (LISC), the Enterprise Foundation, and the recently created National Community Development Initiative have had to fill that void. Pearce and Steinbach (1987:9) note that "there remain too few states and communities in which governors, mayors and private sector leaders understand how CDCs can be integrated into comprehensive economic and human development." In particular there is a need for city governments to come to view themselves as catalysts for community economic development as well as providers of services.

While the CDCs have begun to acquire many new establishment partners, it is not yet clear if these new partners will stay the course. Historically, investors in community economic development projects have had to be extraordinarily patient to see even very low returns. Private-sector capital, in particular credit for small, struggling businesses, remains the crucial ingredient for inner-city economic development, and remains the ingredient hardest to come by. There are only 125 minority-owned banks—the principal lenders to minority businesses historically—operating in the United States, fewer still in inner-city neighborhoods. Only 2 percent of $4 billion in loans backed by the Small Business Administration in 1991 went to black-owned businesses (Thomas 1992:1, 12). Banks remain very reluctant lenders to CDCs, although that is changing slowly (Pearce and Steinbach 1990.52). Mainstream banks that have branch offices in the inner city usually do not have a commercial lending officer in those offices. The few loans made come with extraordinarily high, business-killing interest rates. Some of the reluctance to use CDCs as vehicles through which to invest in the inner city is due to continuing questions about CDCs themselves, particularly their managerial soundness. One observer describes the stability of the majority of CDCs as like that of "a house of cards" (Pearce and Steinbach 1990:65).

CDCs have also become increasingly less likely to work in the most distressed inner-city neighborhoods. Only 23 percent of the neighborhoods in which CDCs are located today are considered "severely distressed" relative to the average neighborhood nationwide (Vidal 1992: 81). Instead CDCs today tend to be located in relatively poor neighborhoods with "substantial" but not overwhelming poverty and social problems. Their activities do still tend to benefit primarily neighborhood residents: an estimated 65 percent of employees in CDC-developed industrial properties and 75 percent of employees in CDC businesses live in target neighborhoods (Vidal 1992:82). Nonetheless it remains to be seen whether CDCs can maintain their historic commitment to the most disadvantaged neighborhoods in cities.

In reviewing the CDC experience one is struck by the creativity and flexibility they have demonstrated as institutions. For example, the CDC experience provides a hint of the innovative uses to which the enormous reservoir of capital in the United States can be put. One is struck as well by CDCs' balance: between activism and pragmatism, between profit and community reinvestment. Community development corporations may not always have a dramatic impact in and of themselves, but they embody some key principles that create a middle ground between laissez-faire and radical reform that has been all too scarce in social problem solving. CDCs have proven to be reliable brokers among different interests inside and outside of inner-city communities, often being the only party to planning processes or negotiations with the community's overall interest in mind. At the same time one is struck by CDCs' fluidity and even vulnerability, almost like that of the communities they serve. Practically every review of the CDC experience cites lack of core support as an impediment to CDCs' ability to strengthen themselves as institutions.

As Pearce and Steinbach (1987:38) point out, issues of scale have once again become central to CDCs. This time around CDC activities are being conceptualized more in terms of partnerships and collaborations among many community institutions. In a later chapter I describe some wholesale community renewal efforts that involve CDCs in key roles, in one case (that of the Comprehensive Community Revitalization Program in the South Bronx) as the primary institutions involved. CDCs also have an implicit or explicit role in many of the new federal initiatives proposed and underway for the inner city, including the recently introduced Economic Empowerment Act of 1993, the proposed Neighborhood Reconstruction Act, and the proposed Community Capital Partnership Act.

NEIGHBORHOOD-BASED SERVICES AS NEIGHBORHOOD-BASED INITIATIVE

HISTORY AND EVOLUTION TO 1960

We have a long way to go, but I see a day when social services in this city are dispensed from comprehensive, convenient, neighborhood multi-service centers, locally-based and responsive to local residents and their needs. —DAVID DINKINS, April 25, 1990

Overview

Since the emergence of the settlements over a century ago neighborhood-based services have played an important role in poverty alleviation and social reform efforts. Indeed they often have served as the most concrete expression of broad reform impulses in American society. For example, they have been viewed as a vehicle for renewing a sense of community, and even for organizing poor people politically. At the same time within the framework of the human service system neighborhood-based services have played a steadily diminishing role. The reasons for this decline include the exhaustion of Progressive reform spirit, discussed in chapter

2, the professionalization of social services, in particular the growth of statutory and clinic-based social work, the submission of community health nursing to the authority of organized medicine, and the general attraction of bureaucratic organization to a wide range of professionals, academics, and some government officials. Neighborhood-based services did not disappear completely. At least until the late 1950s most inner-city neighborhoods managed to sustain a diverse set of recreational and cultural programs for children and youth; public health nurses continued to visit young families; vestiges of street corner social work with gangs could be found; and schools continued to make sporadic efforts to redefine themselves as community institutions. Nonetheless declining public and private resources for the inner city, the flight of private social service agencies, and the growing financial strains on remaining inner-city institutions such as churches combined in the 1950s to undermine what was left of the supportive service infrastructure in inner-city neighborhoods.

Neighborhood-based services reemerged as an important human service strategy in the mid-1960s with the War on Poverty. Federal funding temporarily replaced much of the lost private and local public resources. Established neighborhood agencies such as settlements and youth-serving agencies were revitalized by the new funds and missions, and new programs and service strategies emerged, reflecting the assumptions and strategies of that era. Paradigmatic of these new strategies was the employment of nonprofessional community members as service providers, attempts to link social services to social action, and the deliberate use of neighborhood-based programs to try to change the culture of the larger human service system (Kahn 1976). Many of the innovative neighborhood-based service strategies of that era, for example the community health centers, would survive but never flourish. Others, such as the community mental health centers, would drastically change their mission. Still others, such as the neighborhood service centers, would evolve gradually with shifting policy interests. One particular program, Head Start, eventually became the most important social institution in many inner-city neighborhoods, as important in some ways as the church.

During the 1970s and 1980s neighborhood-based services continued to be generated, idiosyncratically, in thousands of local communities, usually as a local response to some felt community need. Borrowing from the past, and reinventing, individuals and agencies developed parenting support programs, community schools, youth programs, school-based health clinics, and after-school programs. Many of these locally generated programs survived by responding to government or foundation requests to address prevailing social preoccupations and objectives such as intervention with pregnant and parenting teens, diversion of youth from the juvenile justice system, preserving families in which parents were abusive or neglectful, and provision of emergency shelter and services for battered women, homeless families, and street children. Settlementlike programs, housing a range of services, reemerged for specific populations. For example The Door in New York City began in the early 1970s as a collection of health and mental health, emergency, therapeutic, recreational, and educational services for high-risk youth (Curtis 1993:58). During this same period neighborhood-based services steadily accumulated a variety of additional purposes, some old, some new. These included decentralization and decategorization of services; realigning the roles of professionals and clients in human services; addressing a renewed interest in "prevention" of specific problems such as child abuse and neglect and infant mortality; rebuilding presumably deteriorated informal social support systems for families, through family support programs; and serving as the conceptual engine, organizing principle and vehicle for completely remaking the human service enterprise. With the recently revived interest in inner-city poverty, neighborhood-based service approaches have again been identified as a critical resource in fighting poverty at the neighborhood level. (Interestingly, neighborhood-based services in the inner city, and indeed inner-city neighborhoods as a whole, never became connected to the movement for neighborhood political empowerment that swept through many cities during the 1970s and 1980s, as described by Boyte [1980]. It was as if poor minority neighborhoods had had their turn in the 1960s).

The new and renewed roles for neighborhood-based services in the inner-city heighten a variety of longstanding issues. Different people have always had different things in mind when they thought of neighborhood-based services. Traditionally the term has meant services that are rooted socially and geographically in their neighborhood, that take the community as their referent rather than a particular service field or discipline or categorical domain. Neighborhood-based services are thought to be culturally sensitive, willing to start with local communities' own child-rearing, problem-solving, and coping traditions. They are thought to be friendly, accessible, responsive, nonstigmatizing services, to employ a mixture of community residents and professionals in provider roles (often just the former), and to focus on generalist helping, including assistance and advocacy in linking families to other resources outside the program. Neighborhood-based services have a rich underlife; families draw on programs informally for assistance and support in any area they need, and at any time. Neighborhood-based programs often appear slightly disorganized, a bit vague (or perhaps too global) in purpose and assumptions, but diffusely helpful and supportive of families. They are sometimes seen to include, or even mean primarily, semiorganized and noninstitutionalized activities—unlicensed family day care, sports leagues, church social clubs, volunteers providing homework help for children in church basements, tenant organizations, block clubs. The idea of neighborhood-based services is sometimes associated with specific organizational reforms such as decentralization, service integration (knitting services together), co-location of services, multipurpose centers, and the like. Not least there has always been a political dimension to the concept of neighborhood-based services. Historically, that has meant using neighborhood-based services as a vehicle for organizing poor people to press for better housing or municipal services or access to jobs, or to protect their rights as clients of one or another government program. Since the 1960s the term sometimes has been used to mean community control of specific public institutions, notably the schools, and even to suggest community-level governance of all local services.

Discrete neighborhood-based service programs have themselves struggled continuously, if not always consciously, with issues of identity, role, and boundaries. Are their purposes to provide the best possible services to individual families or to try to alter something larger: to bring new resources into the neighborhood, to reform the mainstream human service system, to seek or provide employment opportunities for community members, to strengthen local democracy? What should the relationship be between neighborhood-based services and the large public service systems such as education and child welfare? Should they try to assume traditional service functions or complement and extend them? What does it mean in practice to take the community as one's reference

point in setting priorities and designing services? How does one determine a particular community's interests? How can families be both partners and clients at the same time? What roles should professionals play
in neighborhood-based programs? What are appropriate roles and expectations of indigenous lay helpers? What kinds of knowledge—whose
knowledge—should shape planning, advocacy and direct services? To
whom ought a program be accountable?

In a different vein, because they are so closely tied to and rooted in
their neighborhoods—and so permeable to the environment surrounding them—neighborhood-based services have tended to incorporate the
difficulties, stresses, and vulnerabilities of those neighborhoods, particularly in staff relations, and sometimes in relationships with families as
well. Working conditions for staff in neighborhood-based programs often
compound the inherent stresses and strains of working with poor families in depleted neighborhoods. These conditions can include low pay,
lack of health or pension benefits, limited job security, a limited career
advancement path, and sometimes physical danger. Because they are
located in isolated neighborhoods neighborhood-based programs themselves too often have remained isolated from the larger society and its
institutions. Poor inner-city neighborhoods are not only ghettos for the
people who live there; they can also be service ghettos. Head Start is a
good example, its strengths the flip side of its limitations. While Head
Start has succeeded in creating new roles for inner-city adults within their
community, it has had much less success taking children or adults
beyond the boundaries of the community, literally or figuratively. It has
not been able to take them beyond where it is itself.

During the 1960s community action agencies and other federal programs created a kind of shadow social and health service system in the
inner city. It was one that was neither designed or equipped to provide
as much or the same kind of direct services as the traditional system it
shadowed (Kahn 1976:33–35). Nonetheless there was often no one else
left to provide direct services. Beyond the schools, the public aid system,
and a rapidly growing child welfare bureaucracy, this shadow system constituted the whole service system in many neighborhoods. The loss of federal funds crippled but did not destroy this alternative service system, and
locally generated program development added to it. Today, as worsening social conditions in the inner city produce growing numbers of mul-

tiply vulnerable families, with a host of complicated problems, neighborhood-based services find themselves struggling alone to serve and help these families, sometimes by default, sometimes by choice and design. Yet neighborhood-based services remain the least adequately conceptualized, funded, and staffed elements of the human service system, unprepared in fundamental ways for this extraordinarily difficult job. Moreover work with multiply vulnerable families tests many of the principles of neighborhood-based services, such as building on family strengths, asking families to take an active role in shaping, and even providing, services.

The Decline and Reemergence of Neighborhood-Based Services

Throughout the history of the human services in the United States neighborhood-based services prevailed only briefly, for a decade or two surrounding the turn of the century, and again briefly during the 1960s. There is some debate in the literature on when the developing human service system ceased to be primarily neighborhood-based, in both the geographic and social sense. Kirschner (1986:chap. 1) argues that Progressive reformers within the human services drifted toward professionalization, by first doing research to support arguments for environmental causes of poverty-related behavior and outcomes, then specializing in a problem area, and from there claiming special expertise in that area. Yet from the outset Progressive reformers were preoccupied with the inefficiency, corruption, and variability of patronage democracy, the prevailing decentralized system of public administration. This preoccupation led Progressives to question the neighborhood as the best level for the governance of public services at the same time that they were trying to make the neighborhood the referent for the organization and delivery of private services. It led Progressives to focus as much energy on administrative reform and scientific management as on social reconstruction (Morone 1990:121–123). Progressives also were concerned with the moralistic and nonscientific nature of prevailing social welfare practice. The new helping professions would convert individual helping from a private exchange between citizens with different amounts of power to a rational, technical, relatively disinterested process requiring specialized expertise. The new human service executive would replace self-interest and factional politics with "objective facts employed for the good of an undivided people (Morone 1990:115).

Progressive reformers discovered that while Americans were deeply suspicious of centralized government power they seemed less reluctant to yield control of decision making to self-proclaimed experts. Nonetheless, it would take some effort to make professionalism fit comfortably with at least some of the tenets of Progressive reform, notably empowerment of communities to solve their own problems. Turning professionals, or quasi professionals, into community residents through settling only masked this contradiction. Moreover an implicit assumption driving the emergence of the helping professions, and the human services as social institutions, was that poor people, at the time mostly immigrants, did not have the ability to recognize, define, and formulate solutions to their own problems (Kirschner 1986), nor even to adequately fulfill such basic family and community functions as socialization of children, provision of social support and social control around child rearing and regulation of community life. In a sense the emerging helping professions derived their very reason for being from the presumption of familial and community inadequacy (Grubb and Lazerson 1980:299), and from the equation of professionalism with the right to label and categorize.

The premise underlying services for poor people—the seeming necessity of justifying services by viewing poor people as lacking the knowledge and ability to meet their needs, to define and address their situation—created contradictions that haunt human services for poor people to this day. From the outset services for poor people embodied aims that were difficult to reconcile: to enable and at the same time to control recipients, to work from poor people's own understanding of their lives and to define and interpret their lives using external standards, to link poor people to mainstream norms, institutions, and opportunities and at the same time to highlight their difference and deviance, by diagnosing and sorting them into categories of dependency and dysfunction. The strong, if implicit, message of distrust of poor people underlying the emergence of formal helping complicated the already difficult task of forging trusting relationships across barriers of class and culture. Not least the whole formal helping enterprise was built to an an even greater extent than before on a foundation of mutual pretense. Poor people, as always, were forced

to acknowledge their incapacity (and thereby their need for professional helpers) in order to gain access to critically needed material support
and assistance in finding housing or jobs. Professionals were forced to
pretend that they had (indeed that there existed) a specialized body of
knowledge and technique that would help poor people with their difficulties and alter their life situation. Poor people were required to act grate-
fully, and professionals would interpret that gratitude as evidence that
they were being helpful. Stadum (1992:136) notes that when a poor
woman "vented her anger with the way life was going or disagreed with
agency directives, she was often labeled `too independent,' `stubborn,'
or `insolent,' descriptions that could put her family at risk of being
deemed undeserving of aid." (Apparently things have changed little. In
describing the anxiety-provoking process of applying for welfare in New
York City, where failure may mean homelessness and loss of one's children, Funiciello [1993:24] notes that the "slightest remark can set your
case back hours, days, weeks, or forever. Occasionally someone loses
it and starts cursing at the top of her lungs. Then she's carted away by
security guards.") The constraints to honesty on both sides of helping relationships, certainly in their initial stages, and too often from beginning
to end, remains one the more unnoted aspects human services.

Professionalization, centralization, and bureaucratization were strong
currents in all fields, but became overriding forces at different points in
time in education, health care, and social services. Education succumbed
first, for a variety of reasons. Katz (1992:58) argues that education had
already become a bureaucratic enterprise by the turn of the century. He
notes that in the latter decades of the nineteenth century alternative
models of organization of schools still vied for dominance: "paternalistic volunteerism, corporate volunteerism, democratic localism, and
incipient bureaucracy." Each differed on such dimensions as financing,
professionalism, and control, and "on the social values or priorities on
which they rested, the importance they placed on community and
democracy, or efficiency and economy" (Katz 1992:59). Bureaucratic organization only seems inevitable in retrospect. Still it won out, because it
met the needs of the emerging profession of teaching, and paralleled the
increasingly dominant culture of corporate capitalism. The idea that
providing education required specialized knowledge and skill served
to legitimate "the divorce of school from community and the subordi-

nation of parents to professionals" (Katz 1992:59). Centralized controls, standardization of curriculum, classification, specialization (i.e., fragmentation) of teaching and learning provided the means for school systems to escape local politics, incorporate new scientific principles of instruction, and process large numbers of immigrant children. The mass production assembly line within schools—particularly at the high school level, where children moved from room to room every fifty minutes to receive a prespecified dose of curriculum—served to prepare children and youth for the new world of factory work. (The fact that this model has not changed in almost a century is a bit terrifying.)

Professionalization and bureaucratization did not lead quite so directly or rapidly to the demise of neighborhood-based organization and service delivery in the health and social work fields. In the case of health services there was actually an increase in multifaceted, neighborhood-rooted work (including advocacy for social reform) through the early 1920s, followed by a decline. Nurses, and to a lesser extent physicians, had been developing a variety of community roles since the last decades of the nineteenth century. For example in Chicago the Visiting Nurses Association (founded in 1889) set up "baby tents" in poor neighborhoods, "portable, open-air clinics that brought comprehensive medical care for infants to the heart of immigrant neighborhoods" (Silberman 1990:11). In the first two decades of the twentieth century there was a rapid growth in the number of public health nurses. Between 1912 and 1924 the number of public health nurses increased from three thousand to over eleven thousand (Melosh 1984). Public health nurses used settlements, milk stations, infant welfare stations, and even schools as a base for a range of neighborhood activities, including home visiting, surveillance of sanitary conditions, and public education campaigns.

In many local communities nurses, in concert with local public health departments, took their activities one step further, creating "neighborhood health centers" (the prototype for the community health centers of the 1960s). The basic idea was to create or use an existing neighborhood base for a concerted, comprehensive local public health program: to provide an array of preventive, educational, and diagnostic (but not curative) health services, when necessary reaching out to "recalcitrant" or overwhelmed families to do so, to gather systematic information on neighborhood health and social conditions, and in some neighborhoods to organize neighborhood residents to press for public health and related reforms (Stoeckle and Candib 1969:1,385). The health center was to be "a clearinghouse where preventive nursing, educational and relief work may be done with the least duplication of effort, friction or delay" (Wilinsky 1927:678). Health centers organized themselves around neighborhood boundaries, with the notion that all the families in a neighborhood were clients, at least implicitly. Some local centers actually set themselves the goal of conducting a home visit to every family that had given birth to a new baby within their catchment area. (This goal was recently suggested again by the National Commission on Infant Mortality). Wilbur Phillips, the secretary of the New York Milk Committee's child health stations, pioneered the use of neighborhood residents as "aides" in neighborhood health centers, using them to recruit patients, take household surveys, and even participate in center governance (Stoeckle and Candib 1969:1,387; they note that this idea never gained popularity—less due to political resistance than to lack of community interest and support).

During those same years, between 1910 and 1930, two forces were at work undermining neighborhood-based nursing practice and multifaceted neighborhood-based health centers. Growing knowledge of disease treatment was giving nurses new clinic-based roles in hospitals, making hospital-based practice more attractive. Equally important, physicians wanted to bring "independent" nurses into the clinic and under their supervision and control. Physicians' explicit argument was that neighborhood-based work, especially home visiting, was inefficient, both too expensive and too time-consuming (Melosh 1984). The real issue was economic: physicians took their cue from large corporations, and worked to create their own vertically integrated monopolies. As Starr (1982:196) notes, "Wherever public health overreached the boundaries that the profession saw as defining its sphere, doctors tried to push it back. Yet this was not just true of medicine. It was a cardinal principle in America that the state should not compete with private business." The health centers succumbed to the same forces. As time went on they were forced, and to some extent chose, to become much more preoccupied with efficiency "at the expense of diversity" and responsiveness, and this preoccupation undermined their identity and reason for being (Stoeckle and Candib 1969:1,389).

Throughout the 1920s social work was also becoming professionalized and bureaucratized, the former in new schools of social work, the latter in growing urban systems of private, voluntary child and family service agencies, and an emergent statutory social welfare sector. There were a number of forces shaping the emerging social work profession. One was a search for a new identity to replace that lost with the demise of progressive reform. A second was the growth of the public social welfare sector due to Mothers' Aid, child welfare, and related programs, which together were beginning to alter the axis of social services. The private social welfare agencies were wary of the growing public sector role in social service delivery. At the same time social work as a profession wanted to demonstrate that its skills were critical to public, statutory work, because that would solidify the place of the profession (see Polsky 1991:chap. 5). Expanding the public role and funding of social work was not an inevitability at the time. It required evidence that social work could be both efficient and effective. Bureaucratic organizational principles seemed to meet the need for greater efficiency and accountability, and social workers embraced these, it with some reluctance. Like nurses, they sensed—correctly—that their professional autonomy would eventually be strangled by the very tools they embraced to secure it in the first place. Helping itself could not be so easily rationalized and proceduralized. Indeed the standardization of casework procedure that had been the aim of Mary Richmond's and others' efforts had not proved to be an effective framework for interpersonal helping with poor and vulnerable families (Polsky 1991:112–113). What was thought to be needed was an approach that was scientific but not overly proceduralized and rationalistic.

The emergence of clinical social work during the 1920s, with its strongly psychoanalytic orientation, met this need and at the same time was particularly critical to the demise of neighborhood-based work with poor families. The availability of psychoanalytic theory to the social work profession allowed it to strengthen its claim to being a true profession with a scientific foundation (a claim first made with the publication of Mary Richmond's Social Diagnosis in 1917). It accelerated the ongoing shift in social workers' attention from community to individual maladjustment. Although it was not intended to explain poverty, it seemed to imply that poor peoples' difficulties were largely of their own making. The daily work of most social workers—"arranging foster care, adoption, and job referral; dealing with financial need . . . coping with children's difficulties in school; assisting with problems arising from desertion, separation or widowhood . . . aiding with housing problems"—would not change significantly until the 1950s (Kahn 1976:28). Nonetheless, the new clinical social worker was the model for the future of social work. Instead of going into the community (as well as into other institutions such as the schools) to seek out clients, he or she waited for clients to self-refer themselves (Levine and Levine 1992:158). Instead of "seeing crisis-ridden families, the clinical social workers now saw at weekly one hour appointments patients who were motivated and completely capable of taking care of themselves between appointments" (Davoren 1982: 263). Lubove (1965) notes that no other profession picked up the tasks that social work began to abandon in the 1930s and 1940s—helping families gain access to services, advocating for disenfranchised groups and communities, providing social support to families. The vacuum left by social work helps explain the strength with which neighborhood-based services reemerged in the 1960s.

Settlements and other neighborhood-based agencies themselves began to experience side effects of professionalization and centralization. Both within and across agencies professionalization had a fragmenting effect. For example, settlements increasingly were composed of numerous departments staffed by specialists defining their own sphere: casework, recreation, hygiene, adult education. Large family welfare agencies such as the Children's Aid Society, Travelers and Immigrants Aid, and the like, established district offices in numerous neighborhoods, each with several little departments that mimicked the main agency's administrative structure. As competition for scarce resources and clients grew, different neighborhood agencies that had once tried to be multifaceted community centers fell back on specific services whose inputs and outputs could be quantified for funding agencies. Playgrounds focused on recreation, schools on adult education, health centers on health screening.

A growing proportion of philanthropic resources went first to centralized bodies such as Community Chests and United Funds (the offspring of the Charity Organization Societies). These "federated" bodies tied various bureaucratic requirements to their grants, which occupied an increasing proportion of the time and energy of social agency leadership. Equally important, because they quickly came to serve as the principal filter for corporate funding of social welfare programs, they screened grant applications for ideological correctness, making sure an application did not imply any criticism of the existing social order. Lubove (1965:180) notes that local human service federations employed the rhetoric of Progressive era community organizers, but their real concern was with "the machinery" of social welfare. They transformed the social and political purposes of community organizing into quasi-scientific ones: efficiency, accountability, and the like.

While bureaucratization was a steady, unyielding process in education, health and social services, in each field there were reactions to it almost from the outset. Even as human service agencies deliberately or inadvertently became "detached" from their neighborhoods, they felt a need to reach out to reestablish bonds. One could argue that the majority of discrete innovations in the human services over the course of the century have been motivated by concerns about the dysfunctional effects of bureaucracy. An early example of this is the visiting teacher, who flourished in many poor urban neighborhoods between 1915 and 1925 (Levine and Levine 1992:chap. 5). Their activities and roles varied enormously. They created clubs and special classes, for example reading clubs, provided homework help, started dance and theater groups, did community lectures. Perhaps their most critical role was to bridge home and school, school and neighborhood, to interpret, share information, correct misunderstanding. They called on families to try to get a sense of what in the home situation—illness or death of a family member, overwhelming household responsibilities for a child, and so forth—might be causing school problems. They struggled to convince parents that keeping their children out of school to work was short-sighted. They worked with classroom teachers to help them better understand and meet the needs of children having trouble in school. They intervened with the juvenile court, social service and welfare agencies on behalf of children and families (Levine and Levine 1992:86).

Ironically, as the visiting teacher movement grew it became transformed by the very forces it was designed to counter. The schools could not countenance independent practitioners who spent time out of the office in the neighborhood, and who sometimes pushed for reform of the very institutions for whom they worked. They therefore put visiting teachers under the administrative control of assistant superintendents or other functionaries, who worried about "cooperation with other departments, hours, caseloads, record keeping," and qualifications (Levine and Levine 1992:88). Visiting teachers themselves, concerned about their marginality within the school system, organized an association and attempted to create a profession out of what had started as a mission.

Already in the 1920s a few social service leaders, for example Hyman Kaplan of Cincinnati, were concerned about the harmful effects of bureaucratic organization and the disabling effects of specialized expertise as a basis for social problem solving in poor communities. When residents of poor neighborhoods walked into an agency to sign up for a program or seek help with a problem, they increasingly found themselves confronted with a maze of paperwork and procedures, or forced to go from office to office in search of the right starting point. As agencies centralized and became more clinically oriented, their staff spent less time in poor neighborhoods, causing both individual providers and whole agencies to lose their feel for the context of families' lives. A few leaders already were arguing the need for "generalists" who could act as an advocate and "buffer between client and technician" (Kirschner 1986:84). They argued also for service decentralization as a means of assuring locally appropriate use of funds and of renewing communitarian spirit in poor neighborhoods. They pointed out that as professionals came to appropriate more and more social functions, from socialization of children to provision of social support and social control around child rearing, they ironically further undermined the very family and community capacities that presumably had deteriorated and therefore required deliberate support and strengthening. Professionalization of social problem solving also seemed to undermine community residents' involvement in neighborhood affairs, from neighborhood improvement campaigns to mutual assistance organizations.

Such concerns spurred a variety of efforts during the 1920s, 1930s, and 1940s to return the human service system to its neighborhood-based roots and to recreate generalist helping roles. Hartford, Syracuse, and other cities experimented with neighborhood councils designed to assure citizen input into the planning and provision (though not the governance) of services (Dillick 1953:116). Settlements, innovators as always, promoted various approaches to addressing growing fragmentation of services, including case management and centralized intake. For example Mitchell House in Hartford tried to establish one intake that would serve as entry into the whole complex human service system in its neighborhood. Settlements also attempted to find ways to bring the services of separate institutions together. In the mid-1920s in Cleveland the Hiram House Settlement tried to link up with the schools in its neighborhood, offering to use its staff to recreate the visiting teacher role, starting small clubs, doing home visits, working with teachers to meet the needs of children having school and other other problems, and doing a bit of street corner counseling (Dillick 1953:103–104). By the mid-1930s community organizing, which had been suppressed both by the general spirit of the 1920s and the specific efforts of local philanthropic organizations in social welfare, reemerged in scattered places around the country, most notably in Saul Alinsky's efforts, described in chapter 2. (Community organization also became a distinct branch of social work practice, but most graduates of that track went to work for Community Chests or United Funds; Trolander 1987:140).

Cross-Currents: Setting the Stage for the Neighborhood-Based Services of the Current Era

The 1940s and 1950s were characterized by discrete innovation and sporadic (but when taken as a whole continuous) local reinvention of various neighborhood-based service approaches: a community school started in one neighborhood, an information and referral center or multiservice center in another, a health outreach program in another. As was historically the case, efforts to reach out to vulnerable families with young children, to individual youth, and to youth gangs, served to stimulate innovative programs, taking professionals out of their offices into the neighborhood. Kahn (1976:29) points out that during this period the recognition of "multi-problem" families, who drained public resources with their multiple, complex, endless problems, also stimulated a variety of innovative approaches. These included pioneering efforts to bring the whole array of agency services—assessment, casework, crisis management, and even long-term therapy—into families' homes. The idiosyncratic process of local invention and reinvention both fertilized the field and preserved ideas and approaches, and kept them alive until the inevitable next wave of reform. It provided a kind of dictionary that reformers would be able to draw on, to name and define things, when the time came. It also helped hold together an increasingly fragile fabric of social support in inner-city neighborhoods.

During this same period, particularly through the 1950s, traditional neighborhood agencies such as settlements and youth-serving agencies struggled with changing inner-city populations, the growth of gangs, geographic and physical change in their neighborhoods (see Trolander 1987:chap. 4). Neighborhood-based services continued their critical role of facilitating the adjustment of immigrants to a new world—this time Puerto Rican, African American, and Mexican immigrants. As discussed in chapter 3, settlements and other agencies tried to establish a presence and find a useful role in new public housing projects, sometimes as basic a role as building a sense of community. One common strategy was to encourage those designing projects to designate space for recreational facilities, and then have the local housing authority fund settlement staff positions in those projects (Trolander 1987:83). Nonetheless once a nursery school or after-school program or youth center was located in a project building it became vulnerable to the dynamics of project life—for example the constraints imposed on children's mobility by building-based definitions of gang turf—in ways that a strategically selected free-standing facility would not have been.

Many traditional neighborhood-based agencies—particularly those with a particular religious or ethnic affiliation that no longer reflected the local population—found the changes occurring around them extraordinarily disorienting, and some abandoned neighborhoods that they had worked in for decades. In Chicago's Lawndale neighborhood, for example, the Young Men's Jewish Association simply ceded a local youth center facility over to another youth-serving agency that was expanding its programs for African American youth. Some agencies followed their traditional constituencies to the suburbs (Kahn 1976:28). Others, particularly settlements, a few nonsectarian youth serving agencies, and locally based churches with social programs, stayed on and struggled to play a role in reducing intergroup tensions created by rapid population change, notably in their work with neighborhood gangs (see Hall 1971:226–227; in some respects the Irish and Italian youth gangs' attacks on Hispanic and African American youth mimicked their parents' efforts to stop neighborhood change through other means). Yet even the agencies that remained in their old neighborhoods often found themselves questioning their role and relevance to new realities and populations. Their traditional enrichment activities, such as drama clubs or home economics classes, did not attract youth anymore. Even their efforts to create positive mirror images of gangs, for example providing space for self-organized youth "clubs," only reached a small group of children.

The 1950s also saw the intensification of three related trends within social work that would pull the few remaining social workers out of neighborhood-based work with poor families. One was a rapidly expanding state and federal social welfare system, which meant rapidly expanding public social welfare bureaucracies. These in turn provided an engine for the continuing growth of statutory social work, particularly in public aid and child welfare. A second was the triumph of clinical social work over basic casework. The "prestige jobs, the well-paying jobs, and the socially respected assignments were in child guidance, Veteran's Administration, mental hygiene clinics, and family counselling agencies" (Kahn 1976:28). A third was a shift in the self-defined mandate of private voluntary agencies. While the state was assuming expanded responsibility for the welfare of dependent and vulnerable families, over the objections of the private "voluntary" social welfare agencies, these same agencies were rethinking—some observers said walking away from—their own responsibilities to this population (see Polier 1989:8). This process actually began during the 1940s. For example in 1948 the Illinois Children's Home and Aid Society "decided to refuse to bow to pressure to take an increasing number of unserved children. In so doing it consciously rejected the role it had assumed at its founding in 1883 to care for children who were left without help" (Bush 1988:30).

The old-line agencies argued that they had to restrict their services if they were to maintain quality; that is, to provide specialized therapeutic services, using the best trained professionals. Underlying that argument was reluctance to serve a growing volume of poor black and Hispanic families (Bush 1988:32). This reluctance stemmed in part from financial concerns; traditional donors sometimes did not want their money used for these new populations of children and families. It stemmed also from a belief that blacks and Hispanics would not benefit from what they had to offer. As inner-city neighborhoods changed from immigrant to African American and Hispanic neighborhoods, the private agencies exchanged the traditional "particularism of serving one's own kind for the particularism of serving those people who might benefit from the specialized skills of trained social workers" (Bush 1988:35). From there it was only a short step to an inference that such clients did not reside in the inner city (see Lerner 1972). One correlate of the new discretion in mandate and response assumed by many old-line child and family welfare agencies was a decision to end what remaining noncategorical neighborhood-based services they still provided in the inner city.

No single loss to the traditional human service fabric of inner-city neighborhoods was critical in and of itself. It was the accumulating losses— of youth serving programs, the old-line child and family service agencies, settlements—that eventually would prove so devastating, especially in combination with losses in other domains such as employment, public housing resources, resources for schools. The damaging effects of professional and institutional abandonment would remain masked for almost two decades by the residue of the new service network created in the War on Poverty. In retrospect it was clear that this new network did not replace the old. The enormous investment in renewing neighborhood-based services in the 1960s did not result in a commensurate increase in direct helping services, particularly skilled services. The staffing and posture that were "optimal for mobilization and protest did not prove to be the best prescription for ongoing service delivery" (Kahn 1976:36). Nor did this new network have much influence on the overall quality and quantity of remaining traditional services in inner-city communities; both continued to decline throughout the 1970s and 1980s.

CHAPTER SIX

NEIGHBORHOOD-BASED
SERVICES
IN THE CURRENT ERA

The renewal of neighborhood-based services during the 1960s was stimulated and shaped by a number of factors, some complementary, some leading to tensions about purpose and strategy. The major demonstrations described in chapter 3, Gray Areas, Mobilization for Youth, and the President's Council on Juvenile Delinquency, provided both a rationale and prototypes for many of the specific federally funded neighborhood-based program models that emerged during that period. These demonstrations, particularly the Ford Foundation's Gray Areas, were the first to respond to, if not note, the increasing dysfunctionality of the mainstream human service system, particularly with respect to inner-city children and families. This led all three demonstrations to a strategy of by-passing the mainstream system by creating new services, even as leverage for reforming that system was being sought. The federal government's own subsequent decision to create what in effect was a whole new "shadow" service system in inner-city neighborhoods—in some respects it had no choice—proved fateful to the outcomes of service reform in the 1960s.

In a related vein the demonstrations noted above were the first to articulate the idea, later embraced by Office of Economic Opportunity staff and consultants, that new intervention models were needed to prepare poor children, youth, and adults to take advantage of new opportunities (that is, opportunities soon to be created by the federal government's efforts to change the opportunity structure for poor people; see chapter 3). This perceived need itself derived from a reemergent line of social science research seeking explanations for poverty-related social problems such as school failure in the poor themselves. Sociologists and psychologists were focusing again on the culture of poor families, particularly poor African American families. Social scientists posited a set of orientations and behaviors, for example strongly matrifocal families and distrust of mainstream institutions, that were immediately adaptive but ultimately self-defeating, presumably perpetuating poverty from one generation to the next (for a review and critique see Valentine 1968). The idea of such interventions as preschool education, compensatory education at the elementary level, and various youth programs was to disrupt what was presumed to be a self-perpetuating cycle. (Needless to say this was not the first time that social scientists' theorizing mirrored American society's chronic need for a tidy, self-contained explanation of social reality in the inner city.)

The early1960s demonstrations recaptured and renewed many Progressive era themes and assumptions, rebuilding the deteriorated conceptual bridges back to that earlier era. The federally funded neighborhood-based services of the 1960s themselves drew on these themes, assumptions, and even approaches. As in that earlier period neighborhood-based services were conceived by those living outside of inner-city neighborhoods—this time the federal government and its professional consultants—as a response to the unique and uniquely local problems of those neighborhoods. As earlier the idea was to make the neighborhood the referent and locus for organizing services and supports to poor families. The overriding focus was on things that could be done within the boundaries of the local community. There was an emphasis on assimilation and acculturation of African American migrants and Hispanic immigrants. There was an orientation toward self-help. Many of the objectives of the new neighborhood-based services were also reminiscent: improving women's and children's health, altering poor children's life chances and developmental trajectories, rebuilding the social fabric of the neighborhood, increasing civic participation, helping "immigrants" to the city adjust to the demands of urban life.

At the same time the social, political, and institutional context for neighborhood-based services in the 1960s differed from that of the Progressive era in ways that made the traditional tasks of neighborhood-based services harder to achieve, and suggested new tasks. For one thing neighborhood-based services of the 1960s had to operate in an institutional context of well-established, rigid public bureaucracies whose disparate elements had tremendous control over most aspects of poor families' lives. (One joke had it that the public services suffered from "hardening of the categories.") Neighborhood-based services had to relate to helping professionals—teachers, social workers, physicians—many of whom felt threatened by a potential loss of status and, in some cases, of monopoly in providing a particular type of service, and at least a few of whom wanted to play a role in reforming their professions and/or fostering social change (Galper 1975; helping professionals' own ambivalence toward bureaucracy, and perhaps even toward their self-defined authority, have received too little attention historically as an element of reform).

The inner-city neighborhoods of the 1960s were more depleted economically and institutionally than immigrant neighborhoods had been fifty years earlier (see Clark 1965:chap. 3). Residents and service providers had fewer resources to work with—to build on, mobilize, draw together—and fewer objectives they could realistically strive toward. Neighborhood-based services in the 1960s were faced with groups and individuals who presented challenges far different than those of European immigrants, no matter how poor those earlier groups had been. As a group newly urbanized African Americans brought with them a history of exclusion, discrimination, and denigration, not in some far country but in their own society. A growing number of families could no longer see their way out of the ghetto, not so much because they were trapped by a self-perpetuating culture of poverty as because paths into the labor market were narrowing and receding. (Constructive patterns of coping with discrimination and chronic hardship eventually would break down in the ghetto, seemingly proving the culture of poverty theorists prophetic.)

Other forces shaping neighborhood-based services in the 1960s included the Civil Rights movement, assorted grass-roots protest groups, which focused on issues ranging from welfare rights to community control of schools, and not least the efforts of black and Hispanic leaders to create pride in ethnic identity. The Civil Rights movement created a legal framework and social climate that encouraged attention to the rights of minorities and poor families above and beyond their needs and obligations. As noted in chapter 3, it provided a basis for public interest lawyers and community organizers to question the presumed right of large public bureaucracies to define, label, and categorize poor people. If the Civil Rights and other rights movements provided a basis for questioning the right of professionals to determine what was best for poor people and their communities, a growing sense of pride in separate identity provided a basis for questioning their ability to do so. Because "caseworkers came from outside the neighborhood, from what was indeed an alien culture, they were seen as unable to grasp their clients' experience and aspirations" (Polsky 1991:176). This questioning profoundly affected relations between professional helpers and their clients in America's inner cities. The effects of abandonment of inner-city neighborhoods by traditional human service agencies were exacerbated by repeated attacks during the 1960s on the relevance and usefulness of those few traditional human service agencies and programs that remained.

The very different motives and intentions of different stakeholders, the heightened intensity of African Americans' long struggle for social membership, and the reality of inner-city neighborhoods created an extraordinarily turbulent foundation for rebuilding neighborhood services. A population with increasingly complex and chronic support needs, a growing sense of distrust toward prevailing social institutions, and a growing sense of entitlement created unprecedented challenges for and demands on human services. Questions about the role that social services could and should play in ghetto contexts tore traditional provider-client relationships from their moorings. The rejection of professional discretion in deciding who had access to public resources such as welfare and housing and of prevailing theoretical and cultural bases for helping (by reformers themselves as well as minority community leaders) left vacuums that were not filled by such concepts as maximum feasible participation and community control. If discretion was to be removed from social workers and bureaucrats, to whom should it be given? If their criteria and procedures for rationing out scarce resources were invalid, then what criteria and procedures should be used? Not least creating a separate, locally controlled service system clashed in many ways with the Civil Rights movement's demands for equal treatment for minorities under the law (see Skerry 1983:34).

Rebuilding the Infrastructure of Neighborhood-Based Services

Given the historical differences it was inevitable that there would be important differences in emphasis and orientation in the neighborhood-based services of the Progressive era and the 1960s. In that earlier period, for example, the emphasis on replacing lost customs with new ones, in the process serving the function of acculturation, contributed to an emphasis on recreational and cultural activities, an emphasis much less visible in the 1960s. In a similar vein there was a much greater emphasis in the 1960s than in the Progressive era on services as an equalizer of social and economic opportunity, thus a greater programmatic focus on education and training. The neighborhood-based services of the Progressive era had a more restorative and integrative, if not utopian, orientation than those of the 1960s. By that later period few still believed in the possibility or even the desirability of trying to bring different social classes back together in an inclusive, harmonious community. By the mid-1960s the historic Progressive wish to rebuild a sense of community had been converted into a militant insistence on the rights of excluded groups, an insistence that such groups have a measure of control over reform efforts, translated into the broad calls for participation and community control.

Specific programs provided the infrastructure and defined the priorities underlying efforts to renew and reinterpret neighborhood-based services in the 1960s. These included Head Start, the neighborhood health centers (which would later be renamed community health centers), neighborhood service centers (later called multiservice centers), the Neighborhood Youth Corps, and community mental health centers. The specific programs emerged from task forces or working groups composed primarily of social scientists, consulted and in some cases recruited into government service by the Kennedy and Johnson administrations. For example, the task force that led to the creation of Head Start was composed primarily of pediatricians and developmental psychologists, who concluded that "on their own the poor are incapable of helping their children escape from poverty" (Skerry 1983:27). Specific programs also emerged from efforts by OEO staff to rationalize the sometimes disorganized early plans submitted by community action agencies. For example, many plans included health components, but these often took the form of long lists of specific services: vision screening, immunization, prenatal education (Levitan n.d.:52). There was some sense in Washington that these elements had to be made more coherent. When a proposal was submitted by two Tufts University faculty for a "comprehensive" neighborhood health center, the idea took hold and was converted into a demonstration program and then a national program (Levitan n.d.:53).

Each program had distinct purposes and provided different services. Yet most shared certain generic features: the focus on serving the community rather than on picking individuals out of the community using diagnoses or labels; the focus on a specific target population enveloped in an orientation toward serving the whole family and worrying about the whole community; the employment of community residents in direct service and auxiliary roles; the involvement of community residents as partners or advisors in policy setting; outreach to isolated, overwhelmed, or distrustful families, to bring them into community life; a preventive orientation in services provided; a self-defined role as mediator between families and the large public bureaucracies, and as advocate when necessary; provision of an array of services within the same program; and, not least, attempts to embed the program physically, socially, and even temporally in neighborhood life. These qualities meant trying to be sensitive to local ways. For example, in the neighborhood health center in Boston's South End patients who made appointments would be seen even if, as was often the case, they showed up at a different time.

Each program was seen loosely as a piece of a larger puzzle that the Office of Economic Opportunity and its local community action agencies were trying to piece together. The puzzle was simultaneously conceptual and geographic. In conceptual terms the questions were what array of supports poor children and families needed to escape poverty, which of these OEO should address and which should be left to other federal and local, public and private agencies, what should go into and be part of each program, and how different programs (including old and new services) should work together to create a whole. Driving these questions was a growing appreciation for the large number and interrelatedness of inner-city families' problems and support needs. In describing the origins of the neighborhood health centers Schorr and English (n.d.:45) note that "the question of health first arose quite incidentally, as communities found that job training for a worker who would ultimately be refused employment because of a physical disability made no sense, that educational improvements meant nothing to children whose physical impairments made learning impossible." The argument underlying Head Start's multifaceted model was that even if poor children were given equal access to decent quality schooling, they would start out disadvantaged by patterns of parental care and nurturance that failed to prepare them to compete with more economically advantaged peers, by poor health and nutritional status due to lack of family resources and good community health services, and by lack of parent involvement in children's educational careers.

The neighborhood created both frame and canvas, and provided at least some of the ingredients, for addressing the conceptual questions. For the first of many times in succeeding years the questions were asked: What should the array of services—the "service system"—look like in each poor neighborhood? How should these services work together? What should be the responsibilities of public service systems in creating a more supportive service system for poor families? At the same time the neighborhood focus constrained thinking and planning. No one at the time (and to some extent few even today) asked how services, cultural and recreational resources within inner-city neighborhoods should be tied to those outside, or whether and how services and resources outside the neighborhood—schools, social services, museums, arts programs for children—should be made available to inner-city children and their families. Already by the 1960s many inner-city children had little contact with the world outside their neighborhood.

Within the framework of categorical purposes and target populations (frameworks created by federal authorizing legislation and refined by subsequent regulations and pressure from existing providers), the programs of that era tended to interpret their mandates broadly and flexibly. In reaction to a half-century of fragmentation of people and their problems, everything was now viewed as connected: youth were embedded in families that were embedded in support networks, institutions, the neighborhood. Nonetheless a tension quickly emerged with respect to where and at what level the effort to make things whole again, to create a coherent service experience for families, would be located. Ideally comprehensiveness and coherence were objectives for the local service system as a whole. But as specific programs began working with families, their staff began to experience viscerally the complexity of family support needs and the loss of human service infrastructure in the community.

Those programs responded by becoming more internally comprehensive, adding services and helping functions, in effect nudging aside the more abstract idea of locating comprehensiveness at the neighborhood level. For example, the model that emerged in Head Start included not just preschool education but health screening, meals, service brokerage for the whole family, and in some centers mental health counseling. Neighborhood health centers not only tried to provide all kinds of health and mental health services but helped start day care programs, and even became involved in advocacy in education and welfare reform. The historic settlement idea of bringing an array of services together under one roof was revived in the neighborhood service or multiservice center (March 1968) as well as in specific categorical programs. Any particular program, a Head Start or neighborhood health or neighborhood service center, might sponsor or offer space for any type of activity, from adult education to legal aid counseling to substance abuse self-help groups.

There were other forces impelling programs to become internally comprehensive. One was a commitment to depart from the historic response of specialized agencies to clients or client needs that did not fit what they had to offer, that is, referral to another program. A second was a desire always to have other functions to draw on if one's central function was threatened, by withdrawal of funds or shifts in priorities. Thus when Head Start's effectiveness as a child development program was questioned in the late 1960s, its advocates argued successfully that Head Start was not just a child development program but a child health and nutrition program, parent support program, and not least a community resident employment program (Skerry 1983:19). Still a third was the idea that neighborhood-based programs were inherently better at many functions than specialized agencies. Neighborhood health center staff in many communities were convinced that they could not only provide primary health care and ancillary services better than hospitals, but treatment for many diseases as well. They understood patient beliefs about health better and were more inclined to explain, follow up, be patient, and so forth. They were not driven by profit-related concerns.

Beyond the common problem of programs being distracted from their core mission when they tried to do too much, tensions emerged in many neighborhoods around both key dimensions of comprehensiveness: that is, trying to do everything and trying to serve all families within the neighborhood, particularly in the arenas of health care and social services. Existing providers wanted the new federal programs to focus on services the former did not claim to provide, and populations that they did not claim to serve (see Levitan n.d.:57). Moreover tensions arose over the locus of reorganizing services: each program tended to see the issues with which it was concerned—child development, health care, youth employment—as the best basis for mobilizing neighborhood residents and then organizing them to address the full range of neighborhood concerns.

Participation as a Major Theme

Many of the contradictory pressures shaping neighborhood-based services in the 1960s intersected around the issue of participation. Kahn (1976) argues that in many respects the strategies associated with and priorities resulting from maximizing participation in neighborhood-based services conflicted with the idea of improving the quality of direct services to poor people. Kahn is getting at a tension in identity and basic purpose that has often complicated the work of neighborhood-based services. Participation was meant to address a variety of very real problems. Professional program planners and providers often simply assumed (wrongly) that they knew what inner-city residents wanted and needed in the way of new services. Providers' perceived focus on helping clients adjust to the realities of their lives—that is to hardship, exclusion, insecurity—was viewed suddenly as another form of oppression. For community residents seeking help from or being a client in a prevailing education or social service or health program indeed often felt like just another form of powerlessness and dependency. Community residents needed accessible opportunities to build work-related skills such as punctuality and under-standing of complex organizations. As service clients poor people had no mechanisms to influence the service system.

At the same time children and families with difficulties requiring high-ly skilled help—difficulties such as substance abuse, inattentive or errat-ic parenting, parent-child conflict, learning problems in school, behav-ioral problems outside of school, and the like—were not getting such help. It was less clear how participation might address this lack. At least a few people argued that participation was a strategy for diverting demand for more and better quality services, just as it was seen to divert demand for genuine political power and economic access (see Valentine and Stark 1979:294.)

The alternative to authoritarian helping that reformers saw at the time was democratic helping. One dimension of such helping was democra-tization of information (Katz 1992:61). This implied access for commu-nity residents to the information used in program design and manage-ment, and access to the specialized knowledge providers presumably used to diagnose and label, as well as to help, in other words, access to the decision-making process itself at both program and client level. In many respects there was less information being controlled than seemed from the outside. For example much of the important knowledge pre-sumed to be hoarded by service providers took the form of practice wis-dom and technique, gained and used in the service of teaching or coun-seling or advocating, or managing a program or agency, and integrated into each individual provider's personal helping theories. This fragile, embedded knowledge was what gave many providers their claim to expertise, and it is not surprising that they felt both unable to articulate it and reluctant to share it. (One wonders what would have happened if teachers or social workers had been willing to acknowledge that they needed support and help from the community in doing their jobs.) Democratization of information also had a different, important, impli-cation: bringing in to the service design and provision process, and therefore legitimizing, community residents' own perspectives on their lives. In other words, it raised questions about who could and should make meaning out of the situation of inner-city neighborhoods and their resi-dents, and therefore about the very basis of prevailing services.

In most programs participation meant involvement of community residents in program-level policy setting, as volunteers and as paid staff. As with the community action program generally, there were chronic struggles in many programs about appropriate roles for community residents, particularly in the arena of policy setting. In Head Start, for example, two very different visions of parent involvement (beyond their roles as volunteers and staff) clashed during the early years of the programs. At one extreme was the vision of parents primarily as clients needing guidance in child rearing, home management, and related domains. At the other was the vision of parents actually running the program: planning, hiring, supervising staff, managing budgets (Valentine and Stark 1979:297–298). For example initial guidelines, developed in 1966, gave parents and community residents veto power over staff-hiring decisions through their role in each Head Start center's Policy Advisory Committee (Valentine and Stark 1979:304). Since most early Head Start programs were operated by school systems this created tremendous conflict with local school boards and administrators, and within a year this power was rescinded. Over time other parental governance and policy-setting functions were also curtailed, notably in choice of program components and curriculum, leaving parental influence more informal.

The opposing visions of participation in Head Start, as in other programs, reflected very different analyses of both the capacities of poor people and the core problem in inner-city communities. The two visions were able to coexist more comfortably within Head Start than within other programs and agencies (such as community action agencies), possibly because there never was a great distance between staff and clients, program and community. Also it was easier to obscure the distinctions between community residents as decision makers and as clients in a situation in which those community residents were the parents of the target population. Nonetheless the history of ever more circumscribed parental and community authority in program design, administration, and content within Head Start reflected what occurred in most neighborhood-based programs of the era.

One of the most interesting exceptions to that rule, albeit a rural one, was found in the "neighborhood" health center in Mississippi sponsored by Tufts University (Geiger 1969:138). A strong commitment by the sponsor to genuine participation led to the formation of ten local health associations. A broad definition of health framed a process in which each association set its own priorities (e.g., drinkable water, child care, home care for the elderly). Each of the ten associations also had a voice on an overall health council, which defined an overarching priority, in this case the need for more food. The professional staff of the health center, taking its cue from the council, focused its energy and program resources on organizing a farm co-op. Also making participation work in this case was a clear, multistep process, with rules, parameters and objectives jointly set by community members and professionals, and a trust in that process among all the stakeholders.

Paraprofessionals as Service Providers

In most programs of the era participation came to mean primarily use of community residents in volunteer and paid staff roles. The latter in particular was a departure, if not unprecedented. (At various times community residents were called "nonprofessionals," "indigenous paraprofessionals," or "lay helpers"). Community residents were employed in Head Start, neighborhood health centers, neighborhood service centers, and community mental health centers, as well as in schools, public health departments, and many traditional private agencies. They cooked meals and worked as classroom aides in Head Start programs and in schools; did outreach in search of pregnant women, to instruct new mothers in infant care, and to check that people were taking their medications for neighborhood health centers; counseled youth in mental health centers; worked as "job developers" (i.e., job finders) in employment agencies; led youth in public works crews for the Neighborhood Youth Corps. Community residents provided transportation, served as translators, provided homework help in after-school programs, visited new parents to provide guidance and social support, and even worked as case managers (for example, in the Lower East Side Family Union; see Weissman 1978). In some programs paraprofessionals' roles were clearly defined and delimited. In others they recreated the generalist helping role of the settlement workers and the early social workers.

A diverse coalition of proponents brought very different rationales to the movement to employ community residents in the human services, and saw it serving different, sometimes conflicting, purposes. To some the paraprofessional movement was a vehicle for both creating jobs and bringing community residents into the labor force, providing entrée and opportunities for skill building and attitudinal change (e.g., raised aspirations and self-esteem). Frank Reissman proposed the "helper therapy" principle, which suggested that when people with difficulties were placed in a helping role vis-à-vis others with difficulties, the therapeutic benefits accrued as much to the former as to the latter (Reissman 1965). Thus when a teenager having difficulty in school served as tutor and support for a fourth grader, both began doing much better in school. Kenneth Clark (1965:51) wrote that "many lower-class persons who now refuse the role of client will accept the same therapeautic help if it is offered in a course of training" to be a volunteer or paid worker. To others the paraprofessional movement was envisioned primarily as a way of addressing manpower shortages in the human services, and of saving professionals from having to spend so much time on routine, nonskilled or unpleasant tasks (Grosser 1969:117–118). For example in some health centers paraprofessionals were trained to do health histories, screen for tuberculosis, do vision and auditory screening, and take take blood pressure as well as to do outreach and casefinding (Wingert, Grubbs, Lenoski, and Friedman 1975:850–851).

To still others the paraprofessional movement was envisioned as a vehicle for altering the culture and enhancing the sensitivity of the human service system; and perhaps for improving its image among the poor. As helpers paraprofessionals started with the advantage of shared life experience, presumed to be an aid (indeed by some to be more powerful than theoretical knowledge and professional experience) in understanding and communicating with clients. As members of "recipient" communities gained entrance into the human service system, they could help that system learn more about client culture, perhaps alter preexisting beliefs and stereotypes about clients. As new agency employees paraprofessionals could present a friendlier agency face to the public. To a few the indigenous paraprofessional movement constituted an attack on professionalism per se and on the traditional human service system as a whole. It also served as one manifestation of efforts to increase community control of mainstream social institutions located in inner-city neighborhoods.

Different assumptions about and rationales for use of indigenous paraprofessionals were reflected in the roles they were asked to play in different agencies, and in the same agencies over time. Paraprofessionals rarely were viewed as partners with professionals, in programs with a full complement of professional staff. In a few programs, including many Head Start programs that were not sponsored by school systems, pay scales were such that paraprofessionals constituted most of the staff. (To this day Head Start salaries remain astonishingly low in many local programs— half or less of what public school teachers make.) Different assumptions about paraprofessional roles were reflected as well in the different attitudes toward training, preparation, and competence held by proponents. Were paraprofessionals supposed to learn professional skills, rely on their "natural skills, acquired not through education but through life experience" (Reiff 1969:62), or to combine both? Certainly paraprofessionals' knowledge of the local community and its ways were helpful in gaining access to families and interpreting their behavior. They knew how to approach people, where and when to find them, and were willing to do whatever it took to reach people. They were able to read behavioral cues, and were "skilled in the local art of persuasion" (Larner and Halpern 1987:3). They could draw on personal experience to understand the issues confronting families.

At the same time the presumed natural strengths of indigenous paraprofessionals had a flip side. Many paraprofessionals, like their peers in the community, had had (and continued to have) hard lives. Many were still struggling themselves with the residue of problems they were supposed to be helping others address, including out-of-wedlock pregnancy, parenting difficulties, domestic violence, substance abuse, school failure, lack of job experience. The content and lessons of their life experience often were not available to paraprofessional helpers (being a source of personal discomfort), and therefore not available as tools to be used in the helping process. Paraprofessionals often were selective in what they were willing and able to "see" in families, and in the issues they felt comfortable dealing with. Some were still struggling to come to terms with injuries and losses in their own personal and family histories. (To be fair the same was and is true of many professionals.) The mutual identification that was supposed to occur between paraprofessionals and community residents did not always occur. Conversely some paraprofessionals overidentified with the people they were supposed to be helping, making it more difficult for them to set limits and maintain the perspective needed to be helpful.

In the event, there was relatively little training provided paraprofessionals in the neighborhood-based programs of that era (Austin 1978: 49), and relatively little of the on-the-job support and supervision that would have helped nurture capacity for self-reflection and self-aware- ness. With what they perceived—realistically—to be a marginal toehold in the labor force, paraprofessionals themselves were reluctant to seek help from supervisors and peers when feeling overwhelmed, assuming that doing so would communicate incompetence. The career ladder created for paraprofessionals within community institutions staffed pri- marily by professionals, notably schools and health centers, was extreme- ly circumscribed. Yet that created within such programs as Head Start was in many respects just as circumscribed. It never extended beyond the boundaries of the program, except for those for whom the work expe- rience kindled an interest in completing or furthering their education, and for those who would have found ways into the labor force in any event. For the great majority of paraprofessional staff the next steps on the lad- der were hard to find in the immediate neighborhood, and the labor mar- ket outside the neighborhood was too far away, both psychologically and geographically. (In many communities job opportunities were also con- strained when it came to the not uncommon need to construct or reha- bilitate facilities for programs! For example, many neighborhood health centers needed to renovate existing buildings or build new ones. While the intent was to use community residents for this work, "practices of the building trades made this hard to achieve"; Levitan n.d.:55).

Participation Bound

Eventually the principle of participation would be partially inverted in many programs, with professionals managing to turn community residents back into clients. This process was evident not just in Head Start, with its growing emphasis by the late 1960s on parent education, but in the neighborhood health centers, community health centers, and job-train- ing programs. It proved extraordinarily difficult for those with different amounts of status to "bracket" these status differences and relate to each other "as if they were social equals" (Fine 1993:683). But professional resistance was not the only factor bounding participation. It was also the confusion, disorder, and doubtful decisions that accompanied shoving poor people into complex new roles—in often ill-defined new pro- grams—with little training or support. Media attention to the often chaotic early consequences of participation within the human services contributed to a public perception that the idea of participation within the whole federal War on Poverty was doing more harm than good. By the late 1960s poverty discourse was returning to its historic narrow track (Katz 1989:3), one that focused on the poor themselves. As Schlossman (1978) noted of the growing emphasis on parent education in Head Start, the federal government appeared to be shifting responsibility for the future school failure of poor minority children from itself back to parents. That meant emphasizing parents' (as opposed to Head Start's) importance in preparing children for school. The substantive preoccupations of the new parent education—appropriate infant stimulation (not too much, not too little), maternal language use, socialization of toddlers—eerily mirrored societal fears associated with the language and behavior of black militancy and aggression.

In a sense human services infused with a participatory ethic were not services at all, in the traditional meaning of the word. The emphasis on participation in the 1960s diluted the boundaries between provider and client, program and community, formal helping and informal support. Most of the neighborhood-based programs of the era, as today, had a rich underlife. Families drew on them informally for assistance with almost any problem or need, brushing aside formal program purposes. At the same time the quality of formal activities was buffeted by the attack on historic assumptions, roles, and usefulness of professionals. Little was offered to replace these foundations (for example an approach to helping that made room both for clients' perception of their reality and professionals' theoretical and practice-based understandings). Further, to the extent that what indigenous paraprofessionals provided constituted most of what clients received as services, that meant that clients received more outreach, linkage, basic information, raw social support, and instrumental assistance, and less guidance, modeling, mentoring, reeducation, and therapy (Kahn 1976:33). When paraprofessionals provided these traditional functions their effectiveness was often modest.

The Focus of Service Reform Shifts

Among other things the new neighborhood-based programs of the 1960s were expected to serve as catalysts for systemic change within the human services—in social services, health care, education. This meant both alter-

ing the values of mainstream services and helping to create a more rational, coherent overall system. One strategy to address the former objective—the introduction of indigenous paraprofessionals—was discussed
above. Other strategies ranged from the indirect, for example trying to
present neighborhood-based programs as exemplars that mainstream service providers could look to and learn from, to the the confrontational,
for example organizing community residents to demand changes in
institutional policies and practices (the paradigmatic example here is New
York City's Mobilization for Youth), and in a few cases such as the
schools in Harlem, organizing to seek community control of public institutions. The values and principles of neighborhood-based services eventually would take a more central role in broad human service reform
efforts. In the short term they were dismissed by mainstream institutions
and the professional guilds linked to them, even as the programs to
which they were attached were attacked for inefficiency and ineffec
tiveness. As described below, the idea of using the new neighborhood-
based services as a base for enhancing the coherence of the overall service system from the bottom up also experienced short-term difficulties
and a long-term revival.

Neighborhood-Based Services and the Lure
of Service Coordination

Throughout the 1960s the human service landscape in inner-city neighborhoods was steadily repopulated. In addition to the various federally
funded programs, scores of small, idiosyncratic programs emerged, seed-
ed by community action or foundation funds, located in storefronts,
church basements, and anywhere space could be found (Kahn 1976:30).
As the decade wore on the large human service bureaucracies and old-
line agency networks reluctantly responded to a variety of pressures
from below, both by adopting participatory rhetoric and by reentering
the neighborhood-based services arena themselves, through the mechanism of decentralization. Decentralization seemed to address the criticism of irrelevance and the demand for community control while further buffering downtown headquarters from accountability to address difficult local problems (for an overview of decentralization purposes and
strategies, see Yin and Yates 1975).

One by-product of all this new program development and old program refinement was an even more complex, fragmented, and incoherent local service system for poor children and families. There were more entry points, service sites, categorical programs and specialized roles than their had been a decade earlier. Different types of programs provided almost identical services. Multiple programs served the same family at cross-purposes, and no one provider had overall responsibility for a particular child or family. Problems too often were not identified until they became critical, and even when they were identified services too often did not materialize due to lack of follow-up or failed connections. When a child or family slipped through the cracks of the system there were no mechanisms even to examine that failure, let alone figure out who might be responsible. Many programs were committed to improving community well-being, but dozens of uncoordinated efforts to do so failed to add up.

Strategies had already been incorporated into Office of Economic Opportunity programs to address fragmentation at the individual client level (e.g., case management) and at the program level (e.g., co-location of services and interagency agreements). Programs such as the neighborhood centers and Model Cities (discussed in chapter 3) were initiated specifically to "knit together" the dozens of categorical programs in inner-city neighborhoods. However there was no vision of what a more coherent local human service system would look and act like from individual clients' perspectives, or how it might be governed and funded. Further, as was the case with community action agencies, new human service agencies or programs did not have the credibility or leverage needed to alter prevailing patterns of collaboration or to influence negative provider attitudes toward and practices with poor families. Their staff did not have funds to purchase client services, nor did they have control over a flexible grant-funding stream. Established service providers tended to collaborate only to the point at which their autonomy in funding, problem definition, eligibility determination, record keeping, and helping approach was threatened, or at which demands on them began to increase.

In the health care arena, for example, black physicians practicing in the ghetto, private for-profit clinics, and pharmacists often were antagonistic to neighborhood health centers, viewing them as a threat to their livelihood (Feingold n.d.:95). The antagonism of established practitioners sometimes stemmed also from being by-passed by local health center program planners working out of public health departments or medical schools. Neighborhood health centers also threatened nonhealth care providers, including housing authorities, schools, and welfare authorities, with their broad and holistic definition of health and the causes of health problems. A patient's bronchial asthma might be treated not only by providing drugs but by trying to pressure housing authorities to investigate the landlord who was providing inadequate heat in a patient's apartment.

In his study of the Lower East Side Family Union, a coordinating agency created by local settlements for that neighborhood's high-risk families, Weissman (1978) describes how participating agencies—those that had signed a contract to serve families collaboratively through the union—were reluctant to sign a contract specifying what services they would provide a family. They felt that their word should be trusted. While the union's family case managers were helpful in breaking families' complex problems into manageable pieces, they often had fewer credentials and less specialized skills than other members of union-created family service teams. This made it difficult for them to perceive themselves or be perceived as team leaders. For example, they sometimes were reluctant to call a team meeting, feeling that someone with less status could not call others together. Participating agencies each felt that their relationship with a particular union case-managed family was unique, and were reluctant to sacrifice that relationship to the objective of creating a coordinated service approach and package for each family.

In his study of the Roxbury MultiService Center in Boston Perlman (1975) describes how other agencies that had initially been convinced to base staff at the center, including the welfare department and visiting nurse association, withdrew soon after the center opened and (presumably) demands for collaboration became concrete. Even the legal aid lawyers working out of the center (lawyers who came from a sister federal program) declined to participate in the centralized record-keeping system. The center also was forced over time to adopt bureaucratic strategies for "selecting" its clientele, for example handing off or returning difficult clients or clients with difficult-to-meet needs (such as a job or housing) to other agencies, undermining its coordination mission. Such practices were a response to the use of the center itself as a kind of agency of last resort. Employment agencies would refer clients for assistance in locating jobs, health care agencies for assistance with health services, family service agencies for assistance with mental health services.

Increasingly the Roxbury MultiService Center staff found themselves struggling to directly address problems for which they had neither the training, nor the authority, nor the resources. Over time as the complexity and number of demands increased the focus of staff energies shifted from the external service environment to the internal environment of their own agency. They concentrated more on providing services themselves, principally supportive counseling and problem solving. As caseloads grew intake workers became more selective in deciding who was appropriate to serve. In other words, rather than helping to reshape the local human service environment, the Roxbury MultiService Center found itself increasingly shaped by that environment to behave in ways that resembled traditional services.

For all their difficulties these and other similar service coordination efforts of the era yielded important lessons. One was that differences in objectives or perceptions among providers could not be swept under the rug. They had to be recognized by all parties as legitimate and reconciled within that framework. In a different vein, though many providers during that era made a genuine effort to discern and be responsive to the preferences of community residents and program clients, it was not always easy to get representatives of client groups and clients themselves to articulate what good services would be like, other than being community controlled (in the arena of schools), geographically accessible, having minimum "red tape" and respectful staff (Perlman 1975:chap. 1). One criterion that multiservice centers such as the Roxbury Center found to be important was acting on the particular problem or specific request for assistance that a person brought to a program rather than converting it to whatever the program happened to offer, or using it as entrée to delve more deeply and widely into that person's life, without invitation.

Another lesson of the era was that in poor neighborhoods the combination of service system fragmentation, families with many and complex support needs, and an overall context of scarcity and disorganization interacted in ways that dramatically heightened the difficulties of service provision. Providers sometimes put themselves in a difficult position when they offered to be a resource in linking poor families to whatever the latter said they needed, since this often turned out to be services or resources the linkage agent had little control over, whether access to direct services such as a preschool program or health care, or such resources as jobs or housing. At the same time people with pressing problems often wanted the program that they walked into itself to address whatever concerns they brought with them, regardless of program mission. They did not want to be referred around from agency to agency. The pull to provide services oneself, no matter what one's mandate, was strong when working with poor families, but those services most needed were usually most difficult to provide.

By the early 1970s there was a growing perception among those concerned with service reform that discreet local efforts to make the human service experience of poor families more coherent and useful had to be reinforced by changes at the state and federal levels. The Nixon administration's primary concerns were extricating the federal government from policies and programs associated with community action, promoting more careful use of resources devoted to services for poor families, and decategorizing at least some portion of federal funds going to states and cities. Elliot Richardson, secretary of the Department of Health, Education, and Welfare (HEW), which had taken over the OEO programs, was particularly drawn to state-level administrative reform as a means to accomplish both objectives. Richardson and his team tried unsuccessfully to get federal legislation passed that would combine decategorization of federal and state human service programs with a variety of management reforms. As a result they chose an opportunistic strategy, freeing planning, demonstration, and evaluation funds from existing categorical programs to stimulate reform where conditions seemed ripe.

Federal demonstration funds were used by states like Florida as leverage for reorganizing their major bureaucratic systems. (Florida consolidated departments and functions and regionalized management.) Federal funds were also used to support discreet initiatives such as computerizing management information systems to better track clients through various programs and encouraging community health centers, community mental health centers and schools to work together. As Kahn and Kamerman (1985:115) note, the principal effect of federal service integration initiatives in the early 1970s was the rediscovery of "the possible techniques and technologies of service integration: co-location, shared core functions, information/referral/follow-up mechanisms, case management." As with the neighborhood-based service integration efforts, the leverage was just not there to influence largely autonomous categorical systems. The service system was loosely coupled not only at the community level but at each succeeding higher level as well. New organizational charts, management information systems, and cross-system priorities were no more able to alter the character of the service system for poor families than were case managers or multiservice agencies. There were just as many failed connections as ever; just as many families fell through the cracks, and just as many families received whatever the first provider they contacted happened to offer (Kahn 1976:27).

Loss of Faith in Services and the Search for New Helping Paradigms

By the mid-1970s whatever vision remained of a seamless, coherent service system for poor children and families was eclipsed by budgetary constraints and growing public frustration with the inability of the major service systems to effectively address social problems. This period marked the beginning of a long decline in inflation-adjusted resources granted to human service agencies, even as the difficulties and support needs of poor families grew. After what seemed like half a century of reform efforts it was difficult to identify new service approaches, especially within the boundaries of a social contract that emphasized private responsibility, and within a system of social provision that had solidified as two separate systems, one for poor and one for nonpoor families.

Once more proponents of service reform drew on the surprisingly sturdy principles embodied in neighborhood-based services, reinterpreting them in light of the social and scientific preoccupations of the moment. They responded to the public image of services as unhelpful, even destructive, to families by arguing that the new "family support" programs they had in mind would be participant-shaped, easy to gain access to and use, provide sustained support when needed, promote informal social support among community members, build on family strengths rather than just respond to deficits, provide advocacy in gaining access to specialized services, reinforce parents' primacy in children's development, and preserve family integrity (see Kagan, Powell, Weissbourd, and Zigler 1987). By-passing the history of the intervening seventy years—the creation of the ghetto, the construction of public housing projects, the public abandonment of the inner city, the ghetto riots—reformers reached back once again to Progressive-era interpretations of social reality, focusing on the decline in family and community. They argued for the need to deliberately reintroduce into inner-city communities, through service programs, the natural social support mechanisms presumed to have broken down. Services would become vehicles for organizing community residents to support each other, under the diffuse supervision and guidance of professionals.

Another thread in the renewal of neighborhood-based services involved efforts to rejuvenate youth services in the inner city. Many of the models that emerged were designed to serve a growing population of marginalized and troubled inner-city youth. Historic problems, such as gang affiliation and delinquency, were taking a more self- and socially destructive turn because of drugs and deterioration of family supports. Aggression and violent behavior were increasing, as was adolescent childbearing, running away, dropping out. Paradigmatic of the new generation of youth service models was The Door, mentioned briefly in chapter 5, which was located in lower Manhattan. The developers of this program basically collected a wide array of individual services in one site, including health, mental health, employment related, recreational and cultural, legal, and educational services. They then tried to create a program structure and climate that allowed youth to use the services collected on their own terms—to drop in or out, to pick and choose—with complete confidentiality, and within the framework of a set of rules dealing with behavior on site (Curtis 1993:58–59). The idea underlying the new youth programs was to create both a safe place, a haven from the pressures of home, street, and school, and an alternative family attractive enough to compete with the lure of gangs.

Still another reinvention was schools-as-community centers. Selected inner-city schools were opened up to the community, housing a wide range of public and private services from recreational programs and social services for children and youth to primary health care and adult education. This expanded use of schools required waivers from rigid union contracts and bureaucratic rules and unusual collaboration between city agencies. One of the first and best known of the new generation of school community centers was based at the Martin Luther King middle school in Atlanta. The school was actually designed and built with a broad community role in mind. A more recent example are the Beacon schools in New York City. A distinct element in some of these schools is the management of the new activities and services by community-based organizations. "Community" ownership of schools has required both flexibility on the part of school staff and courage on the part of community members, unaccustomed to viewing themselves as partners and equals to professional educators.

During the 1980s the service principles and approaches associated with the renewed neighborhood-based service thrust made modest inroads into the specialized, categorical systems that dominated services for poor children and families. Much of the public reform action during that period was state by state and, later, city by city. A number of states, including Minnesota, Michigan, Washington, Maryland, Oregon, and Iowa, used the idea of local networks of neighborhood-based services as the foundation of efforts to reorganize parts or all of their human service system. In California a bill was passed (Assembly Bill 831) to create pilot Neighborhood Family Service Organizations (NFSOs). These organizations, implicitly designed for poor neighborhoods, would consolidate "responsibilities and resources of numerous public programs under unified direction and management," in a sense creating a coherent service system by fiat. Legislative requirements called for services that responded quickly to families, were located to the extent possible within walking distance, were responsive to the cultures and language of the neighborhood, and fostered self-help and mutual assistance (California Assembly 1991:19).

Soon after being elected mayor of New York City David Dinkins gave a speech in which he outlined a vision of New York blanketed with "comprehensive, convenient, neighborhood multiservice centers, locally based and responsive to local residents and their needs" (quoted in Budes 1990:B12). Dinkins's vision built on a proposal presented to him by a citywide coalition of public and private agencies, foundations, and advocacy organizations. Under an umbrella called Agenda for Children Tomorrow, this coalition had developed a plan to create what would be in effect separate little service systems in each of New York City's fifty community districts. Each would have its own governance body (with authority to negotiate with the large public bureaucracies), discretionary resources, and case management system for children and families. Each would focus on the question of what the full array of services should look and feel like in that particular local community.

Few of the legislative bills, executive proposals, or concept papers from private groups developed during those years (or since) spelled out exactly how massive public service systems with thousands of employees, complex rules rooted in state law, processing thousands of children and adults every day, could be frozen, taken apart, redistributed to local neighborhoods, and rebuilt in midstream. The problem was akin to trying to rebuild a ship at sea. In a number of local reform efforts it proved difficult to sweep away the web of cross-purposes and narrow preoccupations simply by naming new principles and objectives. Baker (1990) described the problems Action for Boston Community Development (a multipurpose agency with roots in the community action program) experienced in encouraging its own Head Start and job training divisions to "join forces" to offer more integrated services, with balanced attention to social support and economic self-sufficiency. The job training staff, who viewed adults as workers, were uncomfortable with the lack of clear expectations for parents within the Head Start program culture. They did not understand why Head Start could not change its daily and weekly schedule to provide full day child care. Head Start staff, who viewed adults primarily as parents, were unconvinced that employment was always appropriate or possible for parents, noting that some were not ready for jobs, some were in crisis. They feared that parents would be pushed into low-paying, dead-end jobs without supportive services, and would lose Medicaid benefits. No one created the conceptual bridge between the two cultures, for example trying to turn parent involvement requirements and activities within Head Start into the first steps on a path toward self-sufficiency (see Herr and Halpern 1993).

It also proved difficult to reform services in the numerous states and cities preoccupied by fiscal and institutional crisis, in other words, in just those contexts in which the need for reform was greatest. For example, it was impossible to implement flexible and individualized helping under conditions in which already high caseloads were increasing—to get agencies to work together in rethinking roles and responsibilities when agency directors were preoccupied with budget cuts, and in some cases with survival. Not least, renewed interest in locally rooted service reform coincided with an escalation in the rate of deterioration of inner-city neighborhoods (Wacquant and Wilson 1989:11), including loss of remaining institutions and communal social controls, the thinning out of informal support networks, and increases in survival-oriented patterns of coping and relating. The renewed human service infrastructure from the 1960s had long since dissipated in many ghetto neighborhoods, leaving little to build on in efforts to use human services reform as a vehicle for strengthening community.

As throughout the century, local necessity—individual agencies or communities feeling a need to do something—has remained the key to the continued nurturance of neighborhood-based services within poor neighborhoods. And outside those neighborhoods the rationales for neighborhood-based services, particularly the more conservative ones, continued to resonate with Americans. In an argument terrifying for its continuity with Progressive-era themes, Husock (1992:66–67) advocates bringing back the settlement movement and its "commonsense" approach:

Those who believe that the prospects for upward mobility of the poor can be enhanced by acculturation—by introduction to middle-class norms—can find value in clubs and tutoring. Others, who believe the prospects for bringing the poor into the economic mainstream are bleak notwithstanding individual effort, are alive to the ways in which settlements can at least make life in poor neighborhoods safer and more pleasant. If there is a cultural assumption that unites these diverse efforts—and links today's settlements to the past—it is the implicit belief that . . . those with middle-class means and values should disseminate those values in society through direct, personal involvement.

Conclusion: Strengths and Limitations of Neighborhood-Based Services

Neighborhood-based services have always embodied multiple purposes—to assist poor people in coping with the hardships of poverty and economic insecurity, to guide and monitor them in their roles as parents, to teach them middle-class ways and link them to mainstream opportunities, to provide basic health care, to counsel, encourage, organize, advocate for. At the same time the primary role of neighborhood-based services has been different in each historical era, reflecting the situation and composition of inner-city neighborhoods themselves. In the early decades of the century neighborhood-based services were conceived as a means of bringing mainstream society into poor neighborhoods, and later as a means of compensating for the effects of bureaucracy within the expanding service system. In the 1960s they became a vehicle for the poor themselves to use, to organize, to control public resources, to create their own little society within the larger one.

The federally funded neighborhood-based services of the 1960s helped buffer the effects of a deteriorating social and institutional fabric in inner-city neighborhoods. Those who designed, managed, and provided these services also struggled with but could not resolve the problem of recreating good quality human services in the inner city. To some extent their efforts were constrained by competing purposes, forced upon and embraced by them, conceptual confusion, specific strategic errors, lack of support from the helping professions and traditional human service institutions. The efforts of neighborhood based services also were constrained by worsening social conditions in inner-city neighborhoods. The tasks of neighborhood-based services seemed to become more ambiguous—even dissonant—as the situation of inner-city communities changed fundamentally from port of entry to isolated and excluded enclave. Many programs found it impossible to ignore community organizing, advocacy, and related tasks, even though these often distracted a program from its primary mission. Providers of neighborhood-based services increasingly found themselves in over their heads, feeling compelled to address the causes and consequences of all sorts of social problems they were ill-equipped to handle. The staff of neighborhood-based programs came to believe that no one cared about the children and adults they worked with but themselves. This belief provided fuel for working under very difficult conditions. But it complicated individual helping efforts enormously.

To some extent there were also inherent obstacles to creating conceptually clear, internally healthy, and helpful services for devalued populations in devalued communities. Neighborhood-based services draw their identity, resources, and sustenance primarily from the neighborhood in which they operate. This can be problematic in isolated, depleted, and disorganized neighborhoods. In commenting on the various neighborhood-based programs of the War on Poverty, Rainwater (1970:410) argues that they had "the effect of emphasizing the special status of the poor, and catering to it," in part because they were "based on an assumption of the continued existence of the poor." Neighborhood-based services in poor neighborhoods have helped both to sustain and inadvertently to maintain those neighborhoods. They are now one of the few remaining sources of structure and institutional support in many inner-city neighborhoods. Yet too often they seem as isolated and stressed as the neighborhoods in which they are embedded. Too often they have internalized the sense of stigma of the community in which they are embedded. Neighborhood-based programs have tended to be not just socioeconomically but racially homogeneous (because they draw from a community), reinforcing racial separation.

Historically neighborhood-based services have appeared to be a creative response to the difficulties of inner-city life. One can argue that along with the community development corporations they have constituted a series of natural experiments concerning the means of rebuilding community in the ghetto. Nonetheless neighborhood-based services—through no fault of their own—do not address the core issues facing inner-city communities and their residents. Friendly, responsive services cannot help devalued, excluded people feel valued and included. The notion of rebuilding a sense of community through networks of neighborhood-based services can only be taken so far when the majority of poor children and families are geographically and socially isolated from the rest of society.

CHAPTER SEVEN

EMERGING
NEIGHBORHOOD-BASED
INITIATIVES

The process of social and economic disinvestment in inner-city communities that began in the 1950s slowed only modestly during the 1960s and 1970s and intensified again during the 1980s. Over the past two decades hundreds of thousands of blue-collar jobs have been lost from the inner city. Between 1969 and 1987 the unemployment rate for inner-city males with limited education went from 19 percent to 50 percent (Kasarda 1989:42). Little effort was made by public authorities to maintain the older housing stock of central cities or such public institutions as schools and hospitals. Cities received a declining share of federal spending. During the 1980s the percentage of city expenditures "covered by federal aid fell from 22 to 6 percent" (Weir 1993:8). To the extent that there was any federal urban policy during the 1980s, it was focused on tax cuts, regulatory relief, and privatization. These presented elusive targets for local urban social movements trying to link government policy and public institutional practices to neighborhood decline and elusive handles for those who wished to use government programs to support neighborhood renewal (Fainstein 1987:324).

Between federal neglect, the loss of the local tax base, the continuing constriction of municipal budgets, and the outmigration of remaining middle-class families, inner-city communities no longer had the resources to support even a minimal network of social, religious, economic institutions critical to both daily life and long-term social mobility. One can question whether there ever was a "golden age" in the African American ghetto. Even in the 1950s, when the majority of household heads worked, few earned enough to escape poverty (Stein 1993:222). Already in 1959 the African Americans and Hispanics who populated the ghettos were three times as likely as the general population to be chronically jobless (Stein 1993:238). Nonetheless as Wacquant and Wilson (1989:15) write,

Today's ghetto inhabitants comprise almost exclusively the most marginal and oppressed sections of the black community. Having lost the economic underpinnings and much of the fine texture of organization and patterned activities that allowed previous generations of urban blacks to sustain family, community, and collectivity even in the face of continued economic hardship and unflinching racial subordination, the inner city now presents a picture of radical class and racial exclusion.

After having observed the well-being of poor minority families and the fabric of their neighborhoods deteriorate over the past decade, government, foundations, and increasingly the corporate community have once again become interested in efforts to address that deterioration. Much of the renewed attack on persistent poverty is going into programs designed implicitly or explicitly to help people escape the inner city through education, welfare to work initiatives, and social services. There is growing interest in addressing what has been called spatial mismatch, that is the mismatch between where entry-level jobs are located and where the people who most need those jobs live. Two types of strategies have been proposed to address this mismatch. The former, called dispersal strategies, is exemplified by the Move to Opportunity program, a new federal demonstration (based on Chicago's Gatreaux Program) that will provide families on Section 8 and public housing waiting lists rent subsidies and other help in moving to the suburbs. (Each family that participates in this program, run by the Department of Housing and Urban Development, will get a voucher worth three thousand dollars, and the equivalent of five hundred dollars' worth of information and counseling.) The second, sometimes called mobility strategies, does not try deliberately to move people out of the inner city (in a sense depleting it further), it rather tries to help link inner-city residents to jobs in the near suburbs, through transportation and provision of job information. Presumably mobility strategies leave inner-city residents the choice to stay or leave once they have found jobs.

Meanwhile the idea of transforming inner-city residents' lives by transforming inner-city neighborhoods themselves once again is receiving attention (perhaps in deference to the fact that some six to eight million people continue to make their lives in the inner city). Initiatives are underway in scores of inner-city neighborhoods, including South Central In Los Angeles, Liberty City in Miami, Belle Glade in Palm Beach County, Frogtown in St. Paul, Sandtown-Winchester in Baltimore, Bushwick, East Harlem, and the South Bronx in New York, Harambee in Milwaukee, Upper Albany in Hartford, and Dudley Street in Boston. The Carter Center in Atlanta is sponsoring an "Atlanta Initiative," and Walter Rostow is spearheading an "Austin Initiative." This flurry of activity has been given a variety of names, including geographically targeted grant-making and place based strategies. Neighborhood-based initiative, if not yet the neighborhoods targeted, is experiencing a revitalization.

As ever the new generation of initiatives builds on and is shaped by earlier ones—the social housing of the 1930s and 1940s, urban renewal (at least its ideals), Gray Areas, Community Action, Model Cities. Hallmarks of the new initiatives include comprehensiveness, that is, an effort to address all aspects of neighborhood life and residents' support needs, attention to both tangible and intangible aspects of neighborhood life (i.e., to pride and psychological investment in the neighborhood as well as to housing, services, etc.), partnerships between neighborhood-based organizations and either or both government and the private sector, and the development of some type of representative governance entity. Many initiatives are starting with strategic planning exercises that assess strengths and weaknesses in different domains of community life and then develop "action plans" in each domain. Most new initiatives have a participatory ethos, reminiscent of community action. Most include traditional community organizing among their core activities. Yet most also remain firmly in the hands of professionals with project management experience, and funders frequently play an active advisory role.

The defining characteristics of the emerging initiatives reflect a number of assumptions. One is that, especially in poor neighborhoods, physical, economic, and social, individual and collective, adult and child well-being are all interconnected. A second is that government, mainstream institutions such as schools and housing authorities, and not least major foundation and corporate funders, cannot be viewed and treated as adversaries that have to be pressured to reform. In addition, the new initiatives reflect a belief by government itself that it is not the best front-line problem solver. Rather it should be putting public resources, and in some cases government functions as well, into the hands of locally based organizations. (In at least a few cases federal, state, or local governments are using the opportunity afforded by the new initiatives to by-pass their own categorical rules and programs, an updated and more benign version of 1960s efforts to by-pass City Hall and go directly to communities.) A third assumption is that professionals' experience and residents' own understanding and perception of their lives and neighborhood have to be combined to create a shared understanding of neighborhood revitalization tasks.

Those involved with inner-city neighborhood initiatives have long been sensitive to the interconnectedness and mutual influence of different domains. The Progressives viewed the neighborhood organically, as a complex whole. They also believed that individual, group, and physical environment shaped each other in an almost cyclical manner. So-called housers have always believed that people affect the quality of housing just as housing shapes them. As early as the late 1950s there was recognition that simply building public housing would not unmake the ghetto—not alter the way ghetto residents thought about and approached their lives (see Clark 1965:32). Today's comprehensiveness also echoes the 1960s' call for attacking the poverty cycle at many points simultaneously.

Historically in poor neighborhoods the mutual influence of people and neighborhood, individual and collectivity, tended to work to the benefit of both. The values, institutional structures, and networks within the immigrant neighborhood encouraged at least a measure of upward mobility. An established immigrant already entrenched in a trade learned quickly about jobs, and more important could vouch for his nephew or landsman. Immigrant ghettos were also at least moderately heterogeneous economically and, contrary to popular perception, often heterogeneous ethnically (Massey and Denton 1993:32). There was enough fluidity of people and porousness of identity and boundaries that the influence of people on their environment and environment on its inhabitants was diffuse and ambiguous. In contrast the absolute lack of opportunity, the sense of exclusion, and the closed isolation of many of today's inner-city neighborhoods create a different, more toxic dynamic. There are no networks that can provide entrée to the world of jobs. Adults' and children's lives and aspirations are figuratively and sometimes literally restricted to the boundaries of their neighborhood. Children can grow up twenty minutes from the downtown business and cultural districts and never see those parts of the city. According to Massey and Denton (1993:12), the inner-city ghetto has passed a threshold of isolation and problem density beyond which "each actor who makes a decision that undermines neighborhood well-being makes it increasingly likely that other actors will do the same." Played out over time, the influence of the individual on the neighborhood and vice versa create a downward trajectory that is increasingly difficult to reverse.

Almost thirty years ago Kenneth Clark was already noting a variety of damaging effects of urban residential segregation combined with physical neglect and social exclusion. People in the ghetto, he wrote, "seem to have given up in the little things that are so often the symbol of the larger things" (Clark 1965:27). People no longer tried to keep parks and streets clean. Shop owners no longer painted their stores. Little effort was made to sustain any kind of cultural life. He went on to note that "human beings who are forced to live under ghetto conditions and whose daily experience tells them that almost nowhere in society are they respected and granted the ordinary dignity and courtesy accorded to others will, as a matter of course, begin to doubt their own worth (Clark 1965:64). If anything residential segregation and social exclusion has worsened in the intervening years.

Part of what makes the situation of today's inner-city neighborhoods so unprecedented is the lack of balance between risk and protective factors. Risk factors are present in every dimension and corner of family and neighborhood life, activating each other, exacerbating each other's effects, and leaving little space for the protective factors that buffer the effects of risk. A young parent with a poor nurturance history might be able to overcome the effects of that history with support of a spouse, professional help, and general well-being in her surroundings. But too often such protective factors are absent from the inner city today. That parent's young children might be able to find nurturance and guidance from other family members or in high quality social programs, but too often those protective factors are not there, at least not consistently. A child might be able to cope with inattentive parenting or family conflict with support from teachers or other school staff. But when too many children bring worries and preoccupations to school, teachers themselves cannot cope. Lack of support and reward for school success in the neighborhood environment also limit the potential of school success as a protective factor in children's lives. Schorr (1988:15) writes that not only do the interconnected child and family problems associated with inner-city poverty—difficulties in school, juvenile crime, substance abuse, school-age childbearing, maternal and child health problems, neglectful or abusive parenting—cluster together in individuals, but "increasingly the individuals also cluster, and the damage that begins in childhood and becomes so visible in adolescence reverberates throughout a neighborhood as part of an intergenerational cycle of social devastation."

Stark (1987:895) describes a complex ecology of crime in the inner city, with density, material hardship, physical dilapidation, and social stigma feeding parental neglect, moral cynicism, increased opportunity for crime and deviance, increased motivation to deviate, and diminished social control, which in turn feed the former variables, in a vicious cycle. For example density and dilapidation in homes (along with family factors) push children and youth into the neighborhood, making supervision of children more difficult. The density of people within the neighborhood in turn increases exposure, opportunity, and pressure to engage in crime. More crime leads (ironically) to laxer crime enforcement and weakening of social controls, greater moral cynicism (as those who are most deviant seem to be the most successful), and so on. The same kind of dynamic can be seen in housing, in both maintenance and lending decisions. When one property owner or tenant decides not to take care of a property, it increases the likelihood that others will begin neglecting their homes or apartments (Massey and Denton 1993:13). In calculations of future risk in housing loans, risk is attached both to the borrower (likely ability to pay) and to the house itself (likely value as a function of the future of the neighborhood). The decision not to lend devalues people, which in turn devalues the neighborhood, further decreasing the likelihood of future loans in a worsening cycle (as noted in chapter 2, Bartlet 1993:147). Eventually disinvestment leads to real deterioration of both individual and neighborhood, further undermining future lending decisions.

Not least this dynamic can be seen in employment. It is evident that available work shapes social norms; people do what they can and must to earn a living. The extraordinary levels of unemployment in many inner-city communities cannot be ascribed solely to the movement of jobs to the urban periphery and the suburbs. The effects of that movement have been exacerbated by hardening discrimination against ghetto males, partly a continuation of historic racism, partly a result of experience with the job-related behavior of those males. One can argue that the patterns Schorr describes above extend into adulthood for men, contributing to inner-city male unemployment. A formative environment characterized by erratic nurturance, exclusion from the mainstream social world, and constant social depradation leads to attitudes and behaviors—walking off jobs, threatening employers, refusing to put up with unpleasant working conditions—that simply reinforce racist stereotypes, further heightening reluctance to hire African American men. Worsening male unemployment further worsens community conditions, further undermining men's formative experiences, and so on. In other words, the mutual destruction of people and neighborhood has so intensified in inner-cities that the tasks facing the current generation of inner-city initiatives are qualitatively different than those of the past.

Funders and designers of emerging neighborhood initiatives are responding to the concentration of risk factors characteristic of inner-city communities by working or intending to work on many fronts simultaneously: community economic development, job training and referral, housing, land use, safety, schooling, day care, health care, substance abuse, recreation, youth services, family support services (including case management with multiply vulnerable families), community organizing, leadership development. In some cases they are being selective about the neighborhoods they choose to invest in, seeking those considered to be hard-pressed but still viable as communities. The Annie Casey Foundation's neighborhood initiative will target "neighborhoods which are experiencing serious social and environmental decline, but are not devastated and have some potential for revitalization (Annie Casey Foundation 1992:6). Taking a page from the history of community organizing, the new initiatives also are focusing attention equally on long-term rebuilding and visible, short-term improvements: reclaiming a block from drug dealers, cleaning up a garbage-strewn lot, starting an after-school program. This dual strategy in turn is reflected in some initiatives by a strategy of directly funding service providers or neighborhood groups with innovative ideas, as well as the core institution or governance group (usually with the acquiescence if not blessing of that core institution or group).

Three Examples of New Initiatives

Dudley Street Neighborhood Initiative

The Dudley Street Neighborhood Initiative (DSNI) in Boston is the best established of the newer neighborhood initiatives. It emerged in 1984 as a community response to the planning efforts of the Riley Foundation, a local foundation. The Riley Foundation originally pulled together thirty community agencies to develop a neighborhood revitalization plan. After developing the plan the agencies called a community meeting to present it. The residents who showed up rejected the plan, in part because they had not been involved in developing it (Eisen 1992:20). This led to the formation of a "collaborative" among neighborhood residents, human service agencies, businesses, and churches, and eventually to a second planning process with residents involved. The collaborative has a governing board with representatives from different ethnic groups in the neighborhood, two community development corporations, local human service agencies, businesses, and religious organizations. There is also a core professional staff. DSNI currently has about eighteen hundred members and a budget of $650,000.

The Dudley Street neighborhood comprises one and a half square miles at the borders of Roxbury and Dorchester. The population of twelve thousand is 40 percent African American, 30 percent Hispanic, 20 percent Cape Verdean, and 10 percent white. The neighborhood has twenty churches (some in storefronts), five parks (mostly neglected), four large and dozens of small community gardens, three elementary schools, a middle school, library, a shelter for homeless people, and a multiservice center (nearby). It is also served by two nearby community development corporations. At the same time "there are no major supermarkets in this neighborhood, no banks, no community centers, no swimming or recreation facilities . . . staggering amounts of vacant land—more than four million square feet—grown over with weeds. . . . Buildings and storefronts are abandoned, some are boarded up, some even burned out" (introduction to the Dudley Street Neighborhood Initiative n.d.:n.p.). Much of the vacant land—the highest concentration in Boston—is a result of landlord-sponsored arson (Eisen 1992:19). Over the years the Dudley Street neighborhood had also become a dumping ground for illegal waste (with three illegal trash transfer stations) and abandoned autos. As a result of the history of dumping, the soil in some of the community gardens contains toxins. The human toll of the neighborhood's long-term neglect is high; for example some fifteen hundred neighborhood residents are on waiting lists for substance abuse treatment, presumably only a portion of all those with substance abuse problems.

Between 1985 and 1987 the nascent DSNI and its staff organized neighborhood residents to tackle a number of the discreet problems resulting from the years of neglect, exploitation, and resident apathy. Early accomplishments included cleaning up many of the vacant lots (one initiative report notes that "the stench, which for so many years had hung over the neighborhood, was lifted"), towing away hundreds of abandoned cars, getting the illegal trash transfer stations closed down, getting new street signs and lights installed, and getting a rail stop to downtown Boston restored. These accomplishments were only partly about physical renewal. They were also about changing residents' perceptions of their neighborhood and what was possible in it.

A second, more inclusive planning process got underway in 1987, resulting in a five-year strategic plan for the neighborhood. The plan included objectives for land use, housing, jobs, youth development, community services, safety, and environmental health. The plan used the metaphor of an "urban village" to describe the planners' vision for the transformation of the neighborhood. The idea presumably was to create (or recreate) all the elements of traditional communities—housing, retail space, light industry, human service facilities, a community center, and a town commons area. As would be the case in subsequent initiatives, new and rehabilitated housing was the anchor for the larger plan. The plan was particularly innovative in its conception of land use as the key to the future of the neighborhood.

A central concern of neighborhood residents since the outset of the initiative had been gaining control of the future use of vacant land, owned by 130 separate individuals as well as by the City of Boston. DSNI board and staff felt that the way to accomplish this was to address housing and land use "wholesale rather than one lot at a time" (Keenan 1992:45). In an unprecedented move DSNI asked the City of Boston to grant it the authority of eminent domain, in effect giving DSNI (in consultation with the city) the right to decide how to redevelop much of the vacant land in the neighborhood. An agreement with the city was signed in October 1990 that gave DSNI eminent domain authority over thirty acres of privately owned land in an area called Dudley Triangle. In March 1992 the Ford Foundation's Program Related Investment (PRI) division provided a $2 million loan to DSNI (at 1 percent interest) to buy vacant land for redevelopment. (Ford's deputy director for PRI called the loan a "high-risk" venture, in part because it was unclear if the city was going to come through with housing funds, tax breaks, loan guarantees, and the deeding over of city-owned land, all needed to make redevelopment work; Keenan 1992:45).

Anecdotal reports suggest that DSNI is making modest progress in achieving its objectives for the Dudley Street neighborhood. Construction has begun on a modest number of low-rise housing units to be sold to low- and moderate-income people. Mortgage subsidies will be provided by the Department of Housing and Urban Development's Nehemiah Opportunity Grant program as well as other local programs. A "leadership academy" has been developed to teach neighborhood residents "skills ranging from public speaking to grant proposal writing and accounting" (Eisen 1992:21). At the same time there is already a sense among local stakeholders that the master plan for the neighborhood was too ambitious in both scope and time frame. Objectives with respect to economic development, human services, community centers (planned and designed with input from youth), and housing itself have been put in a longer-term time frame. DSNI's first executive director, Peter Medoff, notes that "deep, grounded, real community-building takes time. . . . You have to have patience and you have to have faith in the people who live in the neighborhood" (cited in Boston Foundation 1992:3).

Comprehensive Community Revitalization Program

The objective of the Comprehensive Community Revitalization Program (CCRP), initiated in early 1992, is to examine how, with technical and financial supports, community development corporations can become institutional bases and engines for broad neighborhood renewal. The proposal for the initiative argues that CDCs that have implemented large-scale housing programs are well-suited, by virtue of wide community ties, broad mission, and prior experience with large, multifaceted projects "to weave together the many separate programmatic strands essential to a cohesive [neighborhood] revitalization strategy" (Miller 1991a:8). Moreover having struggled to manage and maintain rehabilitated housing, CDCs understand intimately the human challenges to neighborhood renewal. At the same time "CDCs committed to holistic revitalization strategies face a formidable challenge. Their local environment is always changing and unstable. There are few, if any, models from which they can learn and no readily available sources of flexible money with which to attract and knit together many categorical programs" (Miller 1991a:9)

In physical terms—especially in recovery of abandoned housing and land—the South Bronx has been on the mend for at least a decade. Some eighteen thousand apartments in abandoned or vacant buildings have been or are in the process of being rehabilitated. In human terms there has been less progress: one-third of adults do not have a high school degree, one-quarter cannot read at a fourth grade level, one-half have no history of labor force participation. (At least some of the human needs arise from the use of the South Bronx as a location for rehousing the homeless.)

The CCRP initiative involves six CDCs, all with a strong history in housing, and will focus on geographic "core" areas surrounding rehabilitated housing. The overall initiative is directed by Anita Miller, who has played a key role in conceptualizing it and pulling in core resources. CCRP has raised about $5 million from ten foundations and corporations. The idea underlying CCRP is to use CDCs as local intermediaries, setting priorities, identifying and mobilizing resources, bringing organizations and people together, and serving as a vehicle for others (including government) to carry out their particular missions. Within each CDC the project is staffed by a program developer/manager and an outreach worker. A strong focus on assuring an adequate array of human services in the core areas has emerged in the early stages of the project. Foci include primary health care, day care and early childhood education, welfare to work, and youth development. Because work in these areas is new for at least a few of the participating CDCs, provision has been made for them to receive technical assistance and training from individuals or organizations with experience in each human service domain. In a number of cases, for example in the day care area with Child Care, Inc., long-term relationships have evolved from the initial contacts. Another way of addressing the capacity-building challenge has been to expose the CDCs to (and thereby implicitly encourage them to adapt) particular program models that come with their own training system, materials, and so forth (Miller 1991a:3). For example, three of the CDCs are looking at the HIPPY program, a home-based preschool education program for three and four year olds and their parents, which has a well-developed and tested set of procedures that guide implementation.

The CDCs are playing a variety of roles in securing and managing grants for particular purposes and in implementing direct services. The commonest pattern seems to be that of joint application and overall administration with a substantive organization, with the latter actually providing and overseeing direct services. For example the CDCs have worked closely with area health providers, including Montefiore and Bronx Lebanon Hospitals, to plan and secure funding for new primary care practices, and will run these practices jointly with those established health care providers. In welfare to work the CDCs have established a relationship with a well-known New York City program called America Works, which finds jobs and then provides follow-up support to welfare recipients. They also have managed to make the South Bronx one of a handful of sites nationwide to participate in a Department of Labor demonstration/replication of the Comprehensive Employment Training Program (CET), a "deep skills" training model that has had considerable success in California (Miller 1991a:3).

As with other initiatives CCRP is serving as a kind of magnet or depository for the particular problem- or geographically focused interests of different funders. For example, the Edna McConnell Clark Foundation has a program for housing homeless families, and "earmarked" its grant to CCRP to fund outreach workers to get formerly homeless families housed in CDC buildings in the target neighborhoods involved in CCRP activities (Miller 1991a:2). The linking of the six CDCs in one project has contributed to this magnetic effect. For example, it has increased the project's competitiveness in applying for grants. Four of the CDCs applied successfully as a group for a competitive Project HOPE grant from the Department of Housing and Urban Development. The CDCs have also provided support for each other, sharing ideas, contacts and so forth.

Leadership of CCRP, particularly Anita Miller, view the demonstration as an opportunity to learn. The proposal for CCRP was one of the few among those for emerging initiatives that raises as many questions as it makes promises (Miller 1991a:21–22). Central among these is the question of what additional capacity CDCs will need to play a leadership role in neighborhood revitalization. Other questions include: How will the CDCs relate to and work with municipal agencies? In particular, what will it take to turn their energies to neighborhood renewal? What approaches make the most sense in trying to create a more coherent local human service enterprise? How can CDCs rebuild paths to self-sufficiency for neighborhood residents? How should helping professionals in human service agencies relate to community residents? What balance of "traditional social work" and community organizing makes sense?

One of the early themes emerging in the CCRP initiative is the challenge of balancing external guidance and assistance to participating CDCs with the need to let each CDC grow by finding its own way and solving its own problems. Miller (1991a:3) notes that it has been difficult "to create a program with sufficient substance to satisfy funders at the same time [to] leave participants sufficient latitude to design their own efforts" (Miller 1991a:3). The six community development corporations involved in CCRP are all accomplished organizations in one way or another. Most of the six were already doing substantive work in one or more areas related to the initiative. For example the Banana Kelly Community Improvement Association has a large contract with the city to train youth in the construction trades and place them in jobs. Promesa, Inc.

already was a multifaceted organization when it signed on to CCRP, running substance abuse treatment programs, shelter programs, and youth services as well as doing housing. All six CDCs have their own established networks to draw on. Nonetheless evidence from the first full-year progress reports suggests that all are needing a good deal of help in shifting gears and taking the initiative to generate their own ideas and contacts in the service of CCRP objectives. Anita Miller has had to be very active in feeding them ideas and leads to funding and technical assistance. In effect she has modeled the process of identifying, pulling in, and using an array of external resources. For example, Miller describes how she linked one of the CDCs that wanted to strengthen its community credit union to the National Association of Community Development Credit Unions.

Community Building in Partnership

Community Building in Partnership (CBP) is an initiative focused on Baltimore's Sandtown-Winchester neighborhood. It began in 1990, and is a collaborative effort overseen by the city of Baltimore. The Enterprise Foundation, Sandtown residents, and two neighborhood organizations, Baltimoreans United in Leadership Development (BUILD) and the Sandtown-Winchester Improvement Association (SWIA), are key participants. Mayor Kurt Schmoke and developer James Rouse (creator of the Enterprise Foundation) were instrumental in conceiving the initiative and getting it started. Initiative staff proclaim it to be "the nation's first neighborhood transformation initiative" (Community Building in Partnership 1993a:1), by which presumably they mean the first to aspire to completely remake an inner-city neighborhood. The vision guiding the project is "the transformation of every dysfunctional system in the neighborhood—housing, education, human services, health care, public safety, employment and more" (Community Building in Partnership 1993a:1).

Sandtown-Winchester is a seventy-two-square block area of West Baltimore with a population of about ten thousand. The community has a rich, and in many respects positive history, although that history is built on the foundations of residential segregation. Unemployment is close to 40 percent; 83 percent of children live in poverty in single parent families; almost half of all adults do not have a high school diploma or a

General Equivalency Degree; 79 percent of housing units are in sub-standard condition. The community has six hundred vacant structures (some owned by the city) and one hundred vacant lots used for dumping of garbage. One planning document for the initiative describes "debris-strewn streets, alleys and backyards; poorly stabilized abandoned houses littered with trash; and rat infestation" (Community Building in Partnership 1992:37). Drug dealing and drug use are pervasive; drug- and other-related violence is commonplace; various family problems, including child abuse and neglect, "plague the community" (Community Building in Partnership 1992:40).

Like the Dudley Street Neighborhood Initiative, CBP emerged in part from community residents' response to an externally generated proposal for the neighborhood. Neighborhood leaders reportedly confronted Mayor Kurt Schmoke after a news conference in which he announced "two conventional housing projects. They said, 'We welcome new housing, but we don't need it if other changes cannot be made' " (Rankin 1992:xx). Schmoke, together with James Rouse and his organization, and the leadership of BUILD and SWIA, used this as an opportunity to create a task force that eventually led to a strategic planning and "visioning" process. Community residents, with support from professional staff (including city agency employees), chaired work groups in each of a number of substantive domains: residential development, recreational facilities, land use, health care, sanitation, family support services, education, youth services, substance abuse, sanitation, public safety, business development, retail goods and services, employment and training, community pride and spirit. The resulting analysis of the prevailing situation, pressing needs, opportunities (including potential resources that could be tapped), and recommended actions were assembled in a report that has come to be called the "Puzzle Book," because each substantive domain is depicted visually as a piece of a puzzle in the shape of the Sandtown-Winchester neighborhood. (The visual message communicated is that the kinds of discreet domains where deliberate action can be taken, when put together, are what make up a neighborhood. The puzzle metaphor also implicitly communicates how efforts in discreet areas relate to each other; that is, they can be both separate and, when fit together, create a whole.)

The strategic planning work groups identified well over a hundred discreet opportunities for action and potential resources and made perhaps half that many specific recommendations. Just a few examples:

Heighten city efforts to condemn and acquire vacant housing for redevelopment by non-profit and for profit developers. . . . Develop planned parks and play areas throughout the neighborhood. . . . Improve programming and utilization of the Lillian Jones Recreation Center. . . . Develop a comprehensive land use plan for Sandtown-Winchester to serve as a blueprint for community revitalization efforts. . . . Use zoning to cluster complementary land uses. . . . Repair and install new street lighting. . . . Develop an integrated, neighborhood-focused primary health care delivery system. . . . Monitor families with high truancy records. Reinstitute truant officer visits to families. . . . Improve communication and cooperation between community residents and the police. . . . Improve accessibility to conveniently located, competitively priced, clean, high quality retail goods and services. . . . Facilitate the provision and marketing of information that will help to make local people aware of and marketable for job opportunities outside the Sandtown-Winchester area.

(COMMUNITY BUILDING IN PARTNERSHIP 1992:19–66)

When taken as a whole, the exhaustive listing of problems, pressing needs, opportunities, and recommendations in the CBP Strategic Plan provides a detailed picture, a kind of blueprint of the way in which communities deteriorate. As if in confirmation of Kenneth Clark's observations, long-term political and economic neglect in Sandtown-Winchester created a climate in which the multitude of small and large elements that make a community viable fell away, one by one.

In the spring of 1992 professionally led program design clusters were set up for four program areas: health and human services, education, physical/economic development and community-building. The team drew on the strategic plan to develop specific programs and "implementation steps" in each of those broad areas. A set of guiding principles framed the design process, including: involvement of community residents in increasingly central roles in all initiative activities (providing training for those roles when necessary); a focus in service design on ease of use, a preventive orientation, and creation of a coherent overall local system; encouragement of flexibility around program management and funding requirements on the part of public and private sponsors and funders; use of existing resources to finance initiative activities to the extent possible; a focus on sustainability in service and activity design (Community Building in Partnership 1993b:10–11). Not surprisingly, the proposal resulting from the design process recommended creation of a new local institution, to be called Community Building in Partnership, Inc., to manage and provide an organizational base for the initiative. The board would have a majority of neighborhood residents; the chairman, initial president and majority of the board would be appointed by the mayor (since the city would be providing a lot of the resources for the initiative).

As in other initiatives, housing rehabilitation and improvement is to provide an important foundation for other activities. Program leadership also are committed to assuring that the resulting construction jobs go to neighborhood residents. One element of the operating plan calls for creation of a "neighborhood development center" that will focus on assembling financing for housing and land use issues. Other foci include creating mechanisms for service providers to cooperate more closely, at both the systems and individual family level, and renovating and filling out a market area, which will offer foods, crafts, cultural activities, and other retail goods. An early step in the local service reform will be to make an existing community center run by the city the focal point for services integration. With respect to long-term job creation the initiative will focus on customized, industry-linked training, responsive to the evolving demands of the area labor market, and on linking residents to jobs created by neighborhood renewal activities (Eilers 1993:personal communication). One area, which is addressed only lightly in the proposal that has been developed but eventually will have to receive fuller attention, is substance abuse. The proposal itself acknowledges that community residents report drugs and drug-related crime as the biggest obstacle to neighborhood transformation. (The initial plan proposes a prevention curriculum, general esteem-building efforts, and improvement of an existing residential treatment program.)

The planning of the CBP initiative provides a reminder that all the new initiatives have to fit into an already existing neighborhood in which, however depleted the neighborhood, renewal and maintenance activities are already going on. For example a good deal of housing activity was already underway in Sandtown-Winchester, including construction of 210 units of Nehemiah housing, of which nearly 50 percent were sold to area residents, and modernization of almost 600 public housing units. Habitat for Humanity has also been working in the community, rehabilitating a handful of houses every year. The community already had a variety of discreet innovative human service programs in maternal and child health, one elementary and one junior high school (being run by a private company), youth services, and so on. Efforts were already underway to foster participation in community life. For example, a program called SHARE (Self-Help and Resource Exchange) provides thirty dollars' worth of food for thirteen dollars plus two hours of community services. Part of the challenge facing the initiative will be to capitalize on these for the larger purposes of creating a coherent community renewal strategy while at the same time acknowledging their own integrity as discreet activities.

Framing CBP's ambitious objectives is the idea that for the Sandtown-Winchester neighborhood really to change, a critical mass of neighborhood residents have to take some responsibility for the effort: "While outside help is essential, ultimately inner-cities can be saved only if the people who live there accept personal responsibility for their fate" (Rankin 1992:xx). In order for this to occur the initiative has to help renew community residents' sense of "belonging, caring, self-respect, pride, joy" (Rouse, cited in Rankin 1992:xx) and, equally important, their belief that change for the better can occur at all. In turn the renewal of these feelings will be based in part on concrete evidence: improved housing and amenities and better services. The initiative has been successful in involving community residents in planning and implementation: in the focus groups that set initiative priorities, in management of community gardening, building maintenance, the community newspaper, crime and safety organizing, and so forth. Still, many residents simply are in no position to take an active role in a neighborhood renewal initiative, by virtue of age, situation, or level of personal well-being and functioning. Some simply remain skeptical, having seen community renewal programs come and go in the past.

Other Emergent Activity

In addition to funding discreet initiatives foundations, the corporate sector, and the federal government are relying increasingly on intermediary institutions to gather and then deploy in a coherent manner a critical mass of resources for neighborhood renewal. The Ford Foundation's Local Initiatives Support Corporation (LISC) has raised over $400 million, which it has used in turn to leverage another $1.4 billion. LISC has focused primarily on supporting CDCs' efforts to rehabilitate and build housing, but is now attempting to broaden the thrust of the projects it funds to include social services. A newer intermediary is the National Community Development Initiative (NCDI), funded by seven national foundations and the Prudential Corporation, which, like LISC, is focusing on both physical and human renewal. James Rouse's Enterprise Foundation is also playing the role of intermediary, bringing in resources to be deployed in initiatives around the country.

As this chapter is being written the Department of Housing and Urban Development, under the leadership of Henry Cisneros, is in the process of formulating the Clinton administration's policies for addressing urban poverty. It is likely that those policies will be organized around what HUD is calling a national community development initiative. One feature of this initiative will be a proposal to support ten Empowerment Zones and one hundred Enterprise Communities, in which the federal government will concentrate a variety of categorical waivers, tax breaks and incentives, and new federal funding. There will be capital investment incentives such as accelerated depreciation for tangible investments; "empowerment" incentives that permit neighborhood residents to accumulate wealth without the usual penalties for people dependent on means-tested public supports; employment and training credits for employers; HUD funds for crime and drug prevention and HUD matching funds for CDCs; and concentration of other federal funds such as Small Business Administration loans, Department of Labor training funds, Department of Education funds for community schools, and the like. Applicants for this initiative will have to prepare a comprehensive strategic plan "that brings together the community, the private sector and local government and demonstrates how the community will reform the delivery of government services." An Enterprise Board made up of cabinet secretaries will provide communities a single point of contact as well as authority to use categorical monies in flexible ways (Department of Housing and Urban Development 1993:6–8).

The Potential of The New Initiatives

Are the leadership of today's initiatives finally putting all the pieces together? Clearly breaking down the historic wall between physical renewal and social services is an important development. Reading the best of the strategic plans created by the new initiatives—for example that of Community Building in Partnership—one can begin to visualize what a multifaceted change process would be like. The ability of many of the new initiatives to balance a holistic, long-term vision of the community and immediate action to address discreet needs (including physical blight and lack of amenities and services) is exemplary. In other words, the new initiatives have not been overwhelmed by the pressing imperative to do everything at once, rather they have learned to hold some things in abeyance without abandoning them. Still, to a large extent comprehensiveness so far seems to mean making sure that one is addressing or planning to address a critical mass of the many obstacles to individual, family, and community well-being in the inner city. Moreover, to some extent the new initiatives are more like umbrellas for existing or planned investment than like catalysts for significant new investment in the inner city.

Underlying the multifaceted nature of emerging initiatives is a heightened search for the ingredients of a sufficiently powerful neighborhood renewal strategy. Having recognized that such a strategy cannot come from either housing improvement or community economic development or social services reform alone, nor from participation per se, it is not yet clear what the power of doing these things together might be. One can see clearly in the inner-city context how interrelated different domains are in fact—how problems in some domains constrain possibility in others, indeed strongly contribute to undermining others. Where a business decides to locate depends on availability of a reliable workforce, quality of physical surroundings, safety, and so forth. It is difficult to talk a small business man or woman into starting a new business in a neighborhood full of abandoned buildings. A child's motivation to stick with schooling depends in part on evidence in his or her community environment that doing so will pay off economically. It will be difficult to convince a child to stick with schooling if no one that child knows has a regular job. A child whose single parent is preoccupied with her own lack of well-being or with basic family survival will not get the parental nurturance, protection, and vigilance that might fortify him or her against the lure of gang association.

The argument, in part, is that if problems in one domain strongly affect possibilities in another, then that mutual influence should also be able to be used in a positive way. One can easily see the synergistic benefit of discreet efforts to connect domains and objectives: using a housing rehabilitation project to train young adults in various construction skills, adding a variety of social services to a housing project, designing a new housing development in a way likely to maximize parents' ability to supervise children when the latter are outside playing (getting adults involved in neighborhood watch also raises their awareness of what is happening to their own children outside the home). One can see the potential benefits of encouraging collaborations among formerly autonomous organizations and programs: after-school programs and the park district of a city, libraries and elementary schools, primary health care providers and high schools, police and youth serving organizations.

A variety of discreet questions generated by the new initiatives will not be answerable for at least a few years. These include the appropriate roles for CDCs versus those of social service agencies, the dynamics of public/private partnerships, what it takes and what the costs and benefits are of transferring government functions to private, neighborhood-based organizations, and related to that, what sorts of local governance arrangements seem to work best (Annie Casey Foundation 1992:13–14). The new initiatives seem particularly ambivalent toward existing human services, or at least do not seem to know how to use them as a resource for their broader community development aims. At a different level it remains to be seen whether the new initiatives will be able to lure adequate public sector reinvestment to inner-city neighborhoods, especially under the difficult financial conditions facing most cities in the early 1990s. (To some extent the private sector will only be lured back to many neighborhoods if it sees public sector commitment to the infrastructure, institutions, and people of those neighborhoods.)

Given the tight links among individual, family, group, and neighborhood in the inner city, another important question has to do with the calibration and timing of intervention in relation to those levels. A further question implied by this one is whether and how the types of deliberate interventions proposed and underway in new initiatives will affect the more subtle things that make a neighborhood what it is—beyond housing, parks, social services, even economic development. These may have to do with neighborliness, interdependence, important common institutions, sense of identification, beliefs about the future. Strategic planning documents and other analyses underlying current initiatives tend not to start from a very textured understanding of community residents' lives—what their daily lives are like, what relationships are like, the meaning they make of their lives and their community. It is not clear if the lack of detail—how one gets a mother to wake up early enough every day to get her children off to school, what to do, if anything, about the breakdown of marriage as an institution, how one can help children acknowledge and cope with the pain of constant worry about (and disappointment with) their families, how one gets gang members to affiliate with something different, how people learn to construct a future for themselves—will hurt the development of implementation strategies. There is also a measure of denial, as there has to be with any intervention into difficult circumstances. For example, drug dealers are described as if they were intruders who have to be pushed out, not people's brothers and cousins and fathers, in other words, not part of what defines a particular neighborhood.

A key question is whether proponents have arrived at their new level of commitment and understanding in time. A dilemma facing all current initiatives is how to address—indeed how to think about—the extraordinary degree of deterioration and loss in the inner city. While this situation suggests an effort to try to remake the whole neighborhood, to return it to some past condition, it also creates enormous obstacles to doing so. Some inner-city neighborhoods no longer collectively embody even the minimal resources—the little bit of extra food and money, the time, the personal energy, the caring—needed to maintain a sense of community amidst exclusion and hardship.

It seems particularly clear that it will be extraordinarily difficult to bring significant numbers of jobs back to the inner-city. Beyond the marginal role of microenterprises there simply has been too little success in even the most thoughtful efforts to try to create jobs in the inner city over the past twenty years. (Even in poor Hispanic neighborhoods such as San Antonio's West Side, where there tends to be plentiful informal economic activity, such activity creates few jobs relative to the total need; Chapas 1993:xx). The implication is that the model of a viable inner-city neighborhood will have to be focused elsewhere, perhaps on an adequate array of retail services, on the presence of cultural institutions and recreational opportunities, on the renewal of community rituals and opportunities for civic participation, on optimism about the future of the neighborhood, as well as on the more obvious physical infrastructure, human services, and safety. As one long-time resident of Baltimore's Sandtown-Winchester neighborhood notes, "This couldn't be the [economically diverse] neighborhood I grew up in no matter what. The role models left. You can't get them to move back. But you can take what you have and work with it" (Barringer 1992:A1).

The dark ghetto is institutionalized pathology; it is chronic self-perpetuating pathology; and it is the futile attempt by those with power to confine that pathology so as to prevent the spread of its contagion to the larger community. —KENNETH CLARK, Dark Ghetto

The demands of those days and nights on the streets, the smoke and the flames, are simply not be to taken in. The most radical reorganization of our lives could hardly sat-isfy them. —ELIZABETH HARDWICK, commenting on the Watts Riots

The American preference for addressing poverty and social exclusion through neighborhood-based initiatives has left a mixed legacy. The responsive human services and community development activities stim-ulated by neighborhood initiative have tempered the hardship resulting from societal neglect, and more recently exclusion, of poor neighbor-hoods and poor people. The participatory aspects of neighborhood initiative have helped tap the energies and imagination of community residents, played a modest role in building community-mindedness, provided a modest number of entry-level jobs, and provided new outlets as well as a training ground for civic activism and leadership development. The local planning and governance functions of neighborhood initiatives have made government more sensitive to inner-city community conditions and provided mechanisms for residents of poor neighborhoods to express their interests (Fainstein 1990:235). The emergence of another notably entrepreneurial generation of initiatives in the early 1990s points once again to the vitality of this problem-solving approach, the innovative ideas, energy, and resources it can draw to itself and generate. The new initiatives remind us of the theoretical logic of neighborhood initiative—its appropriate scale and governability, its consonance with American ideals, its holistic approach to understanding and addressing problems, its tendency to mediate between the structure of opportunity and people's ability to take advantage of opportunity.

Neighborhood initiative frequently has embodied broad societal objectives as well as immediate local ones. Beginning with the Progressives there has been an expectation that neighborhood initiative would reconcile competing values (e.g., those underlying capitalism and community), diffuse political power, redirect capital, regulate broad social change, and generally improve society. The means for achieving these broad objectives would include example, contagion of values, connecting people and interests, the collective influence of services provided, and bottom-up pressure of various sorts.

Neighborhood initiatives in fact have striven to understand and convey to the larger public the complex reasons for family poverty, and to question the accepted bases of inequality. They have struggled to restore the principles of community to American life, to give that vague term a substantive meaning, to restore and maintain the idea of locality as a basis for social participation (Martinez-Brawley 1990:11). Working against the grain, they have kept alive the practices of participatory democracy: "face-to-face" interactions in which people "can learn from each other, reason with one another, and search for common interests" (Berry, Portney, and Thomson 1993:3). The leaders of neighborhood initiatives have played an important role in setting the terms of reform debate in each era. Community organizers time and again have managed to create enough bottom-up pressure to induce modest institutional and legal reforms that affected those living outside the inner city as well as in. Neighborhood initiatives have fostered and sometimes forced modest redistribution of public and private investment in poor neighborhoods.

Nonetheless the historic experience with neighborhood initiative suggests that it is at best an ameliorative, not a transforming, problem-solving strategy. With respect to poor families' concrete needs, local political machines, mutual assistance associations, charity organizations, and public aid bureaucracies frequently have had more to offer than discreet neighborhood initiatives, although the quid pro quo was greater. In terms of poor people's and poor neighborhoods' interests, the leadership of neighborhood initiatives have always been constrained by the fact that while they could create a new negotiating table, and bring established interests to that table, they were were negotiating from a position of vulnerability. They were coming to the table with less political power and fewer resources to start with. They have been constrained also by the fact that neighborhood initiative often is only loosely connected or unconnected to the traditional political processes that determine how public resources are distributed. Neighborhood initiatives have been accommodated and themselves transformed by local political institutions, human service bureaucracies, and private interests. They have been used to maintain social and physical order.

Neighborhood initiatives also have been far more shaped by than have shaped the beliefs, social dynamics, and problem solving tendencies of American society. Principal among these has been our tendency to bound urban poverty and its correlates, to locate their causes and solutions in the people who are experiencing them, to interpret them in terms that do not require adjustment by those who live outside the inner city. In spite of evidence to the contrary, for example the persistence of wages and means-tested supports too low to meet basic family needs, we continue to believe that people singlehandedly create and perpetuate their own hardship. We continue to view, or at least to treat inner-city neighborhoods as if they were autonomous entities—not really part of society—created by residents who were masters of their community's fate. "The people are going to solve their own problems" becomes "The poor are going to solve their own problems." Yet there is now abundant evidence that the beliefs, priorities, and practices of people and institutions rooted outside poor neighborhoods have had a profound effect on creating and then undermining the quality of life within them, and on constraining neighborhood residents' efforts to improve their individual and collective lives.

The idea that poor neighborhoods contain the resources and capacities for their own regeneration can be, and often has been, used to promote self-help without the requisite external supports and linkages. Even under the best of conditions only a small portion of residents act as community custodians (Suttles 1972), and fewer still as community developers. Life in the inner city—at least today—appears to sap rather than promote the energy and sense of identification needed for community-mindedness (as well as the flexible and innovative thinking needed to overcome reality). Scarce resources are viewed primarily in terms of personal and family survival. Competition around existing and any new resources is heightened. Belmonte (1989:49) writes that "all men yearn for relationships founded on an achieved trust. . . . But trust fails in a world of poverty and socially generated scarcity, and so the relations of community also fail, in terms of what they might otherwise provide."

The experiences related in this book suggest that while the principles and practices of neighborhood initiative can provide residents of poor neighborhoods a voice, and strengthen local feelings of social relatedness, they also can exacerbate the vulnerabilities of a local community. In a society given to categorizing, dividing, and distancing as mechanisms for responding to social needs, emphasizing the integrity of a local community can contribute to the separation of that community and its residents from others. Even when a sense of connection and solidarity can be built within a marginal community, that is not the same as a sense that oneself and one's community are connected to and valued by the larger society. Civic participation in poor urban neighborhoods has often meant mobilizing to protest one or another form of perceived injustice, or to defend the neighborhood from external redevelopment plans formulated without consulting neighborhood residents. Such participation sometimes has yielded victory against further or continuing harm and injury. At the same time it rarely has done much to improve community residents' lives and life chances. Not least, creating local governance bodies and mechanisms can seem somewhat empty when the local community has few public resources of its own to govern. (Local control appears to have more meaning for suburban communities than urban neighborhoods for just this reason.)

The history of neighborhood initiative also reflects more subtle contradictions and disproportions. Reformers have not only asked the poor to solve problems that they did not cause, but have distrusted either or both their capacity to do so and the motives of the indigenous leadership that emerged with self-help efforts. Reformers also often have disliked the consequences of community mobilization, whether articulation of specific demands or expression of anger and frustration (Marris and Jackson 1991:11). The tendency to trust the residents of poor communities halfway is as old as neighborhood initiative itself. Morone (1990:126) described the Progressives' approach to local control as "protoparticipatory," since middle-class reformers themselves both set the reform agenda and determined courses of action. Lack of trust for residents of poor neighborhoods particularly undermined government- and foundation-sponsored initiatives in the 1960s. Neighborhood initiative has been viewed as consonant with American problem-solving traditions only when the dynamics and demands that it presented seemed reasonable to those living outside of poor neighborhoods.

The Changing Role and Meaning of Neighborhood Initiative

Although basic assumptions and purposes have remained consistent, the ground under neighborhood initiatives has shifted dramatically over the course of the past century. In particular the role and meaning of neighborhood initiative has been strongly influenced by the changing meaning of residence in the inner city. Historically, neighborhood initiatives were catching poor people in an early stage on their way to the mainstream. There was at least a loose kind of consonance between the assumptions and strategies of initiatives like the settlements and the preoccupations of residents of poor neighborhoods. Even when there was dissonance, around such issues as the validity of traditional values and practices, tenement reform, and compulsory education, the gap did not matter so much because poor people had their own functional mechanisms for mutual support, because the reforms being sought benefited poor people as often as not, and because the fault lines of society were more in the developing relations between wage laborers and the corporations for which they worked.

The context, and the stakes, for neighborhood initiative changed dramatically in the 1950s. Minority immigrants from the rural South found that their neighborhoods were not so much way stations as premature end-points for their imagined journey into the mainstream. As Gregg (1992:358) notes, black migration after World War II was different in motive and dynamic than earlier black and European migration. It was far more "a movement of resignation and despair," the participants as much "refugees as migrants." Major initiatives like urban renewal and public housing became interwoven with the most important changes occurring in society at the time. The neighborhood initiatives of the 1960s had to cope with cross-currents that were only partly perceived or understood: the emergence for the first time in American history of a class of economically superfluous people, the breakdown in the black community of historically adaptive patterns of coping with hardship and discrimination, the hardening of residential segregation in urban areas, the extension of civil rights struggles into the black ghettos, and the ambivalence of the federal and local governments in the face of all these social trends.

Beginning in 1949 with the passage of the Federal Housing Act, federal policy played an important role in shaping the life of inner-city neighborhoods. Marcuse (1993:362) argues that "with redevelopment and urban renewal government powers were for the first time clearly and openly placed at the service of private interests." The professed aim of such practices as granting private developers powers of eminent domain was promotion of the public good. The result, of course, was the opposite.

In the 1960s the federal government made a different kind of promise: if residents of poor neighborhoods prepared themselves for the economic and social mainstream, there would be a place for them there. The government assumed that, with education and training programs, inner-city residents would come to participate in the dramatic economic growth American society was then experiencing. Community action and its human service programs would mediate between the structure of opportunity—the marketplace—and individuals' ability to take advantage of opportunity. Some have argued that the failure of the War on Poverty was due to a lack of will and follow-through. The education, health, nutrition, and other social programs initiated in the 1960s never served more than a modest percentage of those who might have benefited, and struggled chronically to balance quality and coverage. Yet the limited effects of the War on Poverty also were due to misestimation. Creating bridges between poor people and the marketplace proved extraordinarily difficult in communities that were already outside the market. Indeed the economic growth of the 1960s—like that of the 1980s—had perverse effects, increasing inequality (see Orfield and Ashkinaze 1991:11)

One can argue, then, that the history of inner-city neighborhoods since the 1950s is not just one of private disinvestment and abandonment but of expectations engendered and then betrayed by government. This perceived betrayal (along with expectations raised by the Civil Rights movement) In part explains why each succeeding generation of neighborhood initiatives has found it that much harder to find the motivation and trust needed to achieve its objectives. It fueled the black militancy of the later 1960s and (beneficially) contributed to the emergence of community economic development as a grass-roots neighborhood renewal strategy.

Urban Racial Segregation as a Critical Impediment

As this book illustrates, the history of neighborhood initiative to address poverty has been strongly interwoven with, and in recent decades constrained by, practices and attitudes toward racial and ethnic minorities. In the first decades of the century race consciousness and "nativism" were used in part to sanction "the gap between vast accumulations of corporate wealth and squalid immigrant slums" (Dawley 1991:255). Like the neighborhoods in which it operated, neighborhood initiative was a two-edged sword that both demonstrated the gap between immigrants and native-born Americans and tried to close it. Beginning in the 1920s racism and racial fears in urban communities focused increasingly on African Americans. A distinct and new kind of ghetto emerged, created by white hostility, and maintained by coercion and violence. The so-called institutional ghetto was built (for the most part reluctantly) by African Americans on the assumption of the need to build a sep-

arate society, apart from the larger one. The institutional ghetto func-
tioned adaptively for decades, but the fact that it was created by and
built on segregation and exclusion eventually caught up with it. As
Massey and Denton (1993) point out, the dynamic of the ghetto was
always in the direction of concentrating poverty and vulnerability. The
twin forces of massive migration and a changing and receding labor
market in the 1950s and 1960s exacerbated this dynamic.

Fair housing laws and class action suits have done little to reverse
the persistence of extreme urban residential segregation in recent
decades (see in particular Anderson and Pickering 1986, Massey and
Denton 1993:chap. 8). One-third of all African Americans in the United States now live in intensely segregated ghetto communities (Massey
and Denton 1993a:77). What accounts for this? Ninety-eight percent
of housing in the United States, and therefore most housing decisions
and actions, are private (Massey and Denton 1993:229). Anderson
and Pickering (1986:392) argue that urban residential segregation has
evolved in the minds of white Americans in recent decades from a
problem to a self-justifying fact of life, just "the way things are." At most
there is a vague belief that somehow something will happen to reduce
such segregation in the course of time—perhaps the social equivalent
of market forces. As mentioned briefly in chapter 1, the two authors
label this set of beliefs "racist realism," and go on to point out that
"there never was a realism that did not have a moral universe of some
sort embedded in it and, consequently, enacted through it" (Anderson
and Pickering 1986:398). In particular, the seemingly simple and inno-
cent principle involved—that people like to live with their own kind—
only works for the included, those with power and choice. For the
excluded it is profoundly, yet subtly coercive (Anderson and Pickering
1986:380).

Still, what purposes do distancing and exclusion serve, particularly
residential segregation? Historically, they were used by ethnic immigrants to protect social and economic gains. In discussing whites'
resistance to efforts to integrate Chicago's Southwest Side in the early
1960s, Ralph (1993:xxx) notes that "southwest siders were not doctors,
lawyers and professors, but men and women who had scrimped and
saved and sacrificed to buy homes in desirable neighborhoods. They

trembled at the consequences of opening up the southwest side to black residents." As whites moved to the suburbs the same combination of fears and prejudices led them to deny minority entry to their new communities. More recently distancing and exclusion have been used by the white majority to try to "remove the underlying problems of our society farther and farther from daily experience and daily consciousness" (Slater 1976:19). Given the chronic insecurity Americans feel about their place and status in society, another purpose for distancing and exclusion might be to reassure oneself that one is on the inside, that one belongs. But the comfort yielded is a false comfort, the fiction of immunity (Wideman 1992). It is impossible to build a deep sense of belonging on the back of exclusion of others. That sense has to come from and be built on positive things as well as negative ones—a sense of trust, a sense that the cost of stumbling or experiencing a problem will not be the loss of one's place in society.

Already in the nineteenth century it was evident that the costs of maintaining the ghetto could not be contained within its geographic boundaries. Reformers were as or more concerned about the "externalities"—the social costs—of the slum as by its internal hardships. Dawley (1991:viii) writes that "too often it is assumed that the strong are able to control events, while the weak suffer what they must. The truth is that dominant and subordinate groups constrain one another at every turn." The practice of racial exclusion has its costs, for example, "in restricting the movements of others, most whites have lost their own ability to come and go freely" (Anderson and Pickering 1986:387). Certainly the loss of the city as a cultural, social, and even economic resource has been costly to whites. Those who are excluded do not disappear. They may give up, they may lose hope. They also become angrier, more desperate, more willing to threaten and destroy than to try to succeed and contribute. Ultimately, as is already happening, further exclusion becomes a tool for containing the effects of prior exclusion. Massey and Denton (1993:217) note that

as conditions in the ghetto have worsened and as poor blacks have adapted socially and culturally to this deteriorating environment, the ghetto has assumed even greater importance as an institutional tool for isolating the by-products . . . crime, drugs, violence, illiteracy, poverty, despair.

Neighborhood Initiative in Societal Context

It is inevitable that discreet problem-solving strategies will become caught up in larger social dilemmas. In the American context, though, they have been particularly susceptible to these dilemmas. The context in which neighborhood initiative has been forced to operate, especially in the past thirty years, has made it difficult for them to do even the things for which they were suited. A central argument of this book has been that the logic of neighborhood initiative becomes illogic under conditions of community neglect and exclusion, and the lack of political leadership to address these conditions. It is the very existence— the fact—of profoundly depleted and isolated neighborhoods that is problematic and damaging. We cannot continue to move quickly past this idea and and simply focus on addressing its consequences. Each time we do so the stakes are that much higher, the tasks that much more difficult.

I am not arguing that we should disavow neighborhood initiative. Assuring good services and supports in inner-city communities— whether rehabilitated housing, dropout prevention, parent support programs, after-school and youth programs, substance abuse treatment, welfare to work programs—is critical to those who live there. As I argued in the introduction, neighborhood initiative represents an effort by community members to renounce and seek mastery over their hardship and depradation. Yet when we focus our attention inside the neighborhood, on dilapidated and abandoned housing, teen childbearing, inattentive parenting, gangs, drugs, welfare dependence, we have to remember to look to solutions beyond those immediately linked to these problems. The most basic reasons for the prevalence and concentration of social problems in the inner city are not found in the lack of good human services, lack of neighborhood social organization, nor even in the condition of housing stock. They are found in the primacy of the marketplace in defining people's worth and entitlement and in shaping social relations, in a limited sense of social obligation, particularly toward the poor and minorities, in the continued social and political sanctioning of exclusionary housing practices, and in the resulting feelings of exclusion, of being trapped, of anger, despair, depression, futility. Building a reform agenda primarily on initiatives that address the manifest problems of the inner city only masks the underlying social issues, related to the way people treat each other in our society. It does not eliminate the necessity of addressing them.

Wideman (1971:616) describes as moral chaos the result of Americans' "head-in-the-sand disregard for the lives of others who happen to be an inch outside the network of relationships we perceive as necessary to grant our immediate needs." I believe he means that our reluctance to create a somewhat larger frame of mutual interest, if not mutual responsibility, leaves us with no ways to live together as a people and to address societal problems. Our preoccupation with creating and defending boundaries tends constantly to narrow our sense of identity—so does the constant preoccupation with comparing, and with similarities and differences. Wiebe (1975:8) argues that while Americans like to think of themselves as pragmatic, their problem-solving efforts reveal a style that is sectarian: "When Americans encounter [sic] problems they look not for the common ground but for the boundary dividing it." This has been as true of the vulnerable as of the strong. For example, community groups historically have proven incapable of sustaining coalitions that did not necessarily address their immediate community needs but might change harmful policies and practices over time (see Marcuse 1993:364).

Within the framework of an adversarial democracy public policy and social reform seem as often to have conspired to maintain the prevailing balance between the strong and the vulnerable as to alter it. In discussing the history of public housing in the United States, Funnye and Shiffman (1972:202) argue that it followed the path of least resistance. One can

argue that this has been true of reform efforts in general. The Progressives' observations of the damage to people resulting from the demands of corporate capitalism were far stronger than their interpretations of what they observed, which in turn were stronger than the actions they took. The periodic downturns in the business cycle that pushed hundreds of thousands into unemployment, hunger, and sometimes homelessness, mostly led Progressives to redouble their efforts to sort out the loafers from the unfortunate. (Garraty 1978:129)

The Great Depression left deeply rooted anxieties, but did not alter basic societal myths about success and failure at all. Analyses underlying the War on Poverty warned that growing numbers of inner-city residents not only were unprepared for but no longer had access to the labor market. They also indicated that prevailing federal economic and social policy was further weakening urban economies that already were vulnerable (Weir 1993:3). President Johnson chose not to pursue the implications of these analyses in the programs he developed. President Clinton has all the information he needs to call for a major national effort to address both the immediate situation of the inner cities and broader societal attitudes and practices that reinforce that situation. Yet he appears to struggle between his personal instincts, which pull him in the direction of activism, and his political ones, which provide a host of reasons to be cautious. (In this he is not unlike President Carter, who, though mindful of the urgency of leadership on inner-city problems, also feared getting politically and financially trapped by the depth of the needs involved; Fox 1986:13).

We cannot continue to base our problem-solving efforts on the assumption that our culture, political system, social and economic arrangements are basically sound and just need some fine-tuning. We have used our central ideas—family, community, pluralism, individual choice, local democracy—to divide rather than to build common ground for so long that they have lost much of the positive symbolic value they once had. The neglect of inner-city neighborhoods and the exclusion of their residents are not exceptions to American life but important elements of it.

One can argue that, of all the constraints on neighborhood initiative, it has been residents' sense of exclusion that has been the most difficult to address. The "difference dilemma," the dilemma of figuring out what to do in the face of one's exclusion and depradation, has become if anything more profound than historically. What little common life—in beliefs, norms, identity, aspirations, physical contact—once existed between residents of inner-city communities and the larger society around them is gone. The bridges back and forth have almost disappeared. No strategy tried by excluded Americans has worked to resolve this dilemma: neither integration, separate development, self-help, legal action, direct action, militancy, education, social services, community development, collective violence. That is because at heart the dilemma is about the denial of the social membership, the humani-

ty of the excluded, and of the interdependence of majority and minority. We cannot continue to ask the excluded to be largely or solely
responsible for resolving the difference dilemma, for finding a way to
become included. They cannot do so on their own, nor should they be
asked to; from a moral perspective it is largely the responsibility of those
who do the excluding to take some initiative.

Where To From Here?

Addressing inner-city residents' sense of exclusion does not primarily
mean trying to bring large numbers of jobs back into the inner-city. The
CDC experience suggests that doing so is an almost impossible task.
Nonetheless it does mean increasing the percentage of inner-city residents who are linked to the economy through so-called mobility strategies (job information, assistance in gaining entrée to jobs, transportation
support) as well as through job retention and reemployment assistance,
and the like. Discussions emerging between some older cities, such as
New Haven, and their immediate suburbs about how to overcome juris-
dictional and psychological barriers to economic cooperation appear to
offer modest promise to address economic dimensions of exclusion (see
Judson 1993:A1) Among other things, such discussions provide a forum
for ongoing contact between urban minority leadership and civic and
business leaders from around the metropolitan area.

Public policy has to address continuing obstacles to individual
choice in residential mobility (including lack of resources, information,
and ongoing support) so that inner-city residents have the same degree
of choice about where to live as white working-class Americans. At the
same time deliberate residential dispersal strategies will (and should)
play only a modest role in addressing inner-city residents' social and
economic exclusion. For one thing, a primary reliance on dispersal
would communicate the message that, as far as government is concerned, inner-city neighborhoods should simply be written off. For
another, dispersal strategies will never be available to more than a modest portion of inner-city residents (for financial, political, and logistical
reasons). Given the likely limitation of dispersal strategies, the emphasis on trying to strengthen pride in place in current initiatives such as
Baltimore's Community Building in Partnership is an important objec-

tive in that it both propels and ties together discrete initiative activities.

Both local government and private institutions like churches and youth-serving organizations must address the task of recreating a measure of human contact between inner-city neighborhoods and surrounding parts of the city. There has to be more face-to-face contact between children and adults from different communities, so mutual images are not defined by whatever is in the media. Suburban and urban churches have begun programs to foster such contact, and even a few individual schools, for example, Hendricks Academy in inner-city Chicago and Hubbard Woods School in Winnetka, Illinois, have done the same. A major challenge in such contact building is to find an appropriate basis for it. Simply learning about each others' daily lives is one such basis, but it does not carry new relationships very far. Collaborative projects in such cross-community relationships have tended to focus on improving some aspect of inner-city life alone, providing little basis for the reciprocity so critical to sustaining relationships.

Within the inner city traditional institutions of social control and nurturance need enough resources to compete with gangs as bases for community social organization. The costs of the current basis for social organization in the inner city, as adaptive as it may be, are simply too high, particularly since it is tied so closely to the drug trade. Early childhood and youth-serving organizations, churches, and other local institutions in the inner city currently operate for the most part in a survival mode, fulfilling only the most modest portion of their potential to shape and nurture child and family life.

Finally, even the most sensible policies, practices, and investments, if limited to local reform or community renewal, will have only marginal impact without attention to societal context. Among the critical societal elements lacking are a willingness to try to view the world through others' eyes in collective efforts to understand and address social problems, a realistic perspective on and willingness to address legitimate differences in interests, a confident state that can be active when need be, and a unifying ideology more complex than a list of slogans such as strong families and communities.

In spite of all, neighborhood initiative, like the communities it serves, remains strangely powerful, even in its vulnerability. Perhaps I was wrong when I argued earlier that neighborhood initiative is not a transforming strategy. There is a certain transformative value in mobilization and collective action themselves. In a book called *The Magic of Ritual* Driver (1991:184) argues that "rational political methods alone cannot bring about transformation of society from a less to a more just condition, because they cannot fuse the visionary with the actual (the absent with the present). . . . Nor can ideas alone do this for in order to bear fruit ideas require flesh-and-blood performance." More than any other social reform strategy, neighborhood initiative has struggled to fuse the visionary with the actual and translate the result into action. That in part is why neighborhood initiative seems so new each time, even though it follows well-worn paths and faces longstanding obstacles.

Aaron, Paul and Andrew Hahn. 1991 (April). Fighting Urban Poverty in the 1990s: Phil-
anthropy, Knowledge Development, and the Mobilization of Political Will. New York:
Rockefeller Foundation.

Addams, Jane. 1965 [1893]. "The Objective Value of a Social Settlement." In Christopher Lasch, ed., *The Social Thought of Jane Addams*. Indianapolis: Bobbs-Merrill
(1965).

———— 1965 [1894]. "A Modern Lear." In Christopher Lasch, ed., *The Social Thought of
Jane Addams*. Indianapolis: Bobbs-Merrill.

Aikman, Lisa. 1993. "Fighting Urban Poverty: Lessons from Local Intervention Programs."
Background memo for policy conference. New York: Social Science Research Council Program for Research on the Urban Underclass.

Altshuler, Alan. 1970. *Community Control*. New York: Praeger.

Alvarez, Joseph. 1971. *From Reconstruction to Revolution.* New York: Atheneum.

Anderson, Alan and George Pickering. 1986. *Confronting the Color Line: The Broken Promise of the Civil Rights Movement in Chicago.* Athens: University of Georgia Press.

Anderson, Karen. 1982. "Last Hired, First Fired: Black Women Workers During World War II." *Journal of American History* 69(1):82–97.

Annie Casey Foundation. 1992. *Rebuilding Communities: A Neighborhood Reinvestment Strategy.* Greenwich, Conn.: Author.

Arnstein, Sherry. 1972. "Maximum Feasible Manipulation." *Public Administration Review* 32:377–389.

Atlas, John and Peter Dreier. 1992. "From Projects to Communities: How to Redeem Public Housing." *The American Prospect,* no. 10, pp. 74–85.

Austin, Michael. 1978. *Professionals and Paraprofessionals.* New York: Human Sciences Press.

Baker, Paula. 1984. "The Domestication of Politics: Women and American Political Society, 1780–1920." *American Historical Review* 89(3):620–747.

Baker, Ruth. 1990 (April). "Parents as Providers: Integrating an Adult Education and Training Program with Head Start." Cambridge: John F. Kennedy School of Government.

Barringer, Felicity. 1992 (November 29). "A Shift for Urban Renewal: Nurturing the Grass Roots." *New York Times,* p. A1.

Bartlet, David. 1993. "Housing the Underclass." In M. Katz, ed., *The Underclass Debate: Views from History.* Princeton: Princeton University Press.

Bauman, John. 1987. *Public Housing, Race and Renewal.* Philadelphia: Temple University Press.

Bellah, Robert, Richard Madsen, William Sullivan, Ann Swidler, and Steven Tipton. 1985. *Habits of the Heart.* Berkeley: University of California Press.

Belmonte, Thomas. 1989. *The Broken Fountain.* New York: Columbia University Press.

Bendick, Marc and Mary Egan. 1989 (June). "Linking Business Development and Community Development: Lessons from Four Cities." Washington, D.C.: Bendick and Egan Economic Consultants.

Berger, Peter and Richard Neuhaus. 1977. *To Empower People: The Role of Mediating Structures in Public Policy.* Washington, D.C.: American Enterprise Foundation.

Berndt, Harry. 1977. *New Rulers in the Ghetto.* Westport, Conn.: Greenwood.

Berry, Jeffrey, Kent Portney, and Ken Thomson. 1993. *The Rebirth of Urban Democracy.* Washington, D.C.: Brookings Institution Press.

Berry, Wendell. 1987. "Does Community Have a Value?" In *Collected Essays.* Berkeley: North Point.

Birnbaum, Norman. 1988. *The Radical Renewal.* New York: Pantheon.

Blum, John. 1991. *Years of Discord: American Politics and Society, 1961–1974*. New York: Norton, 1991.

Boesche, Roger. 1987. *The Strange Liberalism of Alexis de Tocqueville*. Ithaca: Cornell University Press.

Borris, Eileen. 1992. "The Settlement Movement Revisited: Social Control with a Conscience. *Reviews in American History* 20:216–221.

Boston Foundation. 1992 (Summer). "Building the Dudley Street Neighborhood," pp. 1–3. Boston Foundation Report.

Bowles, Samuel and Herbert Gintis. 1976. *Schooling in Capitalist America*. New York: Basic Books.

Boyte, Harry. 1980. *The Backyard Revolution: Understanding the New Citizen Movement*. Philadelphia: Temple University Press.

Bremmer, Robert. 1972. *From the Depths: The Discovery of Poverty in the United States*. New York: New York University Press.

Budes, Leonard. 1990 (April 26). "Dinkins Describes Plan to Improve Social Services." *New York Times*, p. B12.

Bush, Malcolm. 1988. *Families in Distress*. Berkely: University of California Press.

Butts, R. Freeman. 1909. *The Civic Mission in Educational Reform*. Stanford, Cal.: Hoover Institution Press.

Cahn, Edgar and Jean Cahn. 1971. "Maximum Feasible Participation: A General Overview." In Edgar Cahn and Barry Passett, eds., *Citizen Participation: Effecting Community Change*. New York: Praeger.

Cahn, Edgar and Barry Passett. 1971. *Citizen Participation: Effecting Community Change*. New York: Praeger.

California Assembly. 1991. *Bill 831, An Act to Establish Pilot Neighborhood Family Service Organizations*. Sacramento: Author.

Carlin, Jerome. 1973. "Storefront Lawyers in San Francisco." In M. Pilisuk and P. Pilisuk, eds., *How We Lost the War on Poverty*. N.J.: Transaction Books.

Carlson, David and Arabella Martinez. 1988. "The Economics of Community Change." Report prepared for the Ford Foundation. Texas: Center for Policy Development.

Chambers, Clark. 1963. *Seedtime of Reform*. Minneapolis: University of Minnesota Press.

Chapas, Fernando. 1993 (July 13). Remarks on edited transcript. Roundtable on Family Self-Sufficiency and Community Economic Development. Washington, D.C.: Department of Housing and Urban Development, Office of Policy Development and Research.

Clark, Kenneth. 1965. *Dark Ghetto*. New York: Harper and Row.

———— 1968. "Black and White: Then Ghetto Inside." In H. Samuel, ed., *Toward a Better America*. New York: Macmillan.

Cloward, Richard and Richard Elman. 1973. "Advocacy in the Ghetto." In M. Pilisuk and P. Pilisuk, eds., *How We Lost the War on Poverty*. New Jersey: Transaction Books.

Cloward, Richard and Lloyd Ohlin. 1960. *Delinquency and Opportunity: A Theory of Delinquent Gangs*. Glencoe, Ill.: Free Press.

Cloward, Richard and Frances Fox Piven. 1972. *The Politics of Turmoil*. New York: Pantheon.

Coles, Robert. 1969. "Rural Upheaval: Confrontation and Accommodation." In J. Sundquist, ed., *On Fighting Poverty*. New York: Basic Books.

Community Building in Partnership. 1992. "Phase I Report." Baltimore: Author.

Community Building in Partnership. 1993a (March). "Progress Report." Baltimore: Author.

Community Building in Partnership. 1993b (March 3). "Proposal to Transform the Sandown-Winchester Neighborhood." Baltimore: Author.

Coontz, Stephanie. 1988. *The Social Origins of Private Life*. London: Verso.

Cunningham, James. 1970. "New Approaches to Creating Strong Neighborhoods." In F. Cox, J. Ehrlich, J. Rothman, and J. Tropman. eds., *Strategies for Community Organization*. Itasca, Ill.: Peacock.

Currie, Elliot. 1993. "Missing Pieces: Notes on Crime, Poverty, and Social Policy." Background memo for policy conference. Washington, D.C.: Social Science Research Council on Persistent Urban Poverty.

Curtis, Lynn. 1993. *Doing What Works to Reverse the Betrayal of American Democracy*. Washington, D.C.: Milton Eisenhower Foundation.

Daniels, John. 1920. *America Via the Neighborhood*. New York: Harper Brothers.

Danielson, Michael. 1976. *The Politics of Exclusion*. New York: Columbia University Press.

Davis, John. 1991. *Contested Ground*. Ithaca: Cornell University Press.

Davoren, Elizabeth. 1982. "The Profession of Social Work and the Protection of Children." In E. Newberger, ed., *Child Abuse*. Boston: Little, Brown.

Dawley, Alan. 1991. *Struggles for Justice: Social Responsibility and the Liberal State*. Cambridge: Harvard University Press.

DeForest, Robert and Lawrence Veiller. 1969 [1903]. "The Tenement House Problem." In R. Abrams, ed., *Issues of the Populist and Progressive Eras, 1892–1912*. New York: Harper.

De Lone, Richard. *Small Futures*. New York: Harcourt, Brace, Jovanovich.

Department of Housing and Urban Development. 1967 (December). "Improving the

Quality of Urban Life: A Program Guide to Model Neighborhoods in Demonstration Cities." Washington, D.C.: Author.

Department of Housing and Urban Development. 1993 (July). "Background Information Packet." Prepared for Social Science Research Council Roundtable at H.U.D. Washington, D.C.: Author.

Dillick, Sydney. 1953. *Community Organization for Neighborhood Development: Past and Present.* New York: William Morrow.

Dinkins, David. 1990 (April 26). Quoted in L. Budes, "Dinkins Describes Plan to Improve Social Services." *New York Times* B12.

District of Columbia Redevelopment Land Agency. 1964. *Community Services and Family Relocation.* Washington, D.C.: Author.

Drew, Elizabeth. 1992. "Letter from Washington." *New Yorker* (June 1):80–83.

Driver, Tom. 1991. *The Magic of Ritual.* San Francisco: Harper.

Dudley Street Neighborhood Initiative. "Introduction to the Dudley Street Neighborhood Initiative." Boston: Author.

Eilers, Sara. 1993 (July 14). Personal communication (phone conversation) with the author. Baltimore: Enterprise Foundation.

Eisen, Arlene. 1992. "A Report on Foundations' Support for Comprehensive Neighborhood-Based Community Empowerment Initiatives." New York: East Bay Funders and Other Foundations.

Fainstein, Susan. 1987. "Local Mobilization and Economic Discontent." In M. Smith, ed., *The Capitalist City.* Cambridge: Basil Blackwell.

—— 1990. "Neighborhood Planning: Limits and Potentials." In N. Carmon, ed., *Neighborhood Policy and Programs.* London: Macmillan.

Fainstein, Norman and Susan Fainstein. 1983. "Regime Strategies, Communal Resistance, and Economic Forces." In S. Fainstein and N. Fainstein, R. Hill, D. Judd, and M. Smith, eds., *Restructuring the City.* New York: Longman.

Farrell, George. 1969. "The View from the City: Community Action in Trenton." In J. Sundquist, ed., *On Fighting Poverty.* New York: Basic Books.

Faux, Jeffrey. 1971. *New Hope for the Inner City.* New York: Twentieth-Century Fund.

Feingold, Eugene. N.d. "A Political Scientist's View of the Neighborhood Health Center as a New Social Institution." In L. Judd and W. Manseau, eds., *The Neighborhood Health Center Program.* Washington, D.C.: National Association of Neighborhood Health Centers.

Fine, Michelle. 1993." [Ap]parent Involvement: Reflections on Parents, Power, and Urban Public Schools." *Teachers College Record* 94(4):682–709.

Fisher, Robert. 1977. "Community Organizing and Citizen Participation: The Efforts of the

People's Institute of New York City, 1910–1920." *Social Service Review* 51(1): 474–490.

Flanagan, Maureen. 1990. "Gender and Urban Political Reform: The City Club and the Women's City Club of Chicago in the Progressive Era." *American Historical Review* 95(4):1,032–1,050.

Foglesong, Richard. 1986. *Planning the Capitalist City.* Princeton: Princeton University Press.

Ford Foundation. 1964 (September). "Gray Areas Program Review Paper." New York: Author

———— 1967. "Uniting Two Americas." New York: Author.

Fox, Kenneth. 1986. *Metropolitan America.* Jackson: University of Mississippi Press.

Freeman, Joshua. 1992. *Who Built America?* New York: Pantheon.

Frieden, Bernard J. and Lynne B. Sagalyn. 1989. *Downtown, Inc.: How America Rebuilds Cities.* Cambridge: M.I.T. Press.

Funiciello, Theresa. 1993. *Tyranny of Kindness.* New York: Atlantic Monthly Press

Funnye, Clarence and Ronald Shiffman. 1972. "The Imperative of Deghettoization: An Answer to Piven and Cloward." In R. Cloward and F. Piven, eds., *The Politics of Turmoil.* New York: Pantheon.

Galbraith, John. 1958. *The Affluent Society.* Boston: Houghton Mifflin.

Galper, Jeffrey. 1975. *The Politics of Social Services.* Englewood Cliffs, N.J.: Prentice-Hall.

Gans, Herbert. 1962. *The Urban Villagers.* New York: Free Press.

———— 1965. "The Failure of Urban Renewal." *Commentary 39* (April): 29–37.

———— 1991. *People, Plans, and Policies.* New York: Columbia University Press.

Gans, Sheldon and Gerald Horton. 1975. *Integration of Human Services.* New York: Praeger.

Gardner, Sidney. 1989. "Failure by Fragmentation." *California Tomorrow* (Summer), pp. 3–9.

Garn, Harvey, Nancy Tevis, Carl Snead. 1975. *Assessing Community Development Corporations.* Washington, D.C.: Urban Institute.

Garraty, John. 1978. *Unemployment in History.* New York: Harper and Row.

Geiger, Jack. 1969. "Community Control—Or Community Conflict?" *American Lung Association Bulletin* (November):4–10.

George, Henry. 1911 [1879]. *Progress and Poverty.* New York: Doubleday, Page.

Gettleman, Marvin. 1963. "Charity and Social Class in the United States, 1874–1900." Part 2. *American Journal of Economics and Sociology,* no. 22, pp. 417–426.

Gilbert, Neal. 1970. *Clients or Constituents: Community Action in the War on Poverty.* San Fransisco: Jossey Bass.

Gillette, Howard. 1983. "The Evolution of Neighborhood Planning from the Progressive Era to the 1949 Housing Act." *Journal of Urban History* 9(4):421–444.

Gonzalez, David. 1991 (November 5 and 6). (I) "A Neighborhood Struggle With Despair." (II) "Growth Amid Blight." *New York Times,* p. 1, cont'd p. 14.

Gordon, Linda. 1988. *Heroes of Their Own Lives.* New York: Penguin.

Goren, Arthur. 1970. *New York Jews and the Quest for Community.* New York: Columbia University Press.

Greenberg, Cheryl. 1992. "The Politics of Disorder: Re-Examining Harlem's Riots of 1935 and 1943." *Journal of Urban History* 18(4):395–441.

Greenberg, Polly. 1990. *The Devil Has Slippery Shoes* (Rev. ed.) Washington, D.C.: Youth Policy Institute.

Greenstone, David and Paul Peterson. 1973. *Race and Authority in Urban Politics: Community Participation and the War on Poverty.* New York: Russell Sage.

Greer, Scott. 1965. *Urban Renewal and American Cities.* Indianapolis: Bobbs-Merrill.

Gregg, Robert. 1992. "Group Portrait with Lady." *Reviews in American History* 20:354–359.

Groh, George. 1972. *The Black Migration.* New York: Weybright and Talley.

Grosser, Charles. 1969. "Manpower Development Programs." In C. Grosser, W. Henry, and J. Kelly, eds., *Nonprofessionals in the Human Services.* San Francisco: Jossey-Bass

Grubb, Norton and Marvin Lazerson. 1980. *Broken Promises.* New York: Basic Books.

Gunn, Christopher and Hazel Gunn. 1991. *Reclaiming Capital.* Ithaca: Cornell University Press.

Haar, Charles. 1975. *Between the Idea and the Reality: A Study of the Origin, Fate, and Legacy of the Model Cities Program.* Boston: Little, Brown.

Hacker, Andrew. 1990. "Transnational America." *New York Review of Books* (November 22):19–24.

Hall, Helen. 1971. *Unfinished Business.* New York: Macmillan.

Hallman, Howard. 1984. *Neighborhoods: Their Place in Urban Life.* Beverly Hills: Sage.

Halpern, Robert. 1993. "Poverty and Infant Development." In C. Zeanah, ed., *Handbook of Infant Mental Health.* New York: Guilford Press.

Handlin, Oscar. 1951. *The Uprooted.* New York: Grosset and Dunlop.

Hardwick, Elizabeth. 1993. "After Watts." *New York Review of Books Anthology* (reprinted from March 31, 1966).

Harrington, Mona. 1986. *The Dream of Deliverance in American Politics.* New York: Knopf.

Hartman, Chester. 1993 (November 9–10). "U.S. Housing Policy." Background memo for policy conference. Washington, D.C.: Social Science Research Council Program for Research on the Urban Underclass.

Herr, Toby and Robert Halpern. 1993. "Two Generation Head Start Self-Sufficiency Program." Report to the Department of Health and Human Services. Chicago: Project Match.

Himmelfarb, Gertrude. 1991. *Poverty and Compassion*. New York: Knopf.

Hochschild, Jennifer. 1989. "Equal Opportunity and the Estranged Poor." *Annals of the American Academy of Political and Social Science* (501): 143–155.

Horwitt, Sanford. 1989. *Let Them Call Me Rebel: Saul Alinsky, His Life and Legacy*. New York: Knopf.

Hunter, Albert. 1983. "The Urban Neighborhood: Its Analytical and Social Contexts." In P. Clay and R. Hollister, eds., *Neighborhood Policy and Planning*. Lexington, Mass.: Heath.

Hunter, Robert. 1965 [1904]. *Poverty*. New York: Harper.

Husock, Howard. 1992. "Bringing Back the Settlement House." *Public Interest* (Fall): 53–72.

Jackson, Thomas. 1993. "The State, the Movement, and the Urban Poor: The War on Poverty and Political Mobilization in the 1960s." In M. Katz, ed., *The Underclass Debate: Views from History*. Princeton: Princeton University Press.

Janowitz, Morris. 1969. "Patterns of Collective Racial Violence." In *Violence in America: Historical and Comparative Perspectives*. Staff report. Washington, D.C.: National on the Causes and Prevention of Violence.

——— 1978. *The Last Half Century*. Chicago: University of Chicago.

Jones. Jacqueline. 1992a. *The Dispossessed*. New York: Basic Books.

——— 1992b. Interviewed by Brenda Marder. *Brandeis Review* (Summer):17–21

Judd, Dennis. 1991. "Segregation Forever?" *Nation* 253(20):740–744.

Judson, George. 1993 (June 1). "New Haven's Task: Tying City to Region to Promote Growth." *New York Times* A1, cont'd A9.

Kagan, Sharon, Douglas Powell, Bernice Weissbourd, and Edward Zigler. 1987. *America's Family Support Programs*. New Haven: Yale University Press.

Kahn, Alfred. 1976. "Service Delivery at the Neighborhood Level: Experience, Theory, and Fads." *Social Service Review* 50(1):23–55.

Kahn, Alfred and Sheila Kamerman. 1985. "Personal Social Services and Income Transfer Experiments." In R. Rapoport, ed., *Children, Youth, and Families: The Action Research Relationship*. Cambridge: Cambridge University Press.

Kaminsky, James. 1992. "A Re-history of Educational Philosophy." *Harvard Educational Review* 2062(2):179–198.

Kasarda, John. 1989. "Urban Industrial Transition and the Underclass." *Annals of the American Academy of Political and Social Science* 501:26–47.

Katz, Michael. 1981. "Education and Inequality: A Historical Perspective." In David Rothman, ed., *Social History and Social Policy*. New York: Academic Press.

———— 1986. *In the Shadow of the Poorhouse*. New York: Basic Books.

———— 1989. *The Undeserving Poor*. New York: Pantheon.

———— 1992. "Chicago School Reform as History." *Teachers College Record* 94(1):56–72.

———— 1993. "Surviving Poverty in Early Twentieth-Century New York City." In A. Hirsch and R. Mohl, eds., *Urban Policy in Twentieth-Century America*. Brunswick, N.J.: Rutgers University Press.

Katznelson, Ira. 1981. *City Trenches: Urban Politics and the Patterning of Class in the United States*. New York: Pantheon.

———— 1989. "Was the Great Society a Lost Opportunity?" In S. Fraser and G. Celeste, eds., *The Rise and Fall of the New Deal Order*. Princeton: Princeton University Press.

———— 1990. "Selected Writings." In J. Kling and P. Posner, eds., *Dilemmas of Activism*. Temple University Press.

Keenan, Mathew. 1992 (March 28). "Bringing Back a Roxbury Neighborhood." *Boston Globe*, p. 45.

Kelly, Rita. 1977. *Community Control of Economic Development*. New York: Praeger.

Kenniston, Kenneth. 1960. *The Uncommitted*. New York: Dell.

Kerner Commission. 1968 (March). "Report of the National Advisory Commission on Civil Disorders." Washington, D.C.: Author.

Kirschner, Don. 1986. *The Paradox of Professionalism*. New York: Greenwood Press.

Klebaner, Benjamin. 1951. "Poor Relief in America, 1790–1860." Ph.D. diss., Columbia University. Reprinted by Arno Press, New York, 1976 in Social Problems and Social Policy: The American Experience.

Kobrin, Solomon. 1959. "The Chicago Area Project—A Twenty-Five-Year Assessment." *Annals of the American Academy of Political and Social Science* 322(March): 19–27.

Kotlowitz, Alex. 1991. *There Are No Children Here*. New York: Doubleday.

Kravitz, Sanford. 1969. "The Community Action Program: Past, Present, and Future." In J. Sundquist, ed., *On Fighting Poverty*. New York: Basic Books.

Kravitz, Sanford and F. Kolodner. 1969. "Community Action: Where Has It Been? Where Will It Go?" *Annals of the American Academy of Political and Social Science* 385:30–40.

Kusmer, Kenneth. 1973. "The Functions of Organized Charity in the Progressive Era:

Chicago as a Case Study." *Journal of American History* 60(3):657–678.

Larner, Mary and Robert Halpern. 1987. "Lay Home Visiting Programs: Strengths, Tensions, and Challenges." *Zero to Three: Bulletin of the National Center for Clinical Infant Programs* 8(3):1–7.

Lasch, Christopher. 1977. *Haven in a Heartless World.* New York: Basic Books.

Lears, T. Jackson. 1983. "From Salvation to Self-Realization." In R. Fox and T. Lears, eds., *The Culture of Consumption.* New York: Pantheon.

Lemann, Nicholas. 1989. "The Unfinished War." *Atlantic Monthly* (January), pp. 53–68.

——— 1991. *The Promised Land: The Great Black Migration and How It Changed America.* New York: Knopf.

Lerner, Barbara. 1972. *Therapy in the Ghetto.* Baltimore: Johns Hopkins University Press.

Levine, Murray and Adeline Levine. 1992. *Helping Children: A Social History.* New York: Oxford University Press.

Levitan, Sar. N.d. "Healing the Poor in Their Backyard." In L. Judd and W. Manseau, eds., *The Neighborhood Health Center Program.* Washington, D.C.: National Association of Neighborhood Health Centers.

——— 1969. *The Great Society's Poor Law.* Baltimore: Johns Hopkins University Press.

Lubove, Roy. 1965. *The Professional Altruist.* Cambridge: Harvard University Press.

March, Michael. 1968. "The Neighborhood Center Concept." *Public Welfare* 10(April): 97–111.

Marciniak, Ed. 1986. *Re-Claiming the Inner City.* Washington, D.C.: National Center for Urban Ethnic Affairs.

Marcuse, Peter. 1993. "What's So New About Divided Cities?" *International Journal of Urban and Regional Research* 17(3):355–365.

Marris, Peter and M. Jackson. 1991. "Strategy and Context: Reflections on the Community Planning and Action Programs." New York: Rockefeller Foundation.

Marris, Peter and Martin Rein. 1973. *Dilemmas of Social Reform.* London: Routledge and Kegan Paul.

Martinez-Brawley, Emilia. 1990. *Perspectives on the Small Community.* Washington, D.C.: National Association of Social Workers.

Massey, Douglas. 1990. "American Apartheid: Segregation and the Making of the Underclass." *American Journal of Sociology* 96(2):329–357.

Massey, Douglas and Nancy Denton. 1993. *American Apartheid: Segregation and the Making of the Underclass.* Cambridge: Harvard University Press.

Melosh, Barbara. 1984. "More Than the Physician's Hand: Skill and Authority in Twentieth-Century Nursing." In J. Leavitt, ed., *Women and Health in America.* Madison: University of Wisconsin Press.

Melvin, Patricia. 1987. *The Organic City: Urban Definition and Community Organization, 1880–1920*. Lexington: University Press of Kentucky.

Milgram, Morris. 1979. *Good Neighborhood*. New York: Norton.

Miller, Anita. 1991 (November). "Comprehensive Community Revitalization Program, Proposal and Progress Reports." New York.

Miller, S. M. and Martin Rein. 1976. "Will the War on Poverty Change America?" In Marc Pilisuk and Phyllis Pilisuk, eds., *How We Lost the War on Poverty*. New Brunswick, N.J.: Transaction Books.

Miller, William. 1991. *Pretty Bubbles in the Air: America in 1919*. Champaign: University of Illinois Press.

Minow, Martha. 1990. *Making All the Difference*. Ithaca, N.Y.: Cornell University Press.

Mollenkopf, John. 1983. *The Contested City*. Princeton: Princeton University Press.

Moore, William. 1969. *The Vertical Ghetto*. New York: Random House.

Morone, James. 1990. *The Democratic Wish*. New York: Basic Books.

Moynihan, Daniel. 1969. *Maximum Feasible Misunderstanding*. New York: Free Press.

Murphy, Russell. 1971. *Political Entrepreneurs and Urban Poverty*. Lexington, Mass.: Heath.

Nathan, Richard. 1987. "Will the Underclass Always Be with Us?" *Society* (March-April): 57–62.

National Congress for Community Economic Development. 1990. *Community Development Corporation Profile Book*. Washington, D.C.: Author.

Newman, Linda, Deborah Lynn, and Warren Phillip. 1986. *Community Economic Development: An Approach for Urban-Based Economies*. Winnipeg: University of Winnipeg Institute of Urban Studies.

Newman, Sandra. 1993. "The Role of Housing and Community Development Programs in Fighting Persistent Urban Poverty." Background memo for policy conference. New York: Social Science Research Council Program for Research on the Urban Underclass.

Nisbet, Robert. 1953. *The Quest for Community*. Oxford: Oxford University Press.

O'Connor, Alice. 1993 (October). "The Ford Foundation and the Urban Poor in the 1950s." Chicago: Center for the Study of Urban Inequality, University of Chicago.

Ohlin, Lloyd. 1960. "Development of Indigenous Social Movements Among Residents of Deprived Urban Areas." Mimeo. New York: Ford Foundation.

Olasky, Marvin. 1992. *The Tragedy of American Compassion*. Washington, D.C: Regnery Gateway.

Oliver, Melvin, James Johnson, and Walter Farrell. 1993. "Anatomy of a Rebellion." In R. Gooding-Williams, ed., *Reading Rodney King, Reading Urban Uprisings*. New York: Routledge.

O'Neill, William. 1990. "The Cycle of Reform." *Society* 27(5):63–68.

Orfield, Gary and Carole Ashkinaze. 1991. *The Closing Door*. Chicago: University of Chicago Press.

Osofsky, Gerald. 1964. *Harlem: The Making of a Ghetto*. New York: Harper and Row.

Patterson, James. 1986. *America's Struggle Against Poverty*. Cambridge: Harvard University Press.

Payne, James, Cecil Mercer, Ruth Payne, and Roxana Davison. 1973. *Head Start: A Tragicomedy with Epilogue*. New York: Behavioral Publications.

Pearce, Neal and Carol Steinbach. 1987. *Corrective Capitalism*. New York: Ford Foundation.

———— 1990. *Enterprising Communities*. Washington, D.C.: Council for Community-Based Development.

Perlman, Robert. 1975. *Consumers and Social Services*. New York: Wiley.

Perrin, Constance. 1977. *Everything in its Place: Social Order and Land Use in America*. Princeton: Princeton University Press.

Perry, Stewart. 1985 (November). "Office of Economic Opportunity and the Community Development Corporation." Cambridge: Institute for New Enterprise Development.

———— 1987. *Communities on the Way*. Albany: State University of New York Press.

Philpott, Thomas. 1978. *The Slum and the Ghetto*. New York: Oxford University Press.

Pierce, Neal and Carol Steinbach. 1987. *Corrective Capitalism*. New York: Ford Foundation

Piven, Frances and Richard Cloward. 1971. *Regulating the Poor: The Functions of Public Welfare*. New York: Vintage.

Plotkin, S. 1990. "Enclave Consciousness and Neighborhood Activism." In J. Kling and P. Posner, eds., *Dilemmas of Activism*. Philadelphia: Temple University Press

Polier, Justine. 1989. *Juvenile Justice in Double Jeopardy*. Hillsdale, N.J.: Lawrence Earlbaum.

Polsky, Andrew. 1991. *The Rise of the Therapeutic State*. Princeton, N.J.: Princeton University Press.

Posner, Prudence. 1990. "Introduction." In J. Kling and P. Posner, eds., *Dilemmas of Activism*. Philadelphia: Temple University Press.

Powledge, Fred. 1970. *Model City*. New York: Simon and Schuster.

Rainwater, Lee. 1970. *Behind Ghetto Walls*. Chicago: Aldine.

Ralph, James. 1993. *Northern Protest*. Cambridge: Harvard University Press.

Rankin, Robert. 1992 (May 25). "Helping Residents Re-build a Blighted Community." *Philadelphia Inquirer*, p. xx.

Reed, Adolph. 1992. "Parting the Waters." *Nation* (November):633–641.

Reed, Adolph and Julian Bond. 1991. "Equality: Why We Can't Wait." *Nation* 253(20): 733–737.

Reiff, Robert. 1969. "Dilemmas of Professionalism." In C. Grosser, W. Henry, and J. Kelly, eds., *Nonprofessionals in the Human Services.* San Fransisco: Jossey Bass.

Rein, Martin. 1983. *From Policy to Practice.* Armonk, N.Y.: Sharpe.

Reissman, Frank. 1965. "The Helper Therapy Principle." *Social Work* 10(April):27–32.

Richmond, Mary. 1917. *Social Diagnosis.* New York: Russell Sage Foundation.

Rohe, William and Michael Stegman. 1992. "Public Housing Home Ownership: Will It Work and for Whom?" *Journal of the American Planning Association* 58(2): 144–157.

Rose, Steven. 1972. *The Betrayal of the Poor.* Cambridge: Schenkman.

Rothman, Jack, ed. 1971. "Black Capitalism and Ethnic Economic Development: Portland Blacks Get Their Company Thing Together." In Rothman, Jack, ed., *Promoting Social Justice in the Multigroup Society.* New York: Association Press.

Sarason, Seymour. 1978. "An Unsuccessful War on Poverty?" *American Psychologist* 33(September):831–839.

Scheer, Robert. 1992. "Interview with Sister Souljah." *Playboy* (October):59–72.

Schlesinger, Arthur. 1957. *The Crisis of the Old Order.* Cambridge: Houghton Mifflin.

Schlossman, Steven. 1978. "The Parent Education Game: The Politics of Child Development in the 1970s." *Teachers College Record* 79(4):788–808.

Schlossman, Steven and Michael Sedlak. 1983. *The Chicago Area Project Revisited.* Santa Monica: Rand Corporation.

Schorr, Lisbeth. 1988. *Within Our Reach: Breaking the Cycle of Disadvantage.* New York: Anchor.

Schorr, Lisbeth and Joseph English. N.d. "Background, Context, and Significant Issues in Neighborhood Health Center Programs." In L. Judd and R. Manseau, eds., *The Neighborhood Health Center Program.* Washington, D.C.: National Association of Neighborhood Health Centers.

Sclar, Elliot. 1970. *The Community Basis for Economic Development.* Cambridge: Center for Community Economic Development.

Shelton, Brenda. 1976. *Reformers in Search of Yesterday: Buffalo in the 1890s.* Albany: State University of New York Press.

Sherraden, Michael and Margaret Adamek. 1984. "Explosive Imagery and Misguided Policy." *Social Science Review* 58 (December): pp. 539–555.

Silberman, Charles. 1964. "Up from Apathy: The Woodlawn Experiment." *Commentary* (May):51–58.

Silberman, Deanna. 1990. "Interview with Dorothy Sigel." In *Chicago and its Children: A Brief History of Social Services for Children in Chicago.* Chicago: Chapin Hall Center for Children, University of Chicago.

Skerry, Peter. 1983. "The Charmed Life of Head Start." *Public Interest* 73:18–39.

Skocpol, Theda. 1992. *Protecting Soldiers and Mothers.* Cambridge: Harvard University Press.

Slater, Philip. 1976. *The Pursuit of Loneliness.* Boston: Beacon Press.

Slayton, Robert. 1986. *Back of the Yards.* Chicago: University of Chicago Press.

Spear, Alan. 1967. *Black Chicago: The Making of a Ghetto.* Chicago: University of Chicago Press.

Stadum, Beverly. 1990. "A Critique of Family Case Workers, 1900–1930: Women Working with Women." *Journal of Sociology and Social Welfare* 17(3):73–100.

——— 1992. *Poor Women and Their Families: Hardworking Charity Cases.* Albany: State University of New York Press.

Stark, Rodney. 1987. "Deviant Places: A Theory of the Ecology of Crime." *Criminology* 25(4):893–909.

Starr, Paul. 1982. *The Social Transformation of American Medicine.* New York: Basic Books.

Stein, Mark. 1993. "Poverty and Family Composition Since 1940." In M. Katz, ed., *The Underclass Debate: Views from History.* Princeton: Princeton University Press.

Stoeckle, John and Lucy Candib. 1969. "The Neighborhood Health Center: Reform Ideas of Yesterday and Today." *New England Journal of Medicine* 280(25):1,385–1,391.

Storey, Moorefield. "The Government of Cities." 1969 [1892]. In R. Abrams, ed., *Issues of the Populist and Progressive Eras, 1892–1912.* New York: Harper.

Sugrue, Thomas. 1993. "The Structures of Urban Poverty: The Re-Organization of Space and Work in Three Periods of American History." In M. Katz, ed., *The Underclass Debate: Views from History.* Princeton: Princeton University Press.

Sundquist, James. 1969. "Origins of the War on Poverty." In J. Sundquist, ed., *On Fighting Poverty.* New York: Basic Books.

Suttles, Gerald. 1972. *The Social Construction of Community.* Chicago: University of Chicago Press.

——— 1990. *The Man Made City.* Chicago: University of Chicago Press.

Taub, Richard. 1990. *Nuance and Meaning in Community Development: Finding Community and Development.* New York: Community Development Research Center, New School for Social Research.

Tax, Sol. 1967. *The People Versus the System.* Chicago: Aldine.

Teaford, John. 1993. *The Twentieth-Century American City.* 2d ed. Baltimore: Johns Hopkins University Press.

Thelen, David. 1969. "Social Tensions and the Origins of Progressivism." *Journal of American History* 56(2):323–341.

Thernstrom, Steven. 1969. *Poverty, Planning, and Politics in the New Boston: The Origins of ABCD*. New York: Basic Books.

Thomas, Paulette. 1992 (June 11). "Small Businesses, Key to Urban Recovery, Are Starved for Capital." *Wall Street Journal*, p. 1, p. 12.

Tice, Karen. 1992. "The Battle for Benevolence: Scientific Disciplinary Control Versus Indiscriminate Relief." *Journal of Sociology and Social Welfare* 19(2):59–77.

Trolander, Judith Ann. 1987. *Professionalism and Social Change*. New York: Columbia University Press.

———— 1975. *Settlement Houses and the Great Depression*. Detroit: Wayne State University Press.

Tuttle, William. 1970. *Race Riot: Chicago in the Red Summer of 1919*. New York: Atheneum.

Tyack, David, Robert Lowe, and Elizabeth Hansot. 1984. *Public Schools In Hard Times: The Great Depression and Recent Years*. Cambridge: Harvard University Press.

Valentine, Charles. 1968. *Culture and Poverty: Critique and Counterproposals*. Chicago: University of Chicago Press.

Valentine, Jeanette and Evan Stark. 1979. "The Social Context of Parent Involvement in Head Start." In E. Zigler and J. Valentine, eds., *Project Head Start: A Legacy of the War on Poverty*. New York: Free Press.

Venkatesh, Sudhir. 1993. "Black Gangs and the Reconstitution of Community in an Urban Ghetto." Chicago: University of Chicago Department of Sociology.

Vidal, Avis. 1992. *Rebuilding Communities: A National Study of Urban Community Development Corporations*. New York: Community Development Research Center, New School for Social Research.

Wacquant, Loic and William Julius Wilson. 1989. "The Cost of Racial and Class Exclusion in the Inner City." *Annals of the American Academy of Political and Social Science* 501:8–25.

Warner, Sam. 1962. "Preface." In Robert Woods and Albert Kennedy, eds., *Zone of Emergence*. Cambridge: M.I.T. Press.

Warren, Roland. 1969. "Model Cities First Round: Politics, Planning, and Participation." *American Institute of Planners Journal* (July):245–252.

Weir, Margaret. 1993. "Urban Policy and Persistent Urban Poverty." Background memo for policy conference. New York: Social Science Research Council Program for

Research on the Urban Underclass.

Weissman, Harold. 1978. *Integrating Services for Troubled Children.* San Francisco: Jossey Bass.

Wenocur, Stanley and Michael Reisch. 1989. *From Charity to Enterprise.* Urbana: University of Illinois.

Whitman, David. 1991. "The Great Sharecropper Success Story." *Public Interest* 104 (Summer):3–19.

Wideman, John. 1971. "Fear in the Streets." *American Scholar* 40(4): 611-622.

—— 1992. "Dead Black Men and Other Fallout from the American Dream." *Esquire* (September), pp. 118, 149–157.

Wiebe, Robert. 1975. *The Segmented Society.* New York: Oxford University Press.

Wilinsky, C. F. 1927. "The Health Center." *American Journal of Public Health* 17(7): 677–682.

Willhelm, Sidney and Edwin Powell. 1975. "Who Needs the Negro?" In R. Giallombardo, ed., *Contemporary Social Issues.* New York: Wiley.

Wingert, Willis, Judy Grubbs, Edward Lenoski, and David Friedman. 1975. "Effectiveness and Efficiency of Indigenous Health Aides in a Pediatric Outpatient Department." *American Journal of Public Health* 65(8):849–857.

Wofford, John. 1969. "The Politics of Local Responsibility: Administration of the Community Action Program." In J. Sundquist, ed., *On Fighting Poverty.* New York: Basic Books.

Wolin, Sheldon. 1989. *The Presence of the Past.* Baltimore: Johns Hopkins University Press.

Woods, Robert. 1902. *Americans in Process: A Settlement Study.* Boston: Houghton Mifflin.

—— 1970 [1923]. *The Neighborhood in Nation-Building.* New York: Arno.

Wright, Gwendolyn. 1981. *Building the Dream: A Social History of Housing in America.* New York: Pantheon.

Wright, Nathan. 1968. *Ready to Riot.* New York: Holt, Rinehart and Winston.

Yin, Robert and Douglas Yates. 1975. *Street Level Governments.* Lexington, Mass.: Heath.

Ylvisaker, Paul. 1973 (September). Interviewed by Charles Morrissey for the Ford Foundation's Oral History Project. New York: Ford Foundation.

Young, Whitney Jr. 1972. "The Case for Urban Integration: An Answer to Piven and Cloward." In R. Cloward and F. Piven, eds., *The Politics of Turmoil.* New York: Pantheon.

Designer: Andrea Ratazzi
Text: Optima
Compositor: Columbia University Press
Printer: Maple-Vail
Binder: Maple-Vail